D0593474

LIGHTNING *in a* JAR

A THOROUGHBRED OWNER'S GUIDE

LIGHTNING
in a JAR

Catching Racing Fever

BY W. COTHRAN CAMPBELL

Foreword by D. Wayne Lukas

EP
ECLIPSE
PRESS

Lexington, Kentucky

Library of Congress Card Number: 00-101125

ISBN 1-58150-053-X

Printed in China
First Edition: October 2000

a division of
The Blood-Horse, Inc.
PUBLISHERS SINCE 1916

CONTENTS

FOREWORD

In my forty-seven years as a Thoroughbred racehorse trainer, there are two things that I have found to be true: One, there are many people who have been very successful in our industry and have approached it in a variety of ways. The second thing I have found to be true is most of their stories remain untold. Their successes and failures, their highs and lows, their moments of unparalleled joy, and their huge disappointments remain buried in their hearts. Other than an occasional documentary in our trade magazines, these wonderful stories on people in Thoroughbred racing seldom are shared. Enter Cot Campbell.

In a recent survey taken by the newly formed National Thoroughbred Racing Association, one of the most glaring findings revealed that the racehorse industry is very intimidating to non-participants. Most of the people questioned in the survey stated that they not only were intimidated by this vast endeavor, but they also felt it was something beyond their wildest imaginings. To those surveyed, Thoroughbred racing seemed like a fantasy world visited by oil-rich sheikhs, corporate executives, and people of great wealth, much of which was inherited. These people entwined their lives with a small and select group of old-time horsemen who were in many cases totally unapproachable. Little of their knowledge was shared or their expertise passed on.

Cot Campbell's wonderful journey into our sport should dispel many of these fears. In his magical book, *Lightning in a Jar*, Cot takes you chapter by chapter from his early involvement to the pinnacle of the sport — winning a classic race, the Preakness.

Along the way, as we travel together, we have the opportunity to see the mistakes, the errors, and the pitfalls that so many people who enter the Thoroughbred world experience. But we also find, through reading and completing this journey with Cot, great lessons in how to approach the game, how to be successful at the game, but more importantly, how to enjoy it to the fullest. We find that you don't have to be a sheikh or corporate executive of great wealth to enjoy what so many of us have enjoyed.

Cot Campbell was one of the first to recognize that not everybody could play at the highest level without great financial wherewithal. Through a unique and interesting approach, he tells us in detail about the formation of Dogwood Stable, its use of the partnership as an ownership vehicle, and how these partnerships are accessible to the average person. Through Dogwood, he developed a system that not only allowed people to play at the highest level, but through this entertaining book he shows in detail that there are great associations and friendships that develop when you have a common bond, such as owning a racehorse.

Lightning in a Jar is not only entertaining and informative, but, above everything else, it is educational.

There are no holds barred. *Lightning in a Jar* tells it like it is. And whether you are a complete lay person with a love for racing, a casual racetrack goer, or the seasoned professional, this book offers something for each of you.

I have always been a Cot Campbell fan and have treasured his friendship. Now, after reading *Lightning in a Jar*, I feel that Cot has come full cycle from his innovative way of bringing new people into the game to documenting one of the most successful careers of any entrepreneur in our business.

As you take this journey, I hope that you will recognize and feel the magic of Thoroughbred racing and be touched as we have.

D. Wayne Lukas
Hall of Fame
fourteen-time world champion trainer

PREFACE

One of the strangest, most improbable journeys in the history of Thoroughbred horse racing — or American commerce, for that matter — has been the evolution of Dogwood Stable.

Thirty-three years ago, while sitting around the locker room of the Piedmont Driving Club in Atlanta, I suggested to three buddies that we should buy a racehorse. Two of them went for it, so I arranged for the purchase of a yearling filly for $1,000. We named her Social Asset. She wasn't. Nor could she run much. But this partnership was the start of a new career, and a wonderful life, during which I've bought more than 1,000 horses for about $91 million and have introduced the sport — for better or worse — to 1,200 new investors. There have been two champions, a classic winner, a Breeders' Cup winner, fifty-four stakes winners, thirteen grade one winners, five equine millionaires and plenty — repeat plenty — of others who could not outrun a fat man going uphill!

I'm going to tell you about my splendid life and that of Dogwood Stable. I knew something about racing when I bought Social Asset in

1967, and I know a hell of a lot more about it now, much of it learned the hard way. Perhaps more importantly, I know what I don't know. I think some of my experiences could help you if you are thinking about entering and participating in the sport of horse racing (sometimes enormously intimidating to the newcomer!). This book will attempt to provide you with some dos and don'ts, cover the joys and pitfalls of Thoroughbred ownership, and provide a lot of inside information.

I want you to know this: I will try to address every major element of the Thoroughbred industry in the most factual, informative way. However, after more than three decades of making my living with racehorses and racehorse people (wonderful for the most part), I have inevitably arrived at some strong conclusions; and some of my opinions, concerns, enthusiasm, pet peeves, and unbridled devotion will be found in this work. You may not agree — now or when you are more knowledgeable in the future — but my earnest expressions of passion concerning the racing game are meant to do you a service.

If you have the proper temperament for racing and your mindset is right, if you set your goals realistically, if you don't try to run before you walk, and, Lord knows, if you were to have a little luck, what a great thing it can be. I hope it will be.

W. Cothran Campbell
Aiken, South Carolina
December 1999

"CONQUERING" THE GAME

In a 1925 interview, a reporter asked Samuel D. Riddle, the famous racing man — and owner of Man o' War — about his philosophy concerning the racing game, luck, and the quest for winning race-horses. With a faraway look in his eye, Riddle referred to the Saratoga sale of 1918, and said, "I spent $25,000 for eleven yearlings at that sale...ten of them were duds...but the eleventh was Man o' War!" Considering the animal involved, we would all be overjoyed with that win-loss ratio today! But here's the point:

The great moments in racing are so supremely wonderful that it follows, as it does in life, that one must walk through some exceedingly dark valleys before he or she can expect to scale those fabulous heights. You must be able to enjoy the anticipation, the hope, and the actual journey of finding racing's Holy Grail without being crushed by inevitable disappointments along the way. Remember! If there are twelve horses in a race, eleven of them fail to win. If you're a staunch member of the Bear Bryant-Vince Lombardi philosophy that winning is the only thing, then racing can, and will, make you miserable.

You've got to be able to put today's loss behind you, take some solace from a good effort or focus on the reason for a bad effort, and then look ahead to the next time.

God gave me the perfect temperament for racing horses. One, I refuse to acknowledge disappointment. I may be blown away by a dismal performance for a couple of minutes, but by the time I've gone down to talk to the rider and the trainer, I'm looking ahead to the next time: "We'll put blinkers on him"..."She'll adore the turf"..."He wants to settle in stride and make a late run." The possibilities for rationalization are endless.

But after a period of giving that horse the benefit of the doubt ("After all, he's still a baby!!") do remember this: Just because you own him doesn't mean he has to be good. Everyone's child is not cut out to be a leader of the people.

Through the years, it has always amazed me to observe the great number of intelligent, talented, and super-successful people who come into Thoroughbred racing with the expectation — perhaps subliminal and probably not stated — that they're going to conquer the game, just as they did construction, banking, computers, retailing (*ad infinitum*, just take your pick!) back in Atlanta, Dallas, Seattle, Philadelphia, Sheboygan, etc., etc.

Believe me, many a Board Room Behemoth has been cut down to midget size by this game. No matter how fiendishly clever, analytical, or shrewd your route to stardom in your business, it is impossible to look into the heart of a horse or circumvent the myriad forms of bad luck that can plague a racehorse and horse races. The slightest act-of-God nuances can make for fame for one and failure for the other.

But really, there are two pretty sure ways to achieve success in racing. One is to overwhelm the game. In the past, players on the international stage have gone in, spent enormous sums, and practically cornered the market on truly prime equine prospects. People such as the Robert Sangster-John Magnier-Vincent O'Brien Irish Triumvirate.

In the 1970s and '80s, they bought just about every truly blue-chip, grade AA yearling colt that went through the auction ring. They had the crème de la crème market all to themselves...until the mighty Arab aristocracy — reeking with mystique — entered the fray.

Prince Khalid Abdullah and the Maktoum brothers, Sheikhs Mohammed, Hamdan, and Maktoum al Maktoum, all from a heritage that has for centuries appreciated and understood the racing of horses, started coming to the Keeneland and Saratoga sales. Their 747s set down at Blue Grass Field in Lexington for the first time in the early '80s, creating shock waves throughout the then entire 606 area code (and well beyond), and racing has never been the same. The Arabs, attended by droves of bright, young English advisers, immediately engaged the "Irish Mafia" in a bidding war that sent prices into the ionosphere, much to the delight — make that ecstasy — of the "good ol' boys" who were selling the Northern Dancer, Nijinsky II, Raise a Native, etc., yearlings.

Soon it became apparent that even the deep pockets of both groups could not accommodate the ridiculous prices of the time (one yearling — a fifteen-month-old youngster on whose back there had never sat a saddle — sold for $13.1 million!). The two sides developed an understanding that they would join forces on some young horses, or at least keep one another posted on targeted horses so as to achieve a sort of damage control. In time, the Sangster group became engrossed in other aspects of the business, leaving the Arabs pretty well in control. Soon the Maktoums, Abdullah, and various relatives had the top of the market virtually sewn up. By the 1990s they had created their own "factories" with their great racehorses and race fillies having gone to stud and now producing the Arabs' own homebreds.

Enter Michael Tabor, another Irishman and a prominent United Kingdom bookmaker. He joined forces with the brilliant Irish horseman Magnier (who earlier had helped invent the corner-the-market approach). These two, assisted by an all-star team of vets, bloodstock agents, trainers, and stud managers, plowed scores of millions of dollars into horse flesh, and they, like the Arabs, are now reaping bountifully from that which they have sown.

Here's how they figure: We'll spend about $35 million each year on, say, twenty-five yearlings — the best of the best. Let's say fifteen of them, despite their delicious pedigrees and stunning conformation, are, well, just horses. Fine. Cull them. BUT, five of the twenty-five should be superior racehorses that will make big money on the racetrack. In doing so, they'll become staggeringly valuable as breeding animals, commanding big stud fees, and producing offspring that will bring the same kind of money on the open market.

Then figure the other five of the original twenty-five are pretty good — not superstars but moderate stakes winners. This group, consequently, has significant value.

All in all, this normal case scenario is a viable money-making operation. In no way are these incredible yearling expenditures ridiculous, as they may seem at first blush.

However, to play this game, you'd better be able to come to the table with a couple hundred million!

What's the second "certain" way to achieve success in the horse business?

Get lucky: Buy a John Henry for $1,100 or a Seattle Slew for $17,500. Got the picture?

But what beckons to you at this point?

Do you yearn for the thrills and excitement of seeing your own colors in a race?

Do you want to shoot the moon, race a Kentucky Derby winner?

Do you want your own vehicle for gambling?

Do you secretly want the social wallop and status symbols that can go with owning a "stable of racehorses"?

Do you like the warm, fuzzy feeling of breeding horses, attractively embellishing those ten acres you've got at your place in the country?

Do you think you can make money breeding for the market?

Do you want to "pinhook" — buy weanlings or yearlings, and sell them as finished products as two-year-olds in training; or, in the case of the weanlings, sell them as yearlings ten months later?

Well, whatever your interest, niche, or motivation involving the sport and business of Thoroughbred racing…you'd better like horses. It's a wonderful endeavor, but not an easy one, and you're going to need to get some pleasure and satisfaction out of your association with the horse per se.

I can tell you that before I went into the horse business full time in 1973, I made my living in advertising, one of the most pressurized, fast-paced, nerve-wracking occupations in the history of commercial endeavor.

It was child's play compared with the horse business.

But, I fell in love with racehorses at an early age, and a time arrived when I just had to be closely associated with racing. With me, invention became the mother of necessity (more about business plans in an upcoming chapter).

I was bred to like horses; grew up on the subject. My grandfather, Dick Cothran, was a founding member of the New Orleans Jockey Club. He was a gentleman. And he was a gambler. He also had a seat on the New Orleans Cotton Exchange (a gamble if there ever was one), and among his offices was a large room with wire-service facilities connecting him to every major racetrack in America. You could pick up headphones and hear the "third at Belmont" or another set would provide the call of the "fifth at Churchill Downs." On Derby Day in 1934, while lunching in the old St. Charles Hotel with my grandfather, my mother (his daughter), and my father, the old boy gave me a dollar (not chicken feed back then) to bet on the Derby. He hinted that Cavalcade had a pretty decent shot. I won that bet, and the hook was firmly set when the Brookmeade runner romped home by two and a half lengths that afternoon.

My father, at that time a Coca-Cola bottler in Des Moines, Iowa, had horses, which I showed throughout the Midwest and East. In the late 1930s, I was champion amateur rider of Missouri, Nebraska, and Iowa.

Besotted with horses and strong drink, my dad sold his bottling franchise in 1940. With little real preparation, he decided to plunge (my word, not his!) into the Thoroughbred racehorse business. He bought a farm in Franklin, Tennessee, built a racetrack on it, added a full range of first-class accouterments, and we were in the horse business! He probably would have failed anyway, but the fact that World War II was only a year away certainly did not help.

With the horse's tail and rider's stomach retouched slightly, championship style is demonstrated.

In case you are too young to remember, many racetracks were closed during the early '40s (as non-essential wartime activities), and you couldn't GIVE a racehorse to someone, much less SELL one. My father, you see, was not exactly in a growth-oriented business.

By 1943, he was flat broke. But I had been practically living with racehorses for two years, and the romance had intensified.

I should point out here that I stumbled into racehorse ownership by means of creating the completely unorthodox vehicle of limited partnerships. And I was certainly no stranger to unorthodoxy.

It will perhaps do little to strengthen my literary credentials, but I do have the rare distinction of being one who never graduated from anything — grammar school, high school, or college, although I attended all of them.

My early career was one that charitably could be called "checkered." To use another euphemism, I was known as a rather high-spirited youth, or one who had not yet "found himself." If I had been a racehorse, I definitely would have been considered a "late bloomer." I wouldn't have broken my maiden until I was five, I would have spent much time on the "starter's list" (for horses that are unruly in the gate), and certainly I would have ended up a gelding — for reasons of general obstreperousness.

Until I was thirty, I bounced around from town to town, finding employment as an ambulance driver, master of ceremonies of a Florida water ski show, an apprentice mortician, tire salesman, valet parking attendant at a night club, newspaper reporter, and sports writer…and some other things best not mentioned.

I moved to Atlanta in 1950. I had been living in Huntington, West Virginia, and one night — after a period of intense revelry — I fell asleep with a lighted cigarette in my hand. The upshot was that I burned off the top floor of a rather large boarding house. Prompted somewhat by the displeasure of the other guests, and the disagreeable attitude of the proprietor, I decided shortly after the flames were extinguished that perhaps another town might offer more opportunities for a young man of my talents. Indeed, another REGION seemed to be indicated. I selected Atlanta as the lucky city.

I came to Atlanta with no money, some borrowed clothes (mine having perished in the boarding house blaze), and a bad reputation!

I got a job on the assembly line at the Chevrolet plant, and I toiled there for six months. After my shift ended each day, I would change into a dark blue business suit and call on advertising agencies, seeking a more glamorous form of employment. Finally, one agency became so impressed with my credentials, I was offered a job for $55 per week. I worked for several agencies in Atlanta and New Orleans, and on December 7, 1957, I became a member of Alcoholics

The inappropriately named Social Asset, my first partnership racehorse.

Anonymous, bringing my high-spirited nature under control. This caused my career to begin advancing at a more satisfactory rate. And, in 1964, my friend Jack Burton and I started our own advertising agency — Burton-Campbell, Inc., with headquarters in Atlanta. It flourished in a flourishing market, and soon — 1967 — I was able to own a racehorse by coercing a couple of pals to participate. They leaned heavily on my expertise, pitiful though it may have been at the time.

We bought and raced the bleakly endowed and completely uninspired Social Asset, whose only claim to fame was that she met a ghastly group of maidens at a very cheap racetrack and won in a four-horse photo, paying boxcar figures and making dubious history by being part of the largest daily double in the history of River Downs, near Cincinnati.

Social Asset whetted my appetite. So I went out and bought a big, fat, two-year-old colt who turned out to have a heart of pure hickory. His name was Memphis Lou, and he was one of those wonderful old horses you could stake your life on — IF you didn't get too ambitious. He ran at the $10,000 claiming level, and, boy, did he try! I had four partners in Memphis Lou, and they had the time of their lives. They told every human being who would listen about how much fun they were having.

Next, I caught "lightning in a jar." I went to the 1971 Hialeah two-year-old sale, and late in the session, when just about everyone had gone to the bar, I bought a filly for $5,000. She was smallish, had a crooked ankle, but she had a sharp look and came from one of the finest families in the *American Stud Book*. The bay filly was sired by Yorktown and her dam was Evening Off. We named her Mrs. Cornwallis. She won three stakes races, including the prestigious Alcibiades Stakes at Keeneland Race Course in Lexington, placed in four other stakes, and she was one of the top fillies of her generation.

In the winner's circle with Mrs. Cornwallis.

She put me in the horse business.

Mrs. Cornwallis was a good story, and the fact that she was owned by a limited partnership, unheard of at the time, made it an even better one. Much media attention was suddenly focused on me and Mrs. Cornwallis. Now we were rolling! I looked around one day in 1972, and I had eighteen horses and about forty-five investors. I thought I've either got to be in the horse business or the advertising business but trying to do both is becoming a little tricky.

So I burned my bridges! I sold my interest in the ad agency and went full tilt into the racehorse business. Ninety-nine percent of the people who knew about my decision thought I was a complete idiot. The one — and most important — exception was my wonderful, world-class wife Anne. She believed it — and practically everything I had done before and have done since — was a superb idea. She has had a starring role in "The Dogwood Story."

I started Dogwood Farm on 422 acres in West Central Georgia, about sixty miles southwest of Atlanta. That it succeeded is living testimony to the fact that energy and enthusiasm can overcome most obstacles!

Anne and I in our early Dogwood years.

THE QUEST FOR CLASS

You know, it is indeed startling when you consider that this gigantic industry and major spectator sport essentially revolve around the ability of a large four-legged animal to get from Point A to Point B faster than some other large four-legged animals! Fortunately, there is a little more to racing than that.

If winning is the objective, then the search for "class" is a key component of that quest. What is "class"? It is quality, guts, poise, character, courage…it's just — by God — CLASS. You know it when you see it. And what a wonderful thing it is when you're associated with it — in man or beast.

Good horses, class horses have always had the power to thrill and move the public. At the turn of century when Dan Patch, the great harness horse, would ship from track to track by rail, thousands would gather along the route just hoping to catch a glimpse of the great pacer as his car rumbled across the country. Man o' War was, and still is, a household name. He, along with Babe Ruth, Red Grange, Bill Tilden, and Jack Dempsey, is synonymous with a period of our history — the 1920s. Anyone who saw the mighty Secretariat win the Belmont Stakes (and thus the Triple Crown) by thirty-one widening lengths will never forget the majesty and sheer exhilaration of that big golden chestnut running machine. He was the epitome of the Thoroughbred racehorse.

What does that mean — "Thoroughbred"?

First, it doesn't mean purebred, although certainly the Thoroughbred is, in the most pristine sense. The Thoroughbred is a breed just as a Labrador retriever, or a Dachshund, or a Rottweiler is a breed of dog.

Every Thoroughbred that has started in a sanctioned race since 1873 has been painstakingly registered in the *American Stud Book*, maintained in the staid old offices of The Jockey Club in New York, and now in Lexington, Kentucky.

Thoroughbreds are eligible to be registered at birth (or foaling). They are photographed, their markings carefully detailed. Foal papers are then issued and will follow that animal for the rest of its days. The Jockey Club also must approve a horse's name from requests submitted by the owner. (An owner's first several choices for a name aren't always available.)

In very elementary terms, a Thoroughbred, then, is any horse whose pedigree is recorded in the *General Stud Book*, which was first printed in England in 1793.

Ours was established almost a century later. Interestingly, every horse ever recorded in the English *Stud Book*, and later, in the *American Stud Book*, traces to one of three stallions: the Byerley Turk, the Darley Arabian, or the Godolphin Arabian (or Barb, as he is sometimes known). In early England, breeders were developing horses for the sport of running. And, as it has been since the start of the endeavor, the participants were feverishly looking for "an edge." The Brits noticed that the Arabian horse, perfected by the hard-riding Bedouin sheikhs, had courage, refinement, and, while not very large, could run "a hole in the wind." They also could stay for incredibly long distances. Brisk trade in the importation of these fleet, tough animals sprung up in England. The foreign stallions were bred to the hardy and larger English stock, and John Weatherby soon legitimized the distinct breed with the *General Stud Book*.

Charles II, Turf historians agree, provided the impetus to create the Thoroughbred as a distinct breed primarily by establishing the King's Plate in Newmarket late in the 17th Century. The competition consisted of three heats for six-year-olds carrying 168 pounds for four miles! So Charles II may have been the sport's first racing secretary (the person responsible for setting the conditions of a race).

The breed flourished in popularity, and its prominence was centered in England for the first two centuries of its existence. But during the 19th Century, an increasing number of Thoroughbreds were exported to France, the United States, and South America, as those countries sought to upgrade their stock.

The first recognized racing in the United States took place in

Dogwood's Trippi, a typical example of a modern Thoroughbred.

Virginia, a hotbed of equine activity. With an agricultural-based economy, the early settlers were horsemen, and outdoor life and sports were important. But New York claimed the first formal racetrack, an installation known as New Market situated near the present Aqueduct Racetrack on Long Island. The Governor's Cup was the first prominent fixture on its calendar. Governor Richard Nicholls started the tradition of presenting useful items — punch bowls, candlesticks, plates, etc. — to the winners as trophies.

Before the Revolution, Maryland also was a prominent setting for racing and breeding, with historians listing more than twenty racing centers in the state. South Carolina, Pennsylvania, and New Jersey also had horse racing on their minds.

The importation of Thoroughbreds slowed to a crawl in 1770 due to severe unpleasantness between America and England. The Non-Importation Act stopped it cold. After the Revolutionary War, importation picked up again. In fact, so keen were American breeders, one bought a distinguished English Derby winner, Diomed, whose only drawback as a stallion was that he came across the pond at the rather advanced age of twenty! However, Diomed became a prominent stallion on the American scene, although certainly in the shank of his career. He was followed by the greatest sire of the 19th Century — Lexington, who was foaled in 1850 and later led the sire list sixteen times. During the Civil War, the state of Kentucky — where in Lexington (where else?) this horse plied his trade — was in the thick of the fighting, and both Yankees and Rebels were mighty quick to confiscate high-class equine bloodstock. When Robert Alexander, the master of Woodburn Stud, home of the highly coveted Lexington, got wind that the Yankees were on the advance and that his stallion — and all his racing stock for that matter — was in jeopardy, they were taken to barges on the Kentucky River and poled to the safety of Illinois. The Woodburn horses stayed there until after the war.

Lexington returned to the Kentucky bluegrass in 1865. He was to sire 533 offspring before his death in 1875. His most distinguished descendant was Man o' War.

The *American Stud Book* was started in 1873 through the efforts of Colonel Sanders D. Bruce, a Kentuckian who spent a lifetime researching American pedigrees. He maintained the book until 1896 when The Jockey Club, a centralized group formed to keep the sport organized, took over the task.

Renowned horseman James R. Keene had proposed an organization patterned after the English Jockey Club, whose members would be required to be more interested in the sport, per se, than conducting race meetings for monetary gain. The Jockey Club originally consisted of fifty members and seven stewards, and the current organization is structured the same way.

But the early Jockey Club, based in New York, ran racing with an iron hand. It wrote the rules, licensed jockeys and trainers, appointed officials, allotted racing dates, and, of course, acted as registrar of the Stud Book. Over the years the power of The Jockey Club has been reduced, and this writer feels racing is not the better for it. Individual states have their own politically appointed racing commissions. They write their own rules, set racing dates (often with no regard for what a neighboring state is doing), and issue licenses.

The first Jockey Club-registered foal crop was 3,000. In 1986, it had soared to 51,296. Currently, about 36,000 foals are registered annually. With the objective being top performance on the racetrack, the breed's best specimens have been sought after, and the result is that today's Thoroughbred is far superior to the original racehorses. Typically, he or she stands about sixteen hands. (A hand is four inches, so a sixteen-hand horse measures five feet, four inches at the withers, which is the area where the neck joins the back.) He looks athletic, with a deep, powerful shoulder, strongly engined hindquarters, and good musculature overall.

The writer is certainly prejudiced, but no equine specimen can compare in attractiveness to the Thoroughbred racehorse in racing trim. The five-gaited Saddle Horse may be prettier, the Quarter Horse more muscular, the Arabian more sculptured, but the natural beauty, the athleticism, and the look of class in the countenance of a racehorse when he comes into the paddock on the muscle, on his toes with racing on his mind and ready to fire…well, he will absolutely take your breath away!

But, alas, the racehorse of today is not as durable as were his ancestors of only several generations back, and we're not sure exactly why. Perhaps we've bred too much speed into them. There is certainly an accent today on shorter, faster races from three-quarters of a mile (six furlongs) to one and one-sixteenth miles (eight and a half furlongs). The mile and a quarter and mile and a half races that were quite popular in the 1930s, '40s, and '50s are rarities now.

When I first came on the racetrack, it was normal to work, or

Few sights can stir the soul as much as a Thoroughbred in racing trim.

breeze, a horse every four days. It was not unusual for a horse to run once a week. If you asked a horse for this sort of training or racing regimen today, you would be tarred and feathered. The average trainer now works a horse every six or seven days. The horse runs about once every three or four weeks. Even so, we have more unsoundness — more soft-tissue injuries, more bone chips in knees and ankles, more wind problems — than thirty or forty years ago. Some say this is because with year-round racing, horses don't go into winter quarters as they traditionally did years ago. Back then, racetracks were not open in January, February, and March, with the exception of South Florida, Louisiana, and Southern California.

There's a theory that the relatively foul atmosphere of today, especially in heavy industrial areas where many racetracks are located, has caused numerous horses to bleed from the lungs when put under optimum pressure in races. Others say the racetracks are harder, faster than they used to be, and when a 1,100-pound animal goes thirty-five to forty miles an hour with 115 pounds on its back, the chance of an injury greatly increases.

Whatever the causes, we have better veterinary techniques, better medication, and, in general, have made marvelous advances in procedures for taking care of injured animals. Nevertheless, Thoroughbred racehorses don't stay as sound as long despite easier training and racing schedules.

RACING'S ROCKY ROAD

The history of horse racing in this country has been on a roller coaster. As the new century heralds, we are on a significant upswing with some intriguing and attainable vistas in sight. There's never been a better time to be involved in horse racing...I THINK.

At the dawn of the 20th Century, the populace was captivated by horse racing. The best racehorses were known to every red-blooded American. This was true through most of the first half of the century

— with a fairly significant hiccup in the second decade of the 1900s, when for a brief period racing was outlawed for "moral" reasons. This didn't play nearly as well as Prohibition, and it wasn't long before horses were back in action (some of the better ones having gone across the Atlantic to compete in England and France, not necessarily to the complete pleasure of racing men in those countries). The anti-racing legislation was repealed.

Early wagering was conducted by bookmakers, with racetracks and purses not getting their appropriate share. However, the French system of "pari-mutuel" wagering gained great popularity in this country in the late 1930s, and in short time every racetrack adopted this system, in which the racetrack acts as agent. All the money bet on a race goes into a pool. The racetrack takes its cut — seven or eight percent, we'll say — using that money to pay itself for conducting the whole rigmarole and providing the purse structure to entice the horses to race there (the part we're keenly interested in). Another seven or eight percent goes to the state (the part that appeals to the legislature,

Durable Thoroughbreds like Exterminator (outside) once defined the breed.

as they use it to build roads, pay for education, and so on). The remaining funds go back to the winning bettors, the odds on the horses having been established mathematically depending on the popularity and the amount of play on the entry. An outstanding favorite might go off at 8-5, while a poorly regarded long shot might offer the scrumptiously attractive price of 50-1.

Not many decades ago, if you wanted to gamble, horse racing was just about "the only game in town," and throngs flocked to the racetracks. It was commonplace to have a crowd of 60,000 or 70,000 at Belmont Park or Santa Anita or Arlington Park on a big Saturday when Citation or Tom Fool or Kelso was running. Radio and early television covered the big races, and the public loved it.

But racing, complacent and myopic, turned a blind eye to the opportunity of becoming involved with, and, more importantly, controlling New York legislation that would legalize off-track betting parlors in that state. One could simply go to what would ultimately become a dark, filthy, uninviting "parlor" and bet on horse races. Feeling that this was a recreation that would go nowhere fast, the powers-that-were in the New York Racing Association ignored the legislation, and thus gave away much future revenue for horsemen. This important first step in the evolution of simulcasting set an extremely bad precedent, in that it was controlled essentially by politicians and run by bureaucrats. The OTB system in New York thus became a garden spot for graft, waste, and absence of sufficient, equitable revenue for the horsemen, the guys who were putting on the show.

Along with this problem, which triggered a decline in New York racing, long considered the crème de la crème of the sport, came a torrent of competition. Las Vegas was packing 'em in. Atlantic City followed suit and set up severe competition on the East Coast. Practically every state was clamoring for lotteries. And offshore bookmaking operations made it possible to bet on just about anything.

Suddenly racing was far from the only gambling game in town.

Then another devastating salvo hit our sport and business. Many other states besides Nevada and New Jersey legalized casino gambling and a plethora of casinos went into action. In various states, Native Americans were able to circumvent state and federal gambling regulations and establish casinos on tribal land. This distressing trend (to horse racing, that is) was followed by another shock wave. Slot machines, video poker, and other gaming devices began springing up in convenience stores, gas stations, and, finally, at some racetracks in states such as Louisiana, Delaware, and Iowa.

Surely, never before in any industry had there been such an onslaught of competition. And, remember this: Racing was poorly equipped to fight back and mount any sort of unified, defensive initiative. We're talking about an industry with no commissioner, no central league office, no one voice to speak for it. Instead, the entire industry was made up of numerous fragmented, uncooperative segments, none of which was particularly interested in cooperating with the other. And, in the face of this withering attack of competition, the state legislatures offered no relief to the beleaguered racetracks. Instead, some states welcomed gigantic river boats — owned by some of America's most powerful gaming organizations and docked in some cases right in the heart of town — offering them more advantageous tax incentives.

Is it any wonder that racetrack attendance and handles declined significantly?

The fall in business was offset, and then some, by the increase in simulcasting. Soon you could go to Delaware Park, or Fair Grounds in New Orleans, or Aqueduct, or Prairie Meadows near Des Moines and spend the afternoon seeing and betting on races throughout the nation, and, in some cases, overseas.

Racing was able to strengthen its purse structure, thanks to simulcasting, and by the late 1980s, we began seeing purses that were stag-

Hollywood Park's Casino.

gering for certain big races, and were awfully good for the regular cards offered every day. Never was there a better time to race horses.

So while racing was troubled enough that some of the smaller tracks folded their tents, the game, once America's leading spectator sport and now struggling for space on the sports pages, soldiered on, making surprisingly good progress.

THE NTRA — RACING'S SAVIOR?

In the mid-1990s, an enterprising and persistent advertising man named Fred Pope came up with a plan to establish a "league office" that would control racing and fund a significant marketing strategy that would put racing back in the limelight as the status sport it once was. His plan had merit but did not really get off the ground until John Gaines, one of the brainiest men in this or any other industry (he conceived the idea of the Breeders' Cup), became interested and sold many of racing's leaders on establishing the National Thoroughbred Association. One hundred men and women each volunteered $50,000, and the seed money was there. A hotshot sports marketing firm in Atlanta was engaged to come up with a master plan, elaborating and expanding on Pope's original idea. From this nucleus came the National Thoroughbred Racing Association. The Jockey Club, Keeneland Race Course, Oak Tree Racing Association at Santa Anita, and the Breeders' Cup joined forces with the fledgling association, and for the first time in history, Thoroughbred racing had a central, unified voice. Its mission is to increase public awareness, racing's fan base, pari-mutuel handles, and purses. NTRA was able to hire Tim Smith as its commissioner and CEO. This exceedingly well-qualified "live wire" has considerable experience in television and a sports background with national golf and tennis organizations.

The NTRA has thus far done a commendable job of funding and forming a cohesive advertising-marketing program, with some, but not too many, recalcitrant segments of the racing industry as non-supporting participants. Its national program includes an ambitious advertising campaign, the goal of which is to promote the glamour of horse racing and depict the desirability of spending a day at the racetrack. But its vital "hole card" is a national, interactive television network that will enable in-home wagering on horse races throughout the United States.

NATIONAL THOROUGHBRED RACING ASSOCIATION

This is a program that can put racing back in the "catbird seat." It is a great testimony to racing that it has survived and grown in some ways during devastatingly disadvantageous market conditions. Most of racing's leaders are bullish on the future. Business at the tracks is up, national awareness of racing as a choice for a day or night of entertainment has increased, and the price of horses, long considered one important barometer of the sport, is higher than ever before.

Racing has been around for a long time. Perhaps it is simplistic to say it, but one can't help but be encouraged by the fact that the racing of horses has charmed and attracted such a diverse cast of characters as Queen Elizabeth, Winston Churchill, J. Edgar Hoover, Wayne Gretzky, Magic Johnson, M.C. Hammer, Reba McEntire, George Strait, Berry Gordy, Buddy Ryan, Bill Parcells, Rick Pitino, Burt Bacharach, Tim Conway, Fred Astaire, Bing Crosby, Sam Huff, George Steinbrenner, the Aga Khan, and the various Arab princes, along with some of the families that have played an important part in the development of our country — the Whitneys, du Ponts, Mellons, Vanderbilts, Phippses, Carnegies, and many others.

Any sport with these credentials will continue to survive and flourish.

INVENTION, THE MOTHER
OF NECESSITY

Have a business plan. I repeat: Have a business plan. But do keep in mind that the "business" involves 1,000-pound animals that cannot talk, are fractious to put it mildly, and have no interest whatsoever in striving to meet your projections. The only conceivable way you can do a pro-forma in your business plan and project income is to use a big ZERO. Anything else would be irresponsible.

When we present our Dogwood partnerships to prospects, our material is accompanied by a two-year pro-forma, and the estimated expenses and tax deductions are predicated on the horse's earning nothing. You, too, should budget in this manner.

There are business plans, and then there are business plans. Let me tell you about a "doozie."

After hearing me speak at one of the very worthwhile Thoroughbred Owners and Breeders Association (TOBA) seminars, a certain gentleman decided he was interested in becoming involved in one of Dogwood's racing partnerships. He seemed to be a nice, terribly enthusiastic, rather intense fellow, with lots of his own ideas, and a penchant for numbers and psychobabble. But his interest in the actual horses seemed to be secondary.

We made a date for him to come visit our operation in Aiken. I was at the barn on the appointed hour and day, and we were going to show him those young horses we were currently syndicating.

He and his wife drove in. He burst out of the car, strode over to the walking ring, and while we were shaking hands, with his eyes ablaze and literally quivering with excitement, he thrust a sheaf of papers in a manila folder toward me and asked, "Do you want to see my business plan?"

I murmured something to the effect that it might be better to see the horses first. The six he could choose from were circling the walking ring around our big live oak, riders up, and ready to cross over to the Aiken Training Track to be inspected.

He shot a cursory glance at the yearlings and persisted, "Let me show you how I arrived at some of my projections." Then he opened up the folder with trembling fingers as several sheets floated earthward.

"Look," I said rather firmly, "let's go see these horses train and then we can go over to the office and talk about any of them you like and discuss any details."

The horses did train for him. And when not babbling about various equine organizations he was going to join, racing luminaries he had met or heard, or other foolish minutiae about his business plan, I suppose he actually saw them. But their looks and performances were not very high on his scale of interest.

At the office he became more frantic by the moment and was somewhat agitatedly thrusting the beloved "B.P." in front of me. I feebly protested that it was really of little benefit to anyone for me to see his business plan, but I was defeated and did look at it.

This man had projected that he would invest $30,000 in the purchase of a share in a yearling, he would pay $4,000 in expenses the first (yearling) year, or what was left of it, $9,415 the second year, and $12,357 the third year. BUT — get this — the horse (which horse?) would gross $76,413 as a two-year-old and then $136,942 in the more productive three-year-old year.

With eyes glazing over, I — and a couple of my associates — listened to him drone on nonstop for ten minutes. Finally, I held up my hand and stopped him.

"Mr. Blank," I said, "you and I are not compatible. You don't have the vaguest interest in my horses, but your business plan has already figured out how much money one of them (which one?) is going to make. The chemistry between us is not right. You're going to drive me crazy, and you'll hate me as a result. Let's just forget this whole idea; but thanks so much for coming down here to see our operation."

Unfortunately, as it turned out, his nice wife took over the badly eroding conversation. She suggested a system of communication that would be funneled through her if all else failed, and we went ahead with our partnership transaction. As it is with most bad-vibe beginnings of this sort, our venture was not a happy one. The chemistry was bad.

Here was a guy who loved the "plan" but didn't care that much about the "business."

You certainly would like to make a profit when you go into the horse business. And, if you do make money with Thoroughbred racehorses, the government will surely take the position that you're going to pay income taxes on the profit. Therefore, if you lose money, you are entitled to deduct those losses from your tax liability at the end of the year. This practice is quite well established. This is the way it has been done for a long, long time with little wrinkles in the arrangement introduced from time to time. However, none of us is completely at ease with the predictability of the IRS. Ergo, one excellent reason for a business plan before you take the plunge. But, I still say that other than for cosmetic reasons, projecting income is an exercise in futility.

Your business plan should cover the following points:

• Determine the type of equine venture you will undertake. Leaning on the reasons outlined in Chapter One, state at the beginning whether you'll breed to race, breed for the market, purchase to race, and if so, will you claim horses, buy weanlings, yearlings, two-year-olds, or some combination of approaches.

• An important, logical option to consider is a partnership, an ideal way for the neophyte to "go to school." These opportunities now abound in the industry, and partnerships include racing, breeding, or even "pinhooking" — the purchasing of young stock (raw material) for the purpose of reselling it at a later auction, presumably at a profit.

• Project expenditures. We'll cover typical costs later in the book, and, of course, your adviser(s) can help with this. Decide that you are going to invest a certain amount each year and for how many years. Three-year plan? Five years? No limit?

• Cover the details of your insurance program. With whom will you insure? Will you cover your operation with general liability insurance? Will you then cover your livestock with general mortality insurance? If you are going to breed, will you buy live foal insurance, and if you own stallion shares, will you purchase fertility insurance?

• Expenditures must address such items as purchase price parameters; board, training, or lay-up costs (a lay-up is a racehorse recuperating from injury or getting a break from training); breeding fees; transportation costs; veterinary care; farrier; nominations for stakes or sales; administration expenses; travel and entertainment; and accounting and general consultation fees.

• Where will the business operate? Will your racing or breeding business function regionally, or will you compete or trade nationally or internationally?

It is best to put this on paper in the most official-looking way. This serves two purposes. One, it makes you look at it and pay attention to it. Two, it impresses anyone else who needs to look at it — the

IRS, for instance.

Determine how you will structure your operation. Is it a sole proprietorship, a corporation, a limited liability company, or a general or limited partnership? Each offers certain advantages. Perhaps you'll need to sit down with a lawyer or tax accountant before deciding.

Starting with the purchase of this book, keep track of every expenditure, and from now on save all the bills and receipts. This will include all travel to sales, seminars, races, barn and farm visits, and educational materials. Carefully document dates and hours, remembering that no detail is too small. Being in the horse business is going to exact its economic toll, so be sure you are in a position to ease the pain by being able to defend these expenditures with the tax people.

Farm visits and stallion shows can give prospective owners an inside look.

One very important question that one hears frequently is "How many hours a year must I spend before I am officially considered (by the IRS) in the horse business?" Well, 500 hours is the official magic number. Depending on other circumstances, it could be less. It's a gray area.

The more hours you can log and the more documentation and paper trails you can throw at them, the better tax haven your operation will be.

Done properly, your horse operation is not going to encounter any problems with the IRS. That's not nearly as big a bugaboo as it's cracked up to be, so we'll quit talking about it for awhile.

When I counsel you to have a business plan, do as I say, not as I did.

My business plan just happened, evolved. I saw an opportunity to make my living in the horse business, and I seized it firmly by the throat and never let up on it!

When I began thinking hard about building Dogwood Farm, I realized that the revenue from syndicating horses — at least at the volume I was doing at the time — was not going to be enough. But I wanted to be in the horse business. So, as I paraphrased, "invention became the mother of necessity."

I had business plan on top of business plan, each one designed to augment the already viable but not sizable enough income stream from forming partnerships. Each time I completed what I thought was the big breakthrough, I would write up my plan, make my projections (perhaps somewhat slanted to justify the scheme), catch a plane to Kentucky, and present my newest thoughts to my mentor.

My mentor, John A. Bell, is probably one of the most respected and knowledgeable men in the horse business. Owner of a leading insurance agency in Lexington at the time, he had been recommended to us as a source for insuring our horses. I took up a great deal of this gentleman's time. He showed enormous patience in listening to one ambitious idea after another.

One of the straightest of the straight shooters, John would listen politely and then tell me precisely why my latest idea was flawed, to put it kindly. I couldn't have had a better adviser, but I had no intention of following his good guidance. My mind was made up, and I didn't want to be confused with the facts. Because he was not telling me what I wanted to hear, I decided to switch insurers. I'm sure it was the best thing that had ever happened to John Bell!

I changed to another highly respected insurance agency headed up by Bill Carl, who has been a good friend for a quarter of a century (and so has John Bell, by the way). But I probably knew myself well enough at that point not to burden either myself or my new contact by soliciting advice other than on the subject of insurance.

At this point, my battle cry might have been: ENERGY AND ENTHUSIASM WILL OVERCOME STUPIDITY AND BAD JUDGMENT.

So, it was full speed ahead to launch Dogwood Farm. If there were a plan, it was that I knew — based on the volume of the past year — I could form enough partnerships to account for perhaps seventy percent of the nut. And, hopefully, I could draw enough non-Dogwood horses to break and rehabilitate to take care of the rest of the expenses and maybe make some money. Maybe I thought the "little fairies" would come in and help take care of the problem!

I donated 422 acres my wife and I owned to the newly formed Dogwood corporation, and I recruited nine other investors from the Atlanta area. Each put up $35,000 (since then I have bought out all but one, Dr. Harper Gaston). In the winter of 1973 we started a rather ambitious construction project that included a six-furlong racetrack (I don't ever want to build another one), two training barns with twenty-six stalls in each, four houses for key employees, a dormitory for young girl riders and grooms, a recreation building, miles of black fences, an office; and, on property that was adjacent to the training area, we built two barns for lay-ups, and a guest house. Oh, it was first class! You could have picked it up and moved it to Old Frankfort Pike in Lexington, and it would have fit in perfectly.

When we first started the construction program, in a rainy period in the dead of winter, a friend of mine from Lexington, Jimmy Drymon, who had for many years managed the famous Domino Stud, was visiting his daughter in Atlanta. I invited Jimmy to ride down to the site near Greenville, Georgia, and let me show him around. In a steady drizzle, we rode through the muddy fields and I proudly pointed out that the racetrack would go here, and the two barns would go there, and that I planned to do this and that. We got stuck in the mud a couple of times, and, all in all, it was not a terribly stimulating day for a visiting farm manager, who was probably anxious to get away from farms and horses for a few days.

At the end of the tour, I eagerly looked over at my passenger and

The Campbell family — Cot, Anne, Lila, and Cary — during the early Dogwood years.

asked, "Well, what do you think, Jimmy?" I was brimming with excitement over what I knew would be an encouraging verdict.

Jimmy looked at me, blew his nose, and muttered, "I think you ought to start the car, let's get out of this mud hole, and get the hell back to Atlanta."

Well, anyway, it did look good the following fall. In September, when I got ready to go to the Keeneland September yearling sale, which is like a national convention in the racehorse business, Dogwood had a population of two horses, both unsyndicated yearlings I had bought at the Keeneland July sale, and about twenty-five employees waiting expectantly for action.

During Dogwood's corporate history, which has spanned more than twenty-five years, we have had four farm managers. The last two were wonderful. The first two were not, although all four have been superb horsemen.

At this juncture, the first one was in place. He was a rather irascible older man, who had been one of England's greatest jockeys. While he was known to be a gifted breaker of yearlings and an all-around fine horseman, his career had not exactly taken off — perhaps because he was "bad to drink whiskey," a problem I quite well understood but did not need in an employee, especially at this crucial stage of the fledgling farm's life.

This gentleman (whom we will call George) and I set off for Lexington, seeking to make known that Dogwood was in existence and we were ready to accept horses to break, train, and/or rehabilitate. Our pitch was to be that we offered the finest facilities, personnel, and climate, milder than Kentucky and not as hot as Florida, and that we were right on the main transportation routes between New Orleans and New York and Chicago and Florida…and, furthermore, we were mighty anxious to please.

I don't know that this message was received with much excitement at the fall sale. But try we did — especially me; I don't think George's heart was in it!

As we made the rounds, buttonholing every yearling buyer who would give us a brief audience, the first score came. I'll never forget it, and God bless the kind man who provided us with this accomplishment.

Brereton C. Jones, later to become governor of Kentucky, was a very young man who had a farm in Woodford County and he, too, was trying to get started in the horse business. He and I had become friendly. Brerry came up to me at the sale (while I was standing around trying to look busy, accompanied by the somber George), and he asked, "Do you think you might have room for two yearling fillies at your farm?" I started to scream out, "ARE YOU KIDDING!"

Instead, I suavely struck a thoughtful pose, and looking as if he had created a terrible problem for me, I said, "For you, I think we could handle a couple more," and looked over at George as if for affirmation.

Whereupon George glared at Brerry and blurted out, "Well, I hope they've been vaccinated for equine encephalitis, because, by God, we've got a hell of a lot of it in Georgia!"

We got the horses, but at that point I think it was clear that George's days were numbered.

We got a few more clients out of that sale, but it was tough sledding. I had brochures extolling the virtues of Dogwood, and, of course, I was very proud of them and wanted everyone in Central Kentucky to read and relish every word. At the sale I would make sure that an adequate supply was available in neat little stacks at strategic points throughout the Keeneland sales pavilion. Furthermore, leaving no stone unturned, I visited the leading hostelries of the city (the Campbell House, Springs Motel, and others) and asked permission to leave a supply on registration desks. I would revisit these sites periodically, optimistically counting the remaining ones to determine the demand for this literature. Occasionally, I would find that these precious brochures had been thoughtlessly swept off the counters and onto the floor. Horror of horrors!

Dogwood bought several horses at the sale for syndication, and some other benevolent souls sent two or three down. When we got back to Georgia, other young horses from the area began filtering into our training barn.

One we could have done without came following a phone call from a "Mr. House" from some little town in Alabama. He was a good old country boy, and he informed me in his call that he had a five-year-old stallion that had never been broken, and if he could get him on the trailer, he wanted to bring him to Dogwood. This did not sound like a very promising prospect, and I had a feeling we were going to more than earn our $35 per diem, but I said, "Wonderful, bring him on!"

"By the way, this is one of the fastest horses I've ever seen in my life," Mr. House announced.

"How can you tell that if he's never been broken?" I asked.

"Well, hell, I sic the dog on him and he'll run him for three miles, and he can fly!"

This was our clientele.

That fall we had enough horses to fill up one twenty-six-stall barn, so cosmetically we were looking pretty good to visitors. We did a lot of entertaining at the farm, and, as I expected, just having a good-looking, first-class Thoroughbred horse farm in the Atlanta area — a rarity — was quite a boon in moving shares in our partnerships.

We had what were called "Breezing Parties" where we would invite fifty or sixty visitors to the farm and expose them to our wares. The guests would arrive about two o'clock on a Sunday. We would walk them around the barn for awhile; then, with liquid refreshments in ample supply, we would bring out the young horses we were seeking to syndicate. Armed with a bull horn to help me hold their attention, I would enumerate the attractive features of the horses and the partnership details. It worked quite well, and afterward when we repaired to the guest house for more liquid refreshments and serious (it was

The author at one of Dogwood's "Breezing Parties."

hoped) discussions about participation, we usually did some business.

The term "Breezing Party" was sometimes confused with "breeding party," and this may have accounted for the good turnouts that we had! Although people began to understand that the term "breeze" meant a sharp speed drill of a racehorse in training, word did spread through Atlanta and environs that this was a pretty pleasant way to spend a Sunday afternoon.

At this point, one crystal clear truism was established: If Dogwood was going to make it — and it looked increasingly promising — it was probably because we were in Atlanta, and NOT in Kentucky. Putting a Thoroughbred horse farm in this non-horse, but populous and very affluent southern city, really made a lot of sense. We were THE horse operation in that part of the country. Had we started Dogwood in Lexington, teeming with long-established famous old farms, we would have been a "lost ball in the high weeds."

Things were looking up, but still we needed more outside (non-Dogwood) clients for training.

The following summer the big breakthrough came...but not without its price!

One of the leading trainers in North America was a man named Frank Merrill. He had a lot of horses, and he campaigned in Canada in the summer and went to Florida in the winter. He had been sending his young horses every fall to a farm in Ocala for breaking and early training. I had targeted Frank as an ideal client for Dogwood — lots of horses controlled by only one man, and potentially top-class racehorses that could cast a nice reflection on Dogwood, if they turned out to be high-profile stars.

For some time I had been talking to Frank about giving us his business. I knew he liked the idea, but he was reluctant to leave his Ocala connection. I thought we were making headway, however, and it was a project that was heavy on my mind.

One day in July of 1974, I was due to fly to England to look at a couple of older horses in training that I was thinking of buying. I was at the Dogwood office in Atlanta, had my bags with me, and was set to fly out on a late afternoon plane to London. I got a phone call that morning, and it was Frank Merrill. He said he wanted to talk to me about the training arrangement. Would it be possible for me to fly up to Canada that day and have dinner and discuss the matter? The timing was not convenient, but I absolutely had to go.

I quickly rearranged my plans. My secretary booked me on a flight to Buffalo, leaving later that morning. Frank said I should fly to Buffalo because the current Canadian race meeting was at Ft. Erie, right across the border, and we would spend the night at his cottage near Ft. Erie.

Fine. I made arrangements to fly to England the next day from Canada. It was a hot day, but since I was going to England where the weather is usually cool, I had on a fairly heavy suit. And since I was going to be in England a week, I had packed a big bag, a garment bag, and had my briefcase with me. I also had no time to go to the bank. I only had $21 dollars on me, but I knew Frank would meet me and I could cash a check through him in Canada.

I arrived in Buffalo at 2:30 p.m., but I didn't see Frank or any emissary. My bags came up, but Frank did not. I hung around until about 3 p.m., and then I thought I'd better call his place in Toronto. I got his wife and she said she was sure he must be on the way. "Be patient. You know Frank, he's always late (heh heh!)," she offered helpfully. At 3:30 I called again. Frank's wife told me to catch a cab to the cottage. She promised he'd either be there or would arrive shortly after I did.

So I lugged my bags to the curbside, hailed a cab, and asked the driver how much it would be to take me to 532 Dalton Road in Ft. Erie. Eighteen dollars. Close, but that's OK. Off we trekked to Frank's cottage. I gave the driver twenty bucks since he helped haul the baggage up to the door, and it was hotter in Canada than it was in Atlanta. I had one dollar left…and was a long way from home.

I had no choice but to sit down on the steps in the hot sunshine and hope and pray that Frank showed. I was hot and dejected at this point, and I'm sure I looked the part, sweating heavily in my cavalry twill suit.

In the yard next to his small house, four small children were playing rather noisily. They noticed me, of course, and observed, I am sure, that I was in a foul mood. After awhile it dawned on them that I might somehow fit into the afternoon's recreational activities.

Soon a rock came whistling over my way! With all four crouched behind bushes in the yard, a rock barrage then started in earnest. This was definitely too much!

Summoning up my sternest demeanor, I warned, "Now, see here, you children, this is going to have to stop. We're not going to have any rock throwing!!" Like hell we're not! Now it was like the barrage at Omaha Beach.

At this juncture, one of them yelled out, "Hi there, old Poo Poo Man," a term which seemed to capture the fancy of all the combatants.

Picture this. Here I am on a sizzling hot day, burdened by some very heavy baggage, one dollar in my pocket, no transportation, no idea where any acquaintances are, in a strange land with four tiny children throwing rocks and screaming "Poo Poo Man" at me.

This may have been the low ebb of my life.

I decided to seek a less hostile atmosphere. I picked up my bags and struggled up the street, to what destination I did not know. After about a block I was ringing wet. A pickup truck came by, and when I dropped my bags and began waving frantically, he stopped. I told him I was looking for a motel and he said he was going by one about a mile away — the best news I had heard all day long. He took me there, I checked in with my credit card, and things began to look up, relatively speaking.

After numerous phone calls to his connections, I finally talked to Frank later that night. He seemed only vaguely aware that he had caused me some slight degree of inconvenience. Showing remarkable restraint, I pleasantly made arrangements to meet him at his barn in the morning. We talked, and perhaps in a fit of remorse (although I doubt it), he agreed to send me twenty horses to train.

He continued to send me horses for some years after that. But I DID pay a price — too much of one, I thought at one point.

Get Good Advice

Depending on what phase of the horse business you're going to tackle, you are going to need certain advisers or suppliers or sources. Almost every situation is unique, and you'll use common sense in developing your team.

If you are contemplating a rather grandiose entrance into racing (and more power to you if you are), then you're going to need "varsity" players and specialists at every position. By the same token, if you plan a very modest entry, you certainly don't need a sledge-hammer to drive a tack.

And here's a very important point: This is supposed to be fun! You would like to make money. Sure! And you want to be able to write off your losses if you don't. But the most important consideration is that this venture is supposed to put a little zest in your life. Fun is what it's all about!

So, make sure the chemistry is right when you make a connection. Hook up with people you like because life's too short — and this game has too many downs between the ups — not to make the journey with someone you're fond of.

Many years ago, while considering sending some horses to a certain trainer in New York, I asked Harvey Pack, a veteran and very erudite racing commentator, "What do you think about So and So as a trainer?" Harvey shrugged his shoulders and answered, "He's no better or worse than the average...but he's a hell of a lot of fun." If all things are equal, or close to it, then crank fun or compatibility into the equation.

If you're going to buy weanlings, yearlings, two-year-olds, brood-mares, or older horses in training at a sale, then you'd better get your-self a bloodstock agent.

The Blood-Horse magazine annually publishes a thick but easily referenced tome (*The Source*) that lists all the bloodstock agents in your neck of the woods. Of course, if you're going to the Keeneland sale in Lexington and you live in Perth Amboy, New Jersey, chances are it makes sense to confine your search to the Central Kentucky area where their number is plentiful indeed. Or, if you're going to buy at the Ocala Breeders' Sales in Florida, perhaps you should look over the list from Marion County. And it may make more sense to get the bloodstock agent before you attend a sale, and let him or her tell you

Consider retaining an agent if you plan to buy horses at auction.

what the appropriate sales venue would be for the acquisitions you have in mind.

If you have no one specifically in mind, then I would call several. Lean heavily on instinct; then get references and check them out. Feel free to call the Thoroughbred Owners and Breeders Association in Lexington for help. Certainly they're not going to tell you whom to use, but they will give you guidance in how to go about smoking the person over. This organization has excellent staff, which is there for that purpose — to help people get involved in racing.

One of the first parameters to discuss with a potential bloodstock agent is how much money you want to spend. Make sure the agent wants your business. If he's a guy with orders to spend $3 million for ten yearlings for a billionaire in Chicago, he's not going to turn cartwheels over picking out a nice yearling filly for you to the tune of $15,000. But there are good, capable people who will want that business.

How do you compensate a bloodstock agent? Only one logical, ethical way: He or she gets five percent commission on what you buy; he doesn't get five percent from the seller and another five percent from the buyer. Only the buyer; if he's offered the other, he should tell you about it.

Believe me, after you've seen firsthand the work that goes into selecting and purchasing horses at a sale, you'll understand being a bloodstock agent is no "gravy train," at least not on a modest level. Many of them have ancillary sources of income. They may have insurance agencies or provide services on their farms for boarding, breaking, training, or rehabilitation. So some of them offer sort of a one-stop service center. Nothing wrong with that as long as everyone has a clear understanding from the start. And this brings me to an appropriate place to make a very good point.

If you've bought this book, chances are you're serious about becoming some sort of racehorse owner. So you've got some significant discretionary funds — or should have! — and that means you've almost got to be a practical, intelligent, successful person, so don't let your mentality be insulted when I make this point…because, believe me, it is a valid point.

Because a racing venture is ordinarily undertaken for fun, pleasure, and excitement, even the most intelligent people can — absolutely without knowing it — fall into a rather troublesome little trap of thinking "This is not the same commercial world in which I've been operating. We're all in this in the spirit of companionship and fellowship. The idea of you charging me, or making yourself a profit, is unseemly!!!"

I have had seasoned business people express surprise and concern to me when told of the markup on one of our horses being syndicated. They would never have blinked an eye over a similar, or greater, markup on clothing, an automobile, or a shipment of steel. The fact that we're talking about a four-legged animal whose main *raison d'e-tre* is recreation and pleasure, makes charges from the vendor or supplier go down hard.

Almost thirty years ago — about the time I was driving John Bell to distraction with one enthusiasm-driven scheme after another — it became clear to me that my hometown of Atlanta was not exactly overrun with tax specialists who knew anything about the racehorse business. I decided that I needed a tax accountant who knew the ins and outs of this rather complicated business.

I went to Lexington for an appointment with one of the leading equine tax gurus in the country — Rex Potter & Associates. Because I was a peewee client if there ever was one, they assigned my business to a young new accountant, Nelson Radwan. My association with Radwan to this day has been flawless, and this man has seen to it that we have never strayed from the straight and narrow path in our important quest for a happy relationship with the IRS. He has his own firm now — one of the largest in Kentucky — and it is, in my opinion, the leading horse accounting firm in the country.

Many accounting firms can identify potential problems, but Nelson

Radwan and his people have taken on the role of SOLVING any and all problems. His advice, technical and practical, has been invaluable in our success.

So generally, I advise you to retain the services of a tax accountant who is experienced in horse matters. If your participation is going to be quite modest for some time, then remaining with your present (non-horse oriented, we presume) accounting firm may make more sense. But if your involvement is likely to be pretty significant, then life will likely be smoother if your equine fiscal matters are in the hands of someone who has been to the wars.

There are, of course, other very fine firms of this ilk in other horse-concentrated areas. Here again, The Blood-Horse's *The Source*, TOBA, and state racing associations can help steer you in the right direction.

You were advised in our discussion of business plans to account painstakingly for your horse expenditures and document thoroughly your involvement in the business. Now be sure you turn over this information to an outfit that knows what to do with it.

The important things for you to know here and now are pretty basic:

• Any horse under two years of age must be depreciated in seven years. Older horses — for racing — can be depreciated in three. That applies to any horse that has had its second calendar birthday. Broodmares and stallions, twelve years old or less — seven years depreciation; more than twelve — three years depreciation.

• Any expenses necessary to maintain your horses, and run your horse business, are fully deductible.

• You and your accountant, influenced by the amount of time you spend tending to racehorse matters, the scope of your operation, and the extent of your personal chutzpah, will decide whether you will consider yourself "active" or "passive." If it is the former, you will take your losses in the year in which they occur. If it is to be the latter, you will take any losses (and we're talking about partnerships and limited liability entities here) at the termination of the endeavor.

Most of you are going to be far more in need of accounting expertise (assuming that your entry into the horse business is not of major proportions) than you will be in need of legal help.

That was not true in my case because I was engaged in forming partnerships, and many legal ramifications had to be addressed. I had the good fortune early in the game — even before I went into the horse business — to have a personal attorney in Atlanta who was young, available, and smart as a whip. His name is Kimbrough Taylor, and he is now a key player in one of the largest law firms in America. He learned the racehorse syndication game with me (slightly ahead of me, maybe!) and much of what is being done in this country today in the way of legal vehicles conveying racing and breeding partnerships was masterminded by Kim Taylor. I owe him a great debt of gratitude because — like the aforementioned Nelson Radwan — he not only identified problems, he provided solutions for them. Furthermore, he had a client who was not noted for "sweating the small stuff," and many times this man firmly insisted that I not do something, or at least do it a certain way. He understood that I wanted to deal with the horses and not with what I considered legalistic niggling. In fact, so great did my desire become to simplify legal proceedings in our partnerships that I changed from doing limited partnerships to general partnerships…but more about that later.

If you must ponder what form of legal entity will carry your banner forward into the racehorse campaigns, then you probably will need to consult an attorney. If you go into a partnership, or have any sort of contract to consider and sign, then you might sleep better if your lawyer has looked it over. If he's a lawyer worth his salt, he will inevitably find fifteen things about it that he would like to change.

Lawyers have enough trouble with their image nowadays without my adding to it, but it is germane to remind you that attorneys have a strong inclination to keep reinventing the wheel. And, believe me, when the subject is racehorses, and if they are unfamiliar with that world, they can worry the situation to death. Therefore, depending on the scope of the project, do give serious consideration to going to a good firm that has already gone to school on the subject and understands the practicalities.

As you can imagine, in the early days of Dogwood while we were pioneering what was then a radical approach to owning racehorses, accountants and lawyers representing prospective clients drove me absolutely crazy. In fact, so intense was my frustration with their automatic and incessant negativism with my product — a racehorse partnership that was being painstakingly presented as a highly speculative, tax deductible, pleasure-oriented venture — that I had designed (tongue-in-cheek, of course) a tombstone with a suitable epitaph.

It read: "Here lies W. Cothran Campbell. He wasn't much, but at least he wasn't a damned accountant!" It did not prove to be amusing in all quarters.

The "adviser" not dealt with yet in this book is, of course, the trainer.

Whatever phase of the horse business you tackle, this person is going to have some sort of influence on your life. If you're going to go into racing, the trainer will be a gigantic factor.

If, say, you are going to breed and then sell your yearlings annually at the auction sales, chances are a trainer will have had, to some extent, an influence on how profitable your "crop" turned out to be. Sometimes a public trainer is given a budget by his client and simply told to go to the sale and buy "five or six nice yearlings." In this scenario, he's the sole decision maker on what horses are bought. Quite often, a trainer will accompany his client to the sale, and in this case, he's at least a dominant factor in the purchasing decision.

Within the context of discussing advisers, there are two whose functions can overlap when it comes to counseling you on the acquisition of horses. And they are the bloodstock agent and, of course, the trainer. Supposedly, they are both accomplished horsemen. But the bloodstock agent's living stems essentially from buying and selling horses. And, prior to the yearling and two-year-old sales, he spends many hours poring over catalogs, checking statistics and inspecting horses. That is the crux of his job.

On the other hand, the trainer's job is to train racehorses. BUT — and it's a big BUT — he has a vested interest in recruiting talent for his barn. Most trainers live and die on their ability to attract and keep owners. No owners, no horses.

I suggest this: If you are contemplating a rather modest entry into racing and expect to buy one or two or three yearlings or two-year-olds, then it might make more sense to select a trainer first (based, of course, on the requisites of chemistry, reputation, and size of operation). You'll explain to him that you want to spend around X dollars on three yearlings and determine his interest and availability in going to the sale with you and doing the legwork in the selection process. By the way, his interest and availability will increase in direct proportion to the dollar amount you plan to spend! As well it should.

If Trainer Jones is going to train the horses for you, it's helpful if he's had a part in the selection process. If you're buying yearlings, the young horses will be sent to a farm (probably one with which the trainer is comfortable) to receive their rudimentary training, and then turned over to Trainer Jones six months later when they're ready to go the races and "do their number." If you're buying two-year-olds, they could go straight to his training barn at the racetrack.

So, in modest programs, the trainer might fit in more practically than the bloodstock agent.

But if you're going to make a sizable splash at the sale, then the bloodstock agent should be brought on board to do the organizational work. The horses would be turned over to the trainer later on, your bloodstock person having helped you choose the training farm and, maybe, the selection of a trainer closer to the time when his services will be needed.

Or perhaps at the sale you would have a selection team of blood-stock adviser AND trainer. If your undertaking is large enough, the two of them will certainly make a point of being harmonious!

The trainer is a major force in our industry, and he deserves to be. And, the trainer-owner relationship is a vital — and complicated — one to discuss. I attempt to deal with this subject in Chapter 8, so that you are ready to reckon with one another.

I Ain't Never Been On No Horse That Fast

Meanwhile, back at Dogwood Farm? There was definite progress. We're well into 1974, and the first farm manager, surly George of the unquenchable thirst, has been replaced with a tall, likable man from Florida. Here was a man with a marvelous reputation as a horseman. He could do it all — dentistry, farrier work, veterinary medicine — he could ride a horse, and he could certainly break and train one. This fellow could come close to speaking with a horse in the animal's language. He was always in the barn, usually underneath a horse, working on legs. He would wake a horse up if it was sleeping because he had thought of something he needed to do to it. And no order or request could be made to which he would not immediately respond.

In short, this fellow was almost the ideal farm manager. He was talented, he was immensely personable, he was a true workaholic. The trouble was — he was also a true alcoholic! He worked at Dogwood for about a year and a half. He hid it a lot better than did his predecessor, and the fact that I lived sixty miles away in Atlanta — and maintained the Dogwood offices there — permitted him to schedule his drinking pace quite efficiently. A few surprise visits found him a little the worse for wear, and I began to worry about the situation. However, he was a smooth talker, and he could charm the birds out of the trees. He decided to get married, and I thought this might have a constructive influence on him. So I gave him the benefit of the doubt.

The nuptials came, and nuptial bliss may have followed, but "John Barleycorn" did not depart.

One night, when we were shipping six horses to three different racetracks on the East Coast, our man, handicapped by confusion brought about by strong drink, and aided by several staffers who were similarly impeded, managed to put the wrong halters (identification) on four of them. The result was that three different trainers received — and began training — horses they were not supposed to have. It was several weeks before these blunders were straightened out. To make matters much worse, the horses involved were not Dogwood horses, but were boarders. The owners received the news (in one case PROVIDED the news) with varying degrees of understanding. Shortly after this incident, farm manager number two was discharged and replaced.

There were only two more farm managers after that, and they were both wonderful. The first was Elwood McCann, a good, old Kentucky "hardboot" who had been a racetrack trainer for some years, and had had horses at the track for Dogwood. I hired him away from a fine farm in Virginia, and he stayed with us for six years, until family problems forced him to relocate. We still have the odd horse with him in Kentucky, since he's gone back to the racetrack. I've known him and done business with him for almost thirty years. You can stake your life on him; I'm devoted to him and consider Elwood McCann a very good friend.

The fourth man replaced Elwood in 1981, and he and I have been together ever since. He is Ron Stevens, and he has played a gigantic role in our outfit's success. His name and his fine attributes will appear throughout this book.

As explained earlier, Dogwood Farm set out to offer horse owners a place in a temperate clime where young Thoroughbreds would be taught to be racehorses. In other words, we would offer a curriculum that would start in kindergarten and go through junior high school — a good analogy, I think.

In addition, we would serve as a spot to freshen and provide relaxation for race-weary older horses, and to rehabilitate injured warriors back from the racetrack.

And incidentally — and uniquely with us — the farm provided us with a site for selling shares in our partnership horses. A place to sell the "sizzle" as well as the steak!

The grammar school, or elementary school, cycle of the Thoroughbred world is surely one of the most vital — and one of the most under-appreciated — in our business. Under-appreciated

With Elwood McCann, who was Dogwood's farm manager for six years.

because when a racehorse becomes a star, his renown is credited to the trainer who is handling him. It's always "Shug McGaughey's so and so did this," or " Wayne Lukas enters such and such," "Billy Mott blah, blah, blah." And, of course, the trainer, the guy or gal who took the young horse off the farm, put the finishing touches on him, and brought him to stardom, should receive the lion's share of the credit.

But there are some forgotten characters in the scenario, and they are, in order of recognition due, but not received, the farm trainer (and his staff, of course), the racetrack groom, and the owner. It is the training farm, where the young horse receives his first lessons and where he formulates his first taste of the game in which he's going to be the major participant, that is the crucial starting point in the career of this young animal-athlete.

The farm trainer in Ocala, Lexington, Aiken, Camden, Middleburg, or wherever, is so very important. The farm is the place where the young horse is taught his manners and given his early lessons. Hopefully, he develops a love of training and a sense of competitiveness. The young horse is protected from being intimidated in his early training, and he is introduced gingerly to the starting gate and so many other potentially terrifying new experiences.

When the young two-year-old leaves the farm in the spring, he is like a country boy who shows up in New York, slightly mesmerized by the hustle and bustle, ogling the tall buildings and pretty much in a daze — but not afraid. Instead, he is confident in his own ability to tackle any assignment. This comes after a well thought out, individualized training program that has eased gradually forward over a period of six to eight months.

THE BREAKING PROCESS

Most Thoroughbreds are foaled in the late winter or spring. Let's say our young horse was born on April 1. He is weaned from his mother around September 1. He technically becomes a yearling on

January 1, since, for simplicity's sake, all Thoroughbreds have a birth-day on that day. The following September, when by the calendar he is nineteen months old, comparable in most ways to a ten- to twelve-year-old human, he should go into training and be "broken."

The verb "break" is truly a misnomer. Nothing is " broken," and the process is very gentle, so gradual that the young horse is almost unaware that anything very significant is going on. The autumn of his yearling year is the ideal time to start this process, because the equine individual is strong enough to handle weight on his back, and men-tally he is at a very malleable stage in his psyche. He is quite receptive to new ideas (a human being riding around on his back!), and has not formed too many unshakable convictions and attitudes of his own.

Most of the yearlings that come to the major training farms, such as Dogwood, come from auctions which may have taken place a month or two beforehand. And this is helpful. It means that these young horses have been handled extensively. They have long since been taught to lead, they've been groomed, and, in general, they probably have pretty good manners. Most important, they are certainly not goosy about being around people. At the sale, they have probably been shown with a bit in their mouths. This is a Chifney bit, a circular steel bit that fits around the horse's bottom jaw into the mouth and attaches to the halter. So the student arrives at the farm, having accepted the idea of the bit in his mouth. If he hasn't, it's no big deal, because it doesn't take long to introduce this concept. But accepting the bit is the first step, as this device is the basic conduit to control.

Once the bit is behind us, we address the girth, which goes around the horse's belly. A canvas surcingle (girth) is hung over the horse's back and ever so gradually tightened. All of this is accompanied by a good bit of hand and rub-rag activity around the horse's back and belly. The next step is to place a light training saddle on his back and tighten the attached girth rather firmly.

With one person at the horse's head, the rider-to-be begins leaning

Introducing the bit usually doesn't take long.

over the horse's back. This conditions the pupil to accept weight. Soon the horse is being turned while the rider lies crossways on the horse's back. All of this takes place in the stall. Next, the head man will give the rider enough of a "leg up" to accustom the horse to what will come next.

After a day or two of this last exercise (we're now probably four or five days into the whole procedure), depending to a great extent on how the young colt or filly is handling all of this, the rider will be lifted onto the horse's back. Usually, if all has gone smoothly up to now, there's nary a buck. Maybe a hump in the back as a response to this strange sensation, but that's about it. When the young horse has clearly accepted the idea, the head man begins turning the yearling in the stall, and the rider will exert pressure on the bit, through the reins, so as to indoctrinate the horse to the fact that this is about control — but pleasant, gentle control.

The next day (always concluding each lesson on a good note, and certainly before fatigue and grouchiness come upon the scene), the horse, rider up, is led outside and is walked about, going first one direction and then another. Soon, the head man — usually an assistant trainer, foreman, or seasoned groom — steps away and the rider and horse are on their own.

From there, it's more of the same, but now with other youngsters, moving into perhaps a one-acre paddock, doing "figure eights" at the walk and then an easy trot. At this point, maybe ten days having elapsed, a set of young horses (four to eight, depending on the size of the farm) now proceed to the racetrack, where they will encounter numerous "wondrous" sights to behold and from which to shy. Led by the head trainer on the stable pony (oftentimes an ex-racehorse, Quarter Horse, or a mixed-breed equine nursemaid of some sort), this rather tentative and ungainly procession will make its way slowly and — one hopes — uneventfully around the racetrack. Progress!!

The young horse learns to accept weight with the rider lying crossways.

EARLY TRAINING

For the next two months it's just a matter of putting in the miles. Each and every day around and around we go, picking up the pace and the distance, sometimes two or three abreast, or single file (to experience getting dirt kicked in his face. After their gallop, they're made to stop and stand, all in line and facing the infield, for about thirty seconds. Then it's back to the barn at a walk. The set is given baths by their grooms. Then they are walked and cooled out, and permitted to graze for awhile. At some point during the day they are turned out in individual paddocks for several hours.

The routine continues pretty much this way, except the young horses may go on a trail ride a couple of times a week, and they are walked through the starting gate three times weekly. This "monster" can terrify a young horse, unless he's introduced to it very gradually and in a very relaxed way.

Around mid-January, our now two-year-olds are asked to "pick it up" a little for maybe an eighth of a mile as they finish their gallops. And, at this point you can see the "light come on" in their brains — SOME of their brains, that is. Others don't have a clue — yet.

This is a good time to address the question: "When do you know you've got a racehorse?" Sometimes from the start you're pretty sure you have. But be careful about deciding you don't (or you do!). It is the unwatched pot that sometimes begins boiling, and at a furious tempo, later in the year. How often have I seen a fat, lazy yearling, who might easily have been voted "least likely to succeed" in March, blossom with a vengeance in summer when he — for some reason (maturity?) — suddenly got running on his mind. In fact, Dogwood has just run third in both the 2000 Kentucky Derby and Preakness with Impeachment, who fits that description perfectly.

Believe me, horses are like people! All of us remember the kid in high school who was an absolute star when he was fifteen years old. But maybe he never developed much from that time, and when he was twenty-eight, he was lucky to be the produce clerk in the grocery store. Nothing wrong with that, but we expected a lot more. At the same time, there was another fifteen-year-old who stood six feet two and weighed in at 135 pounds and couldn't get out of his own way! We were flabbergasted when at twenty he was the starting tackle at the University of Nebraska. It took him awhile to get it together — but did he ever!!!! Or, there's the skinny, bespectacled, quiet, "nerdish" boy whom no one ever noticed. He became chairman of the board of a blue chip company.

So, don't arrive at too many firm conclusions when those equine "eighth graders" are still on the farm.

What you are looking for, of course, is young horses that move well, have an economical, flowing stride, who, like all fine athletes, are getting a lot done without seeming to struggle. You want to see classy behavior. That means a young horse that is bright, has a keen sense of interest in life, and is confident and not at all apprehensive about what's going on around him.

You want to see a good appetite, and what is truly a joy for a horseman to behold is a young or older horse, who, when training is over, nestles down in the straw and goes to sleep. That's usually the sign of an effective horse.

In February and March, we are asking the young horse for some speed; or, if he has clearly indicated that he will be a late developer, we have taken him out of training and turned him out so he can grow into himself (like our Nebraska tackle).

The faster pupils are now coming out of the starting gate, and when they ship off the farm in late March or April to Keeneland, Belmont, Laurel, or wherever, they'll be up to breezing a half-mile and close to getting their gate cards (approval by the track starter to run in a race).

Since the young horse first came to the farm, the trainer will have been in touch regularly with the owner and/or the racetrack trainer. Now, with spring approaching, and with much more going on, com-

A group of Dogwood horses going out in a "set."

munications accelerate, and firm plans have been made for when the colt or filly is to be shipped to the track.

I now want to strike a mighty blow for the Thoroughbred industry, and clear up a dreadful misconception brought about — inadvertently — by the widely heralded and wonderful book written by Monty Roberts on his system of "starting" young horses.

Monty Roberts is essentially a cowboy, and definitely a magnificent horseman. Rankled and distressed for years about the traditional inhumane system of breaking cow ponies and mustangs out West, he developed a remarkable technique of "starting" young horses (understandably, he never uses the term "breaking"). He calls this approach "Join up." The details of this exercise are not germane, except to explain that within twenty-five minutes Roberts will have a rider on the horse's back, through a series of movements that involve touching the horse, walking away, ignoring him, and playing on his inclination to want to join up with Monty's "herd."

Queen Elizabeth inspired Monty's book. She and a vast number of other people heard about, and became enamored of, the concept. She invited him to England to demonstrate the approach, and he toured the British Isles, tackling and succeeding with some pretty nasty problem cases that caused him to have some very tense moments — with a hell of a lot of people looking on!

The inadvertent problem he caused the Thoroughbred world, and one that drives me to distraction, is that half the people who read the book assume that Thoroughbred racehorses were, and are, broken in the grossly inhumane manner of the Western horses. Nothing could be further from the truth! Our system is — and always has been — the gentlest, most non-confrontational method.

When someone — usually a lady — asks me, "How do you break your young horses?" I immediately think, "Oh hell! Here's another Monty Roberts reader."

Another point about his method and why it's not vitally suited to the Thoroughbred world, is that we're not in any hurry to get on the young horse's back. Where are we going when we get there? We've got from eight to twelve months to bring this colt or filly to racing fitness. There's no advantage to riding him in twenty-five minutes. Chances are we're going to take him out of training for a couple of months in the winter anyway.

Another service Dogwood and most other training farms provide is the care of lay-ups. A lay-up is a horse that has been racing and needs a break — because he's injured or because he's sour (tired of racing). He may need to be confined to a stall, due to the severity of his injury, but in most cases, this horse will be turned out in a paddock, usually about an acre in size. If all he needs is plenty of sunshine and the services of "Dr. Green," but he is just off the track and in peak racing fitness, then for the first week he must be protected from himself and his own high spirits. He'll be turned out in a small round pen, where he can't cavort, pick up a full head of steam, and run through a fence!

Then, with the help of a mild tranquilizer, he can be moved to a

Round pens can have many uses on farms.

bigger paddock. Soon he will be enjoying life, running and playing, without going crazy and hurting himself. After the prescribed amount of turn-out time (during which he will be brought in to his stall at night), the horse will be put back in training.

The most common racetrack injuries dealt with on the farm that require rehabilitation are knees and ankles from which bone chips have been arthroscopically removed, bucked shins (seen often in young horses and comparable to a shin splint in a human being), torn or pulled ligaments from the knee down to the ankle, and foot problems. Foot problems can include a fracture of a small bone within the hoof, or a quarter crack — a split in the wall of the hoof, painfully comparable to your splitting a fingernail or toenail. There are many more, but these are the most prevalent.

The bucked shins are nothing — almost routine. The ankle chips are usually no big deal. The knee chips tend to cheapen a horse. He may return to competition in fine shape, but the knee is a complicated area and his future potential is often compromised. The pulled suspensory ligaments or bowed tendons are grievous indeed, and the latter is usually career ending. A quarter crack will grow out in time, but it signals a weakness in the foot, and there may be more quarter cracks on the way. The foot is a crucial area, and disease or fractures within it usually spell big trouble.

Racehorses, like all athletes, are prone to injury. Consider that the racehorse is a 1,100-pound animal, with 115 or more pounds on his back, going thirty-five to forty miles per hour, on a pretty hard surface!

The tricky thing for a new owner to balance is the need to be realistic about the injured horse's future while retaining an optimistic outlook, certainly a requisite in this game. If a horse has bowed a tendon severely, and your veterinarian advises that the outlook for the horse getting back to the races and competing are slim or none (And "Slim" just caught the last bus out of town!), wouldn't it be better to bite the bullet — find a nice home for the horse and take the tax write-off? Awful hard to do, but often better in the long run. To look at it commercially, remember that "the first loss is the easiest loss."

Swimming used to be a very popular activity in the rehabilitation of horses. It is quite useful, but it became something of a fad, which ran its course, and you don't see or hear much about it nowadays.

Swimming a horse permits you to get the animal back to a high degree of fitness (some say within a week of a race, but don't count on it!) without pounding that injured leg on the racetrack every day. Also, swimming is effective in bringing a sour horse back into trim, without subjecting him to the monotony of galloping around the oval each day.

Cantankerous horses have found swimming a palatable way to train up to a race.

The truth is swimming can be very advantageous in certain cases. But putting the facilities into a farm operation are hellishly expensive, and it is much more trouble to swim a horse than to gallop one. It takes two people.

Our swimming operation at Dogwood Farm was quite functional.

In the infield of our six-furlong track was a two-acre lake. We simply built a 100-foot dock into the lake, put a drawbridge about twenty feet out and constructed ramps for the horse to enter and exit the lake — and we were in the swimming business.

The groom walked along the dock and led the horse out into the lake. When the horse began swimming, the drawbridge was raised, and an island was created. When the horse had had enough, the drawbridge was dropped, the man walked across it, and out the swimmer came.

Interestingly, the first time did not particularly appeal to the horse, and some urging was required, but he was really swimming (a feat they take to naturally) before he knew that was what he was doing. But, the second time! Now he knew what was happening, and he didn't want any part of it! However, after that, the aquatic equine walked right in; in fact, some would almost drag the handler into the swimming routine. Of course, the best swimmers were the best horses, because they were the best athletes.

Some horses benefit from — and enjoy — swimming.

The horse that christened our pool, and spent half his life in it, was the wonderful grass horse, Johnny D., champion turf horse of 1977. Johnny D. had bowed a tendon and was sent by his owner, Dana Bray, down to us for rehabilitation.

Swimming was just the thing for this great old campaigner. We loved old Johnny, and were proud to have him at Dogwood.

Our boarding and training business was plenty good because early on we had turned out some splendid horses who cut a wide swath on the national racing scene. We had another champion in the fine mare Northernette, who earned her title in Canada. Other Dogwood alumni included the fine stakes winners Queen of Song, Special Honor, Classic Go Go, and A Letter to Harry. These were runners! And the fact that we were being entrusted with this kind of stock was becoming known, and a lot of glamour horses were being sent our way. The Dogwood Stable horses also were beginning to excel at the better racetracks, and, all in all, things were starting to pop for us in the mid- and late 1970s.

Still, west central Georgia was a rather unconventional site for a Thoroughbred training farm. Certainly our climate was a big factor. Most of the concentration of training operations in America is in Florida, South Carolina, California, and Texas. These are mild weather states. You may be surprised that Kentucky is left out. But Kentucky gets plenty cold in the winter time, and training tracks are frozen and unusable much of the time. The really big farms in Kentucky are mostly stallion stations and breeding farms.

A stallion station usually is a smaller farm that concentrates on standing stallions. Such a farm might have twenty-five or thirty studs, with enough land, of course, to provide paddocks for each. The breeding shed (an understatement for such an operation) from February to July closely resembles the air traffic control tower at O'Hare. There's a lot of action, and a lot of important action! There may be forty or fifty mares being bred each day at the height of the season in April.

The stallion station may have acreage and barn facilities to care for many mares on a year-round basis, or it may provide limited facilities for mares that come in that day (with romance on their minds!). I think

Some Kentucky stallion stations have palatial proportions.

the term, "stallion station" implies the latter. If so, you can be certain there are satellite farms in the immediate vicinity to care for and prepare the mares seeking carnal knowledge at the stallion facility.

Breeding farm probably implies that it is a layout of considerable scope in acreage, housing many mares — of its own and belonging to outside boarders. A breeding farm probably stands stallions, too. Whether it does or not, a breeding farm's responsibility is to care for the boarding mare, handle the birth of her foal, and tend to the scheduling of her liaison with the next daddy-to-be. All of this is mighty important, involves animals of staggering value in many cases — and is pretty darned complicated.

There are breeding farms all over Central Kentucky. There are numerous specialty farms of this sort in Florida, and in other states, too. Maryland, Virginia, Pennsylvania, New York, Louisiana, Texas, and California are significant Thoroughbred racehorse states that contain many farms. But farms in these states tend to do it all. They may stand a stallion or two, board mares, take the offspring to the market (yearling sales), break young horses, or do whatever needs to be done in the world of the Thoroughbred.

One of the most lucrative aspects of breeding farm life, and one of the most logically integrated, is the function of sales prepping and sales agency. If you're a customer or client (as we smoothly call them) of the "Ignatz Thoroughbred Nursery," and you have a band of broodmares which is designed to produce foals for the yearling market, you need someone to prepare and sell these youngsters for you. Some farms, like Eaton Sales, Taylor Made, Three Chimneys, and Lane's End, specialize in this, while others offer the services as part of "the menu."

Sales prepping is a fine art. It involves an intense, six- to twelve-week period of boutique grooming, feeding, lessons in decorum, and promotion (if the farm is to act as sales agent). There is much to be said for being a sales agent, as the agent receives five percent of what the young horse brings through the auction ring. It does not take a genius to figure out that some of these agents who are selling $10, $20,

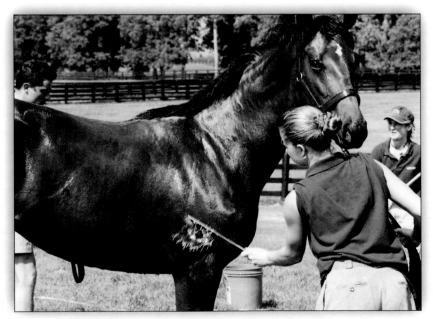

Sales preparation is a specialized service.

Breeding farms board mares and foals.

$30 million in horse flesh are receiving some "heavy brass." Of course, they have to deliver the goods and are under big time pressure.

In order to develop a business plan and budget, you need to have some idea of what these various services cost. The most expensive are those operations in the states with the big reputations. We've checked around the country and have come up with what is probably a reasonable range.

BREEDING FARMS

Broodmare boarding runs $18-$25 per day. After she produces a foal, the cost of the suckling is $2-$5. When that baby is weaned, the per diem goes to $14-$25. Yearlings (after January 1, remember) are about the same as weanlings until they go into training, maybe a couple of dollars more per day. Animals being prepared for sale — a period that spans approximately two months before the auction — would cost $5-$10 more each day, or $20-$35.

Stallions are maintained for $400-$600 per month. Bear in mind that the farm really derives its benefit from standing stallions from the very significant four annual breeding rights it gets. If the stud fee were $25,000, then this arrangement generates one hundred grand, plus the many other tangible and intangible benefits such as boarding mares and offspring. Then, too, there are untold promotional benefits to the farm, including farm name exposure that goes right along with advertising the stallion.

The farm charges for transportation, preparing Jockey Club papers, foaling per se, and various other incidentals.

TRAINING FARMS

Cost for any horse in training — yearling or older horse — at any stage of training and housed in the training barn, will run $35-$55 per day. This can include swimming, or some advanced phase of lay-up status (Aqua-Tread therapy, for instance). Lay-ups run $18-$35 per day. These horses either are confined to a stall or turned out in a paddock part- or full-time.

Dogwood was getting all the outside horses we could handle, and space problems sometimes arose when we had to bring one of our own back from the racetrack unexpectedly. And this revenue was greatly appreciated. But our primary bread-and-butter business was forming partnerships — buying young horses, marking them up a reasonable amount and selling the shares. And, as was stated earlier, having a pretty farm with unique entertainment facilities was highly advantageous.

It was not an easy farm to run — for me, but certainly not for our farm manager. Ron Stevens, the fellow who served the longest time in that job, had to baby-sit and train a large aggregation of expensive horses, most of them intent on committing mayhem. He also had to baby-sit and train (and manage!) around thirty red-blooded boys and girls — and men and women — who made up what was a very good staff. However, some of them were more intent on committing mayhem than the horses!

One family that rather enlivened the domestic and functional life of Dogwood was the Grizzard family, about whom a sit-com could easily be developed. However, its necessarily complex and colorful plot would definitely be denounced for its flagrant exaggeration.

There were three Dogwood Grizzards, and they hailed essentially from the west Georgia area, although you may be sure that during their careers in the horse business they had all ranged far afield, and pursued many interests. In the current vernacular, "We may not want to go there." They were likable (to me, at least), colorful to a fault, good horsemen, effective, and a hell of a lot of trouble generally. I was very fond of all of them but more than a few of my gray hairs were supplied by the Grizzards.

First there was Father Grizzard. He was always referred to as "Mister Grizzard," and he was our night watchman. I am not sure how vigilant he was, but any peccadilloes of his own were minimized by the fact that Father Time had clearly slowed him down and assuaged the voracious, fun-loving appetite one learned to associate with a true Grizzard.

He had a rather laissez-faire attitude about life in general, and since he was already old and tired, he was wise enough to emphasize this inclination especially as it applied to guidance for his two sons, Jimmy and Render.

He had sired five or six Grizzards, and most of them had gone on to be Quarter Horse jockeys, and damned good ones. They all spent their lives working around horses, although they could and did participate — and enjoy — other activities!

Jimmy was perhaps Dogwood's third employee, and I will never forget seeing him for the first time, when he came motoring through the farm gates in a very old, excessively smoking vehicle. He looked to be about fourteen years old. He would have weighed 105 pounds soaking wet; he was clad in Levi's, of course; his head was about the size of a large grapefruit and on top of it was an enormous, white, ten-gallon cowboy hat that looked as if it had belonged to Hopalong Cassidy. Jimmy had heard about Dogwood. He said he could "ride the hair off a horse," and he was seeking employment. We tried him on a few horses the next morning, and he could! We hired him and he stayed with us for a decade. Jimmy was a chatterbox, had a lot of opinions, and, therefore, did not ingratiate himself with every other employee. He was also a con man par excellence. This could be infuriating, but it also had its appeal. I remember well at Christmas time when I would distribute the bonuses, which were fairly significant, most of the employees would nod, stick the envelope in their pockets, perhaps grunt, and that was the end of it. Not our Jimmy. He would clasp your hand with both of his. Pumping furiously, he would look you in the eye, and with tears streaming down his cheeks, follow you around the barn proclaiming his appreciation. It might have been a tad overdone, but it beat the hell out of the other response. It made you like him. That was his strong suit.

Jimmy definitely contributed to the economic development of Dogwood Farm — intangibly and very definitely tangibly. Clear cut; and here's how.

Earlier, we told about our training shows, or "Breezing Parties," as we called them. Around sixty guests — mostly prospective owners of horses being syndicated — were invited to the farm on a Saturday or Sunday in the spring or fall. Aided by the volume of my bull horn, I would ask them to sit down on a grassy knoll overlooking the racetrack. We would then bring out a set of two or three horses, and work them — meaning we would let 'em roll for about a quarter of a mile. And two or three horses going past at full throttle about thirty feet away would definitely get your attention, make the goose pimples come out.

After the horses had zoomed past, they would gradually pull up, turn, and jog back to where we were situated. The horses would turn out, facing the crowd, while I would reiterate their breeding and somewhat matter-of-factly cover the superlative move they had just demonstrated, and, finally, state the cost of a share.

At this point, Jimmy Grizzard would invariably mop his brow with a large, red bandanna, shake his head in wonderment, and exclaim, "Whoee, Mr. Campbell, I ain't never been on no horse that fast!!"

I could have kissed him. People started reaching for check books.

His older brother, Render, was somewhat less effusive than Jimmy. He was some kind of fine horseman. He was possessed of great mystique, had a face like a hatchet and a build like a welter-weight boxer. There were all sorts of unsubstantiated rumors about dark deeds in Render's past. In general, he looked like a man who could "cloud up and rain all over you."

This man was a wonderful rider. The truly noteworthy thing about that was that he only had one leg!

Render had been one of the country's outstanding Quarter Horse jockeys. After a bad accident, and a subsequent operation to repair a broken leg, there had been complications which required amputation.

He was fitted with a prosthesis, and he gamely tried to resume race riding, but he wasn't the same and his "business" — the rides he could get — dwindled to nothing and he had to give it up. For several years he worked at training farms around the country. When Jimmy was pretty well ensconced with us, he touted his brother as a great addition to our riding staff. We hired him, and he was.

A sight that will live with me forever was Render, working a horse past our clocker's stand, enraged over his inability to get what was left of his right leg to perform as he wanted it to, simply reaching down, jerking the prosthesis off and hurling it out into the infield, accompanied by a blood-curdling scream of rage. This happened on several occasions — fortunately not during our "Breezing Parties" — and several of us would routinely walk in the infield, locate Render's "leg," and return it to him. He couldn't go get it.

His demons — their presence understandable — regrettably forced us to part.

All of this may lead you to think that the Dogwood operation was a pretty "loosey goosey" set-up. Far from it. It was a good place to work, high in morale, and greatly in demand.

We ran a smart, clean, sharp, attractive outfit. The head man (me) was a stickler for running either a class operation — or none at all. While there are, of course, some bad actors among the grooms, hot walkers, and exercise riders plying their trades in the racehorse business, they did not work at Dogwood — long. They shaped up or they shipped out.

We had rules, we had standards, and they created a climate that gave us a reputation for excellence. This instilled in the employees a feeling of pride, and we made sure they had a sense of belonging. They thought — perhaps subconsciously — "This is a class outfit and if I'm working here I must be ok."

In Ron Stevens I had the ideal man to uphold this philosophy. He was right with me on some of the demands we made, and he was way ahead of me on others. Our people came to work looking clean and decent. Our riders went out from the beginning — and do so today — in Dogwood yellow and green shirts and helmet covers.

We permitted no dogs on the farm. I love dogs, but without this rule every employee would have had one (or probably two!). And yearling Thoroughbreds combined with dogs are accidents waiting to happen.

No radios in the barn. There's nothing more "bush league" than to walk down the shedrow in a racehorse training barn and every third or fourth stall you come to has a radio hanging on it, one blaring out rap music, the next, gospel music, then whatever. It's bedlam. We did not have it.

We had a profit sharing plan for our employees. If the company made money, they received an amount of fifteen percent of their salary invested for them.

We had staff lunches, letters of commendation, trips to the track, parties, celebrations, and we put out what has become a rather famous newsletter, in which our employees were often included and featured. We had horse-naming contests.

We had certain moral standards (believe it or not!!), and permitted absolutely no profanity.

Ron's job was like being mayor and police chief and school superintendent of a small, potentially contentious town. He did it well, and figured to. This man is a high-class gentleman. He's from Kansas originally, and his background included a life with horses, a stint in the Marine Corps and service in Vietnam, teaching, and then training Quarter Horses and Thoroughbreds. He was managing a farm in Texas when I flew him to Georgia to interview for the job that Elwood McCann was leaving.

It was clear from the outset that we needed each other. He and I got together. He and a most attractive family — wife Julie, and daughters

Ron Stevens, with his wife Julie, arrived at Dogwood in 1981.

Leslie, eleven, and Nikki, seven — arrived at Dogwood in the summer of 1981, and it has been a wonderful and harmonious relationship ever since.

In 1986, the rigors of too many early morning commutes (three or four times a week) from Atlanta to the farm sixty miles away in Greenville, Georgia, had taken their toll. I decided to make life simpler. The plan was to sell the farm and move the horses and our training operation to a horse-oriented community like Aiken, South Carolina. The horse people in Aiken, and the community, in general, made it very appealing for us to make this move. And we did. On June 17, 1986, a caravan of eighteen-wheeler horse vans, loaded with horses, equipment, and personnel, brought us to Aiken.

This move was brought about primarily by fatigue (wear and tear on the head man), but it was also motivated by efficiency. At this point, the business of forming partnerships was long since established and going great guns. We were certainly known to be the leading practitioner of the syndication concept. Business was good. However, life would be simpler without training outside horses; and we didn't have to have this revenue and the headaches that went with it.

During the thirteen years of operation, we had dabbled in other aspects of the Thoroughbred industry. For awhile, we kept a band of broodmares and bred for the market. We also pinhooked horses for a few years, buying yearlings for the purpose of training them and reselling them at the two-year-old sales in Florida. These ventures, while moderately successful, helped me embrace, with greater than ever dedication, a philosophy I have always tended to espouse: Do what you know how to do best.

My pride of ownership in what was truly a beautiful and high-class farm had definitely diminished a little. How could it not? In the early days I would load up any human being who showed the vaguest interest in the operation and whisk him or her to Dogwood, and have the time of my life doing it. By 1986, I was still whisking but not exactly having "the time of my life."

The move to Aiken with the horses, with the Dogwood business office remaining in Atlanta where my wife Anne and I lived, made considerable sense at this juncture. The farm had served its purpose and gotten us well established, but now we didn't have to have it, and it had become a bit of a drag. Relocation was part of a game plan that worked out terrifically, although the future provided some significant and surprising variations — but that's for another chapter.

Ron and his family, living on Dogwood Farm, and well settled in the community, were not ecstatic about moving, but they understood the logic of it, and handled it with customary equanimity. Many of our key employees made the move; of course, some did not. Aiken, a traditional horse town, provided a pool of good horsemen and women, and some were interested in going to work for us. All in all, the transition was relatively painless.

My enthusiasm in the early days, and the diminution after a steady diet of it for thirteen years, were mirrored by Anne, on whose shoulders fell much of the burden of entertainment. And what a star she has always been in that department!!

Nevertheless, after making enough spinach dip, paté, and, numerous other delicacies to fill up several railroad tankcars, packing it in the back of the car — with my help usually! — and supervising the consumption of it during the sixty-invitee "Breezing Parties," she, too, began to "shorten stride" a tad. She has always been a marvelous hostess. And much of the brunt of her hosting came during a time when she was serving on numerous civic boards in Atlanta, and being president of the Atlanta Junior League, the largest in America then. Never have I known her to be flustered or nettled by the need to serve as hostess for the numerous Dogwood-related social functions; and she insisted on preparing all the party comestibles herself.

Well, she DID almost become flustered one day when the entertainment disaster of the century actually turned into a truly delightful and certainly memorable occasion.

It involved Prince Faisal of Saudi Arabia, and his rather sizable entourage. The Prince and his beautiful wife, Asiya, had moved to Georgia — Atlanta and Columbus. The former was for socializing and the latter so that he could be instructed in techniques of making war, at nearby Fort Benning. The Prince, you see, was being groomed to be Minister of Defense, serving, of course, at the pleasure of his daddy, the king.

Well, it was made known to us that Faisal, a sporty type, to put it mildly, would enjoy a visit to Dogwood Farm. This fact did not fall on deaf ears, and we were all atwitter over the idea that this incredibly rich, horse-loving, young Arab Prince — with time on his hands — wanted to be exposed to our racehorses, and vice versa. This could be the big breakthrough of the century!

Faisal's attorney made the arrangements for the visit, and he let it be known, tactfully, that it might not be a bad idea to "kill the fatted calf." Faisal et al. were not ones to be offended when a fuss was being made.

We were given several weeks to prepare, and much discussion preceded the visit (to be a private one, of course; this was no time for a routine "Breezing Party!"). It was decided they would arrive at the farm at eleven in the morning, we would show them around, and then train several sets of horses — ones with shares available in them, naturally. After this, we would repair to the guest house for a delicious lunch.

Led by Anne, much research and consideration went into determining the menu, table seating, protocol, and so on. The culinary fare had to be just right: having about it the feeling of the sporting world, but certainly not nervously ostentatious, and wonderfully flavorful in a creatively casual, down-home way. These were the simple parameters!

We knew the Saudis did not drink, and we assumed that their American connections would not either on this occasion, so that took care of the libations. Was there anything they could not eat? We

Princess Asiya, Lila Campbell, and Prince Faisal of Saudi Arabia with Anne.

checked around in places that should know and were told that they had no dietetic restrictions. Absolutely none.

Earlier we had received for Christmas what would be the ideal backbone of the meal. This was a succulent Kentucky ham, killed, smoked, and cured at the storied, old bluegrass Thoroughbred nursery of our friend, the legendary Warner Jones. Perfect! This met all the prerequisites. We would start with a nice, hot cup of Kentucky burgoo, and a superb, zesty salad with all sorts of goodies in it, including bits of bacon. Topping all of this off would be just the thing to give the meal a touch of sophistication and just the right degree of international personality. What else? Czechoslovakian Cookies!! What a smashing success it would be!

Anne got busy with her part of the presentation, I thought out the exact chronology of the day's activities, and then Ron Stevens met with the farm maintenance and barn crews to assure that the farm and the stock would be presented flawlessly.

The chosen day arrived. And not too long after eleven, a huge, rather ornate motor home, emblazoned with the royal crest of Saudi Arabia hove into view. Disembarking, while we all stood at a sort of quasi-attention (or at least we weren't slouching around!), were first the two bodyguards, then — a secure environment having been established — the Prince. He was a rather jolly, portly, young man, clad in a princely type of beige jumpsuit, also emblazoned with the royal crest of his country. He was followed by Princess Asiya, then came Prince Turki (a visiting potentate) and, lastly, three Georgians in business suits, one being an attorney from Atlanta, whom we knew slightly.

Pleasantries met with, we began our tour of the barns, and then arranged ourselves on the viewing stand and started bringing horses out. They could not have been more delightful. The Prince did love horses, and the entire entourage seemed to be blown away with what they saw (Jimmy Grizzard was mopping at his brow and marveling at the speed of the horses he had been asked to work!!). Couldn't have gone better. Now, we're circling for the kill! It's off to the guest house for further bonding and perhaps an introduction into the Dogwood concept of group ownership. They were charmed by the guest house, a shabbily elegant old Georgia farm house. We milled about in the yard and then went in to lunch, which was arrayed buffet style on the sideboard in the dining room. The Atlanta lawyer was the first to go through the line, preceding the royal couple by design, it seemed.

When he got to the ham, he looked over at Anne and, in a loud, deliberate voice, exclaimed, "Oh, Anne, I see you're serving CORNED BEEF." He saw a problem, and was trying to save the day!

Slightly insulted and anxious to straighten out a grievous error, she briskly shot back, "Oh no, no. That's Kentucky HAM," and quickly began expounding on its heritage. With that, the entire group began to look somewhat crestfallen, glancing surreptitiously at one another.

With a rather sickly grin, the Prince then said, "Oh, I'm afraid we cannot eat any type of pork." But, he threw in, rather lamely, "There are plenty of other good things here."

Like hell there were! The salad had bacon in it, the burgoo was riddled with pork. That left the Czechoslovakian Cookies — and, maybe a little iced tea?

While the rest of them sat down at the table and began dispiritedly pushing around the meager fare that was edible (the Americans continued to honor the eating and drinking habits of their benefactors), Anne was gamely trying to salvage the day. She quickly produced some nice, fluffy cheese biscuits, tossed them into an antique, earthenware serving dish and rushed into the dining room to serve the guests.

She first proffered the dish to Princess Asiya, an exceedingly lovely and staggeringly buxom young woman, clad in a decidedly décolleté blouse. As she energetically urged this plate toward the young woman, inexplicably the plate broke right down the middle and many of the steaming hot cheese biscuits fell into that cavity housing the ample bosoms of the Arabian Princess.

It was pretty terrible. But, you know what? It was so bad, it was good! There was nothing to do but to laugh about it, and we all did, and became better friends as a result.

An hour or so later, when the royal group departed, as the motor coach of state pulled out of the driveway, the prince got on his public address system and was repeating plaintively, "Anne! Next time give me CORNED BEEEEEF!"

They came back many times during their stay in the States and we did become good friends. Did they buy any horses?

No.

PACKAGE DEALS

In 1955, no horse made more news on the racing scene than the mighty bay three-year-old colt Nashua. But he became even bigger news overnight when his socially prominent owner, William Woodward Jr., allegedly was mistaken for a burglar by his wife, Ann. She shot and killed him in their palatial home on Long Island, New York.

This led — very indirectly — to the first stallion syndicate, which some years later sparked the idea of the first racing partnership.

After Woodward's death, the executors of the estate, Hanover Bank and Trust Company, decided to sell Nashua via a sealed-bid auction because of his extraordinary celebrity and his scheduled participation in upcoming big races.

One of the cagiest and smoothest operators in the history of the Thoroughbred horse business, Leslie B. Combs, leapt on this opportunity. He flew in from Lexington, Kentucky, tendered an envelope containing a cashier's check for $1,251,200 (Did he know something?), and got the horse. Combs, a man who made a career out of getting the best out of practically every business deal, and making the loser have the time of his life in defeat, represented a blue-chip "syndicate" of six recreational horsemen.

From this nucleus, Combs conceived the idea of forming a group of thirty-two and selling each a "share" in Nashua. The idea was that a participant would share proportionately in the expenses and earnings of the horse, which had at least one more year of competition. But, more significantly, the purchaser would own the right to one stud service each year for the rest of Nashua's life. Owning a share was exactly like owning a common stock in that its value could go up or down depending on how the horse's progeny fared on the racetrack. In the meantime, the share owner could send a mare to the stallion each year or sell the service, or "season," as it's called, to an outside breeder. Thirty-two was selected as a safe number of mares the stallion could handle in a year. As it turned out, thirty-two was a "piece of cake" for the highly enthused Nashua. But no one at the time could guess the extent of his libido, for Nashua still had worlds to conquer on the racetrack.

Nowadays, most stallion syndicates are forty shares, and the stud is typically bred to seventy mares each year. This means that the thirty additional seasons can be sold outside the syndicate and the income pooled and shared equally by the forty members. The arrangement varies, but this is a typical example. It should be pointed out that the syndicate manager is entitled to four breeding rights, and chances are the trainer has a breeding right.

The difference between a share and a breeding right is that a share is a unit of ownership. It is negotiable. It can be bought or sold. A breeding right is the expense-free right to breed a mare to that stallion annually. That right cannot be sold. For instance, you can sell your 1999 season to the stallion for the published stud fee, or for whatever you can get; but you cannot sell the lifetime breeding right. You — the owner — must utilize it in some way on an annual basis:

breed on it, or sell the stud season annually. But the "right" cannot be sold on the open market as you would a share in a stock (or a syndicate share). And, usually, it's renewable each year at the pleasure of the syndicate. Should it become necessary — because of age, for instance — to reduce the "book" of the stallion (the number of mares he can service), breeding rights are the first to go.

Here's the best case scenario for buying a stallion share:

The share costs $100,000 (leveraged out over three or four years), and the stud fee is set at $25,000. You're a breeder; you buy a share, send your entitled mare each year, and at the end of four years — in a perfect world — you've had three babies and you have a pregnant mare. The first crop of the stallion has gone to the races and they've run like "scalded dogs." Now that share is worth $150,000. And, you've "used" the stallion for four years.

Leslie B. Combs, a pioneer in stallion syndications, and the great Nashua.

Or, let's say the first crop did nothing. The progeny may be late developers. But if the share is now worth only $75,000, you're still way ahead of the game, because you've gotten three foals and your share is still worth seventy-five percent of what you paid for it. Not a bad deal!

When Dogwood became known as the pioneer of racing partnerships, a leading industry publication wrote: "Cot Campbell (Dogwood) is to racehorse limited partnerships what Nashua was to stallion syndication. He is the measure by which other limited partnership ventures are examined." I rather liked the ring of that!

We were the first to do it seriously and successfully. After buying that first pitiful filly (Social Asset) with a couple of buddies, I was hooked. With the stallion syndication scheme frozen somewhere in my brain, I thought, "Why can't this be done with a racehorse?"

The only close-to-legitimate reason was that most racing jurisdictions had adopted rules prohibiting racehorse ownership to more than four people. This was to keep tabs on ownership — through licensing — and make it more difficult for "undesirables" to participate.

The real reason was that up to then racing was made up primarily of huge stables owned by wealthy families, and the concept of a partnership owning a racehorse was a decided break with tradition and very unnerving to racing's Big Wigs. That viewpoint filtered down to the fifth-level bureaucrats who controlled the licensing procedure in most racing states.

Back in the early days, these licensing officials had the authority to waive the four-person ownership rule if a reason warranted it. You can bet your bottom dollar that Nashua, a national hero with the ability to put a lot of behinds in a lot of seats, warranted it! Otherwise, they moved with all the speed of molasses.

The second horse I bought was immediately converted through the sale of three other shares to a limited partnership supported by a rather simple three-page legal document. The truth is that I was on much sounder footing with the racing authorities than with the federal government.

Little did I know — and neither did my first lawyer — that when I started this limited partnership with myself as general partner, giving me complete control over the venture, I was in effect selling securities without having a license. I was in violation with the Securities and Exchange Commission!

Out of ignorance, I had simply run an ad in *The Blood-Horse* or *The Thoroughbred Record* and said, "Here's a colt by so-and-so, out of so-and-so. I am going to form a racing partnership, and would you like to buy a share in him? This is how much it will cost."

Another lawyer — much smarter than the first — said to me one day, "You could get in trouble doing that. You're selling a security."

I asked, "What can they do to me?"

He said, "Well, they can stop you from selling the shares, or they can make you give the people their money back."

"Suppose I don't do that?"

"They can put you in the penitentiary," he gently explained.

Admittedly, this version is slightly dramatized, but only slightly. The point was clear that if I were going to sell shares in racing limited partnerships, the legal procedures would be more involved. I had bitten off much more than I was in a mood to chew, but there was no other choice.

First thing, I had the law firm come up with a document as thick as the Manhattan phone book. This voluminous instrument was to protect the investor, of course. It frightened me, and you can bet it would scare the daylights out of some guy who thought it might be fun to own part of a racehorse. And it terrified his accountant and lawyer.

LIMITED VERSUS GENERAL PARTNERSHIPS

The limited partnerships certainly increased the cost and trouble of doing business, and after some years — and some success — we could indulge ourselves and switch to the simpler general partnerships.

The beauty of the limited partnerships was that the general partner — me — completely controlled the venture. The limited partners had no say in the management of the horse. Since most were neophytes back then, that was a pretty good idea. Their liability was limited to the amount of money they agreed to invest, which certain investors find attractive.

The main concern one would have with a general partnership is legal liability. "Could I be sued if my horse gets loose and injures someone?" The Dogwood answer — and I think a pretty satisfactory one — is that the trainer has mandatory worker's compensation insurance, the racetracks where the horses compete are insured to the hilt, and each of our partnerships is covered to the tune of $20 million.

If you're a "Nervous Nellie" about such things, think about the thousands of high-profile, deep-pocketed people in racing. They

Southjet's partners celebrate a big Canadian win.

aren't worried, and maybe one reason is that some of them race under the protection of a corporate umbrella. A few of our partners are incorporated, but most are not concerned about the liability factor. After thirty years in business, we have not had one liability claim. But, the $20 million general liability policy gives everyone a warm, fuzzy feeling.

For the first fifteen years we did only limited partnerships, with four, eight, ten, twenty, and forty shares. In 1990, after our horse Summer Squall (forty shares, owned by twenty-eight people) won the Preakness, we went to general partnerships. Why?

We had a built-in roster of clients with whom we were quite comfortable and who were quite comfortable with my controlling day-to-day decisions. Therefore, it was a moot point that I needed complete control. We eliminated a staggering amount of paperwork by going to general partnerships, which are (oversimplified) just a group of people who get together and launch a venture, each one having equal say in the undertaking, with the majority ruling. Further, the "equal say" angle gives each partner a better shot with the IRS to take the position that he is "active" rather than "passive" and, thus, to take any write-off at the end of each year instead of at termination of the venture.

From 1990 on, our procedure (exquisitely simple compared with what we had been doing!) has been to buy about twenty-eight young horses each year, keep five percent of each, and sell four shares of 23.75 percent ownership in each partnership. I serve as racing manager, making the day-to-day decisions and keeping close communication with the other partners.

We maintain that it is the best of all worlds for us, and our partners. However, everyone doesn't agree, and you may not.

But, I do think anyone looking into Thoroughbred ownership should strongly consider partnerships. There are many different types and some fine people involved in structuring them.

Some are large, well-established operations, and, at the risk of hurting someone's feelings, I'll list four: Centennial, Team Valor, West Point, and Dogwood. Again, the publication known as *The Source*, published by The Blood-Horse, Inc., provides addresses and phone numbers, and the Thoroughbred Owners and Breeders Association in Lexington, Kentucky, is there to provide help.

The four mentioned are highly reputable and have good track records, although they tend to specialize in different approaches. Some buy very high-priced yearlings and two-year-olds for their racing potential, certainly, but also for their pedigree appeal in the breeding shed. Another outfit goes for established and emerging racing stars and has had good luck doing it. Another pays a good bit for young horses and also seems to have a pinhooking (reselling) operation going.

While we sell only four partnership interests in each horse, some of these syndicators offer a wide variety of units, in some cases as small as 2.5 percent. Some of them put several horses together in a package and sell shares, so they probably have a sizable ownership group in many cases.

Take note, please, that the use of the term "syndicator" is one of convenience within the industry, but our subject is "partnerships." There are insignificant technical differences in the two terms; in verb and noun forms "syndicator" and "syndicate" are easier to use.

It's not my business to know all the details of these partnerships, and if I attempt to encapsulate each of them I'm going to do an injustice to one of my friendly competitors, and I'd just as soon not. They'll be glad to explain why their partnerships make the most sense…just as I would.

In addition to these people, there are numerous other less high profile, more loosely structured partnerships all over the American and foreign racing worlds. Leading breeders, trainers, bloodstock agents — everybody and his dog, it would sometimes seem — are offering all kinds of partnership opportunities. You can pick up the leading trade periodicals and learn of partnership shares available for as little as $500, and I'm sure the Internet is crawling with various deals. The cheapies would not "light my fire."

If you are going to go into racing via the partnership route, look for a substantial, quality outfit, or stay away entirely.

A racing partnership should offer you the opportunity to enter Thoroughbred racing at its highest level. It should pave the way for you to compete at the best racetracks with your horses being trained by the finest talent and ridden by the best jockeys, and the endeavor should be managed by someone with whom you feel comfortable. You are entitled to communication about your horse, and the partnership manager should provide certain amenities when your horse runs (that's why I like four partners; easier than forty!). As previously stated, you're going in it to make money (maybe), have a good write-off if you don't, and, lastly, to have fun. So make sure that you like the people and that the all-important "chemistry" is there.

Partnerships are a wonderful way to "go to school" and learn what you do and don't like in racing while limiting your exposure. We have partners who have been with us for twenty years. They like having someone else tend to the nitty-gritty. They are busy people and not inclined to struggle with the details of the racing game.

Conversely, several of the biggest racing stables in the country started with Dogwood and later decided to "move their own checkers," to use the expression of the late Tommy Valando, one of our most distinguished alumni and owner of the champion racehorse Fly So Free.

You do not have much control in a partnership, and if you want the daily details of dealing with trainers and countless other aspects of campaigning racehorses, don't get in a partnership.

Partnerships are educational, and certainly the manager and his people will provide you with a lot of information, but it is not incumbent on him or her to spend hours each day schooling you on the racing business. And the amenities referred to earlier do not — or should not — include those arrangements that appropriately fall under the domain of a travel agent.

If you are thinking about a partnership, you will definitely want to get references on the person in charge. After you've determined which, if any, horses appeal to you, you should ask to see the prospectus, or partnership agreement. To be prudent, your lawyer and/or accountant should see it, making sure they understand that you understand the proposition is highly speculative. Certainly you must understand the financial arrangements and know how and when the syndicator makes his money.

Back to the horses. How good are they? Where did they come from and how much did they cost? (Did the promoter breed them him-self…a bit of a "no-no," I would think?) Get the names and addresses of some of his current clients and talk to those people. Where are these horses going to be broken, where will they race, and who is to train them? You're not going to be able to control these last three particulars, but you should know about them.

The popularity of partnerships has developed in a rather interest-ing and somewhat erratic pattern. When Dogwood sort of stumbled into our start, we had uniqueness and news value on our side. Soon we came up with a quality filly named Mrs. Cornwallis.

People started writing about us and our unusual concept. Soon *The Wall Street Journal*, *Forbes*, *Fortune*, and many other major publica-tions ran significant features. This brought clients, which delighted us, and it brought competitors, which did not delight or surprise us.

Soon it became clear that some people in the business who had been derisive of us at first had started thinking, "Well, maybe this is not such a terrible idea; and I do have some yearlings here on the farm that I didn't get sold in September…hmmm."

I started getting phone calls that began, "This is Joe Glutz, at Gooberman, Globberman and Lee. I've heard about your partner-ships, and I'd like to see your prospectus." No interest in what horses I may be offering, just wants to see the legal agreement. This was a guy "going to school." Some were good actors (one of today's major competitors would have won the Academy Award!) and some just went through the motions. I knew what they were doing, but I had no protection against it. I had to send the legal agreement. I guess if I had been in their shoes I would have done the same thing.

There began to be a discernible trickle of other partnerships being offered. Nothing big, just a few more every year.

In the late 1970s, the Kentucky Thoroughbred Owners and Breeders Association held "A Day In Kentucky," an annual event to introduce prospective newcomers to the racing game. It was a good idea, and a lot of people attended, including me. But isn't it ironic — after our substantial bloodstock purchases, mostly from Kentuckians — that I was looked upon by some of them like a "bastard at a family reunion"? Invariably, some of the neophytes in the audience would logically ask, "What about this new Dogwood partnership concept that I've been reading about?" At this point, the worst fears of the hardboots had been realized: They were going to have to let me say something. The blood would drain from the organizer's face, and he would mutter, "Well, Cot Campbell is here today and maybe he'd give us a few short comments." I would — and they would be short — but numerous questions would follow because this subject was right down the audience's alley.

It was so silly, because I represented a new and untapped source of yearling sales for these Kentuckians. They should have sent a limousine to the airport to pick me up. They are certainly more enlightened today. And some of the ones who might have asked in a snide way then, "How in the hell do you stand dealing with all those damned people?" are now eagerly trying to do their own partnerships.

The horse business started to explode in an astonishing way in the late 1970s and early '80s. Tax benefits were mighty good, and all the high rollers and wise guys wanted to play the game.

A rash of deals began to spring up as promoters sought to take advantage of a national craze to get in on the racing and breeding business. Brokerage houses, always subject to fads (cattle breeding and feeding, oil and gas tax shelters, boxcar and barge leasing, and so many other gimmicks), decided to tackle horses. We saw some big breeding partnerships and some brokerage house-sponsored racing deals. Some were decently conceived and presented. Others had irresponsible projections. ("We'll buy twenty mares, breed them, sell the yearlings in the summer sale. Let's see, last year's yearling average was $400,000. So, twenty times $400,000? Presto! $8 million a year. Man, where has this been all my life!")

Then came the Tax Reform Act of 1986. The ridiculously high prices of stud seasons, yearlings, and everything else began to plummet...and the chickens came home to roost. Those yearlings conceived at the crest of the boom went to market and did not do too well. Good-bye brokerage houses and big partnerships! What was demonstrated — and always must be remembered — is that anyone involved with any aspect of the horse business had better enjoy horses. A lot of people were led down the primrose path during this time. They were misled, they lost a lot of money, and many were embittered.

A lot of people and outfits were shaken out of the racehorse business, and prices came back down to earth. People began to realize that the end use (the PROPER end use) of a racehorse is to go to the track, run fast, and earn money. Hopefully, earning more than he cost. If that horse does extremely well, then he or she has a future as a stallion or as a broodmare. For a while the Thoroughbred racing business got to be like the Arabian horse industry: You produce one gorgeous animal so he can be retired, go to stud, and produce other gorgeous horses...*ad infinitum*. It's like the old Ponzi scheme, a pyramid. Where does it all end? That trend did end in the racing business at the dawn of the 1990s.

Today's partnerships seem to be guided in the right direction, in my opinion. Most are racing partnerships, but there are a growing number of pinhooking partnerships, in which money is raised by horsemen to buy weanlings or yearlings at auctions and resell them at the next stage of their development, presumably for a profit.

Not much action, not many thrills. But, it's not super speculative, which tends to assuage the mental outlook of the hard-nosed businessman who may be a trifle lacking in "soul" or "madness." We should all have a little of the latter, according to Zorba the Greek.

For our Dogwood racing partnerships, we buy young horses in the $75,000 to $250,000 range and not much at the higher end. It's our way — not necessarily the right way or the only way. My theory is that we want to put ourselves in the position to get lucky, and I don't want us (our partners) to be dangerously vulnerable. I think the $500,000 yearling probably has a twenty percent better chance to be a stakes-caliber horse than the $100,000 yearling, but he costs five times as much, and his chances of getting hurt are just as good.

I maintain that with painstaking shopping, you'll definitely be able to find a well-conformed horse with enough pedigree that if he does pop up and become a good horse, it is no fluke. I do want some pedigree; all I can get. When the going gets tough, and those babies are fighting it out down that long, grueling stretch, I want mine to be able to reach back and call on his mama and his daddy. I want them to have bestowed on him some of that all-important "class."

ANATOMY OF A PARTNERSHIP

Here's how we structure our partnerships:

Let's say I go to the Keeneland September yearling sale and buy a colt for $100,000. He and his stablemates are shipped back to Aiken. We break them, live with them for several months, and then we offer them for syndication. This means we have photographed them (the world's most horrible job!) and prepared a sharp-looking color brochure that is mailed to our clients and others who have indicated through the years that they are interested.

We now have invested about $110,000 in that colt. So, hypothetically, we are going to mark him up to $135,000 (Maybe a little more or a little less. Whatever we can justify and feel good about — no other formula or reason). We are going to keep and maintain five percent of the colt. A share amounting to 23.75 percent ownership will cost you $32,062. You can pay for that in cash, or terms are available, spread out over six months in three equal payments. This buys your interest in the horse. The maintenance will be billed quarterly, in advance, and is, of course, adjusted at the end of each quarter. We simply estimate that it costs about $35,000 per year to keep a horse in training under maximum conditions. This includes training, shipping, insurance, stakes nominations, vet charges, blacksmith, and other incidental charges. If the horse puts money in his bank account, we keep enough there for the upcoming quarter and distribute the rest to the partners.

Our markup compensates us for taking the risk and putting the deal together and for managing the partnership. The only other kicker is that once you have reached positive cash flow, meaning you have gotten all your investment back, we are entitled to ten percent of the net cash flow.

There are two points about partnerships about which I am quite sensitive. One is the occasional reference one reads about "using other people's money" (sometimes cutely referred to as "O.P.M."). We don't do "blind pools," meaning we do not collect money and then go to the sale. We use our money, and we deal in the most perishable commodity imaginable. Every year we end up "eating" a horse or two that came up with a problem before he was syndicated.

The other is complaints about markups, which I admit are pretty rare. I just remember them for a long time! My comments about that are (1) read the last two sentences in the previous paragraph, and (2) refer to comments in the third chapter dealing with the fact that just because horse racing is designed to generate pleasure, one tends to think that fellowship is what it is all about and that any profit taking tends to be on the crass side. The same markup applied to furniture, gifts, groceries, and on and on would never be noticed.

Oh, one other pet peeve. Every now and then some numskull will say to me, "Boy, I wish I were like you, and I could go to the races, have fun, and not have anything to worry about."

The horse business, like every other business, has its own indigenous set of problems. We are dealing with a highly damageable and perishable commodity. Inevitably disappointment rears its ugly head, and vital business decisions are usually made in the least conducive of environments (behind the barn, in a stall with a horse, outside a frantically noisy and pressurized auction ring). Making a living in the horse business is fascinating, stimulating, but certainly no "piece of cake."

If that son of a gun did what I did for a living, he'd have a heart attack, or a nervous breakdown, or both, by 10 a.m. the first day!

Having now vented my spleen, I will go on with our hypothetical case history. Usually, within three weeks after the brochures are sent out, the partnerships are completed, and we have added six or seven new partnership horses to the stable. The partners are advised of each other's identity. We communicate about the progress of the young horse through phone calls and via memo or e-mail. We encourage clients to come to this charming horse town of Aiken and see their horse train. A surprising number do not, and really not many see the horses before purchase. They go by the photographs, which, in our opinion, are the finest money (ours!) can buy. We retain the services of Tony Leonard of Lexington, whom I consider the premier equine photographer in the country.

Communication is key in a partnership. There needs to be a lot of it, and we should take the initiative. People don't get nervous when you let them know what's going on. When the horse gets to the racetrack, information about him flows through us, and there is no line of communication between the partner and the trainer. Our partners get to know the trainer, they see him at the racetrack, and we'll arrange visits to the barn, but it would be disruptive and unthinkable for trainers to be fielding calls from partners all day long. The partners understand that, and the trainers appreciate it.

I have found on occasion that trainer reports need elucidation to avoid causing alarm or needless misunderstanding. We pass on any significant developments to our clients, but we may wait a day or two until we can be definitive about the situation.

I recall a rather unfortunate example of communication that turned out to be excessively direct in nature.

A most attractive couple, Janice and Bruce, were visiting our Georgia farm from Indianapolis. They were involved in several partnerships and loved to come to Dogwood, stay in our guest house, and see the young horses train. They were very genteel; a lovely, soft-spoken, and enthusiastic pair of genuine horse lovers.

One spring they called and asked if it would be convenient for them to come down on a given day the next week. It was, and Anne and I made arrangements to join them on the farm and for us all to have dinner.

At the time, we had a number of horses with a trainer who was located at Gulfstream Park in Miami. This man, Jack Wipowski, was a fine horse trainer but not a man especially noted for his sensitivity or his refinement. In fact, he would get right to the point.

Well, Jack decided this would be a good time for him to fly up to the farm and see how the two-year-olds were training, with the idea that he would try to stake a claim on a few that he particularly liked. He picked the same visitation period as Janice and Bruce. This did not seem like a great idea, but it was the only time Jack could come, and, what the hell, maybe the gathering would be a lot more convivial than I anticipated.

The appointed day came, and all parties convened on the farm in late afternoon. There would be seven for dinner (feeling the need for an additional buffer, I had asked the farm manager and his wife to go with us to the nearby town of La Grange, where there was a nice little restaurant).

Jack Wipowski was built like a rather short longshoreman, and he clearly was a man who did not suffer from lack of appetite. Jack was on the crude side and had a suitably surly manner to go with it. Altogether, he was not the dinner companion you would have selected for this particular function.

All dolled up in a T-shirt and what looked like pajama bottoms that had seen a good bit of use, Jack climbed into the back seat. The motorcade set off gaily for dinner, Anne gamely serving as conversational catalyst for our party of rather disparate backgrounds.

We ordered a drink at the restaurant, and things were going acceptably well. The food arrived.

It should be pointed out here that among Jack's Dogwood charges at Gulfstream was a little filly named Pink Dogwood. And Janice and Bruce owned a share in this filly, and Janice's feelings about all horses, in general, and Pink Dogwood, in particular, were indescribably tender.

Seated across from Jack — not the ideal arrangement — Janice decided that this would be a propitious time both to engage Mr. Wipowski in dinner conversation and get some firsthand comments on Pink Dogwood's progress.

Jack, no such conversational requirements on his mind, was busily shoveling in the groceries, his head about four inches from his plate.

"Oh, Mr. Wipowski," Janice cooed sweetly. "You must tell me how that precious Pink Dogwood is getting along! She's such a sweet thing; such a lovely filly. I do so hope she's going to do well for us. Tell me now. Do you think she'll be a good racehorse?"

Pausing briefly with his spoon inches from his mouth, Jack gave Janice a nasty, incredulous look and barked, "She's a piece of shit!!!"

In a futile effort to save the day, I quickly jumped in and said, "Uh, Janice, I think what Jack means is that Pink Dogwood has not quite come to hand yet."

The day was not saved.

The right sort of communication is vital in a partnership. In addition to routine phone calls and memos, we automatically call forty-eight hours before a race, at which time the entries are taken. We advise our clients that the horse did, or did not, get in the race, the race number, jockey, post position, and other pertinent details. We call after the race is run and tell the partners how the horse fared. With some truth to it, our communication director Jack Sadler likes to say that if the horse won, Cot Campbell takes the calling assignment; otherwise, Jack does the honors.

Jack also maintains a telephone "hot line" providing entries and results on Dogwood horses. This is for the benefit of anyone who is interested and certainly for those running horses that day. If the person goes to the races, we arrange passes, notify the trainer to look for Mr. and Mrs. So and So in the paddock, and arrange for the use of our box. Whether they go or not, we still call after all races.

We also maintain a website (www.dogwoodstable.com), on which we provide stable news, updated weekly.

Three or four times a year we publish the "Dogwood Newsletter," which purports to be an amusing eight-page journal that is sent to every person with any sort of interest in our racing stable.

Jack Sadler has been with Dogwood in one way or another for twenty years, and he is invaluable. After graduating from Washington and Lee, this Baltimorean decided he wanted to go into racing. He went to work as a "hot walker" and worked his way up to assistant trainer before coming to Dogwood Farm in Georgia in the same post. Jack moved with us to Aiken, and about nine years ago he came into the office to take the job that is essentially dealing with our clients.

He is a good horseman, has a marvelous personality, and he's extremely popular with clients. The job and Jack are a match made in heaven. I appreciate him very much.

Other than communications, there are pertinent details in connection with other aspects of life within a partnership, and they should be covered. I emphasize here that other outfits may handle them more beneficially than we do, but I do not know about those details, and I must write about what I do know.

We carry life insurance in the amount of the original partnership price, and this is raised or lowered depending on the horse's performance as his career develops. Should a partnership horse die, the partners will recoup their purchase investment and only be out maintenance money. By the way, partnership horses are the only kind we have. If Dogwood owns them, something is physically wrong with them and they were withdrawn from syndication.

I think an attractive feature in our agreements is that if one of the partners goes into default, which is thankfully quite rare, the other partners are offered their pro rata share of that defaulting partner's obligation and ownership. If they do not wish to take it, Dogwood is obligated to pick it up. If it's a good horse they will want to; if he's bad, they won't, and we have to. Best of all worlds for the partners.

If a partner wants to sell his share, the other partners have the right of first refusal. We do what we can to accommodate the selling partner, with no guarantees, of course. Depends on the horse, naturally.

How do we dispose of horses? Good ones, bad ones? The good ones are more fun. When a stakes-winning colt begins to wind down his career, having lost a step or two, we sell him for stud duty. It makes sense. Making stallions is a game unto itself and is best left to the specialists in that field. Sometimes, if it is the only way to make the sale happen, we will agree to keep a portion of the stud. However, it's cleaner to sell him. Our racing partnerships are just that — RACING partnerships.

If it is a filly, we sometimes breed her and enter her in the Keeneland November breeding stock sale. Depending on when she is retired, we might sell her privately or at auction. In the case of our champion filly, Storm Song, she was retired in July and sold in November "empty" (not in foal) — for $1.4 million, I might add!

I find that people involved in a filly racing partnership will some-times find it charming to consider breeding the filly and selling her offspring or racing them. But when they realize that it is going to be several years before any money comes back, and breeding has its own very real list of problems, their enthusiasm wanes. Let's sell the filly, get the money, and do something else.

When a horse of ours gets good, we will invariably receive inquiries and offers to buy the horse, even though we are not known as "sell-ers." Naturally, these offers are passed on to the partners with any pertinent comments of mine. And they make the decision. The answer is almost always "no." Our partners have gone into racing looking for the "big horse," and when it looks as if he may have arrived they want to hang on.

How do we cull failures, or horses that are "just horses?" First, unpromising horses must be given the benefit of the doubt, after which you've got to be decisive and cold-blooded. If you invest in yearlings in the fall of the year, then I think you must give that horse the chance to get into his three-year-old year — eighteen months later, let's say. Remember the example of the high school "klutz" who went on to be an All-American tackle at the University of Nebraska?

Then, if they are still showing nothing, they should go into claiming races until they find a level at which they can compete. When that happens they will most likely be claimed (or bought) and you are rid of the expense of upkeep. More about claiming races later, but that's the primary avenue for culling (and maybe knocking out a purse or two in the process).

If the horse is injured or has some ailment that will completely compromise his chances of competing at a decent racetrack, then you must get the horse as sound as you can and find a good home for him as a hunter, polo pony, or pleasure horse of some sort.

Several years back "worthless" ex-racehorses were being sold in alarming numbers (anything more than zero is alarming!) to the meat processors for export to horse-meat-eating countries. This practice, which has drawn a great deal of publicity, must be stopped.

Just reflect on the fact that most human beings are not cut out for stardom; most human beings are not even cut out for mediocrity! The same is true for horses, no matter who owns them. The horse doesn't know about his parentage, nor about his cost.

TAX INFORMATION

Our treasurer and his assistant get busy on January 1 preparing tax information for distribution to our clients around February 20. Bill Victor is a bright, thorough, innovative (not excessively innovative, mind you) fellow who is used to fielding a lot of questions from accounting types with varying degrees of sophistication on equine tax accounting practices.

The nature of our partnerships, and, naturally, the participants in those partnerships, have changed drastically though the years. At first we bought cheap horses for larking about and trying to have some fun. Thanks to a steady enough stream of good horses, we have been able to buy better and better horses in this country and abroad (refer to Chapter 6), and we have attracted — if I do say so — a truly blue-chip roster of investors.

In just the past few years, we have had the former or present CEOs of Dow Chemical, Delta Airlines, Ralston Purina, Atlanta Falcons, Visa, NBC Sports, San Francisco 49ers, Marsh and McLennan, Sunkist, the Palm Restaurants, Leggett and Platt, Wachovia Bank, Serta Mattress, E. F. Hutton, Emerson Electric, Textron, and others.

From the horse field, we've had such well-known people as Will Farish, August Belmont, Dick Duchossois, Martha Gerry, George Strawbridge, Lee Eaton, Bob and Beverly Lewis, Warner Jones, Brereton Jones, Reiley McDonald, Tom Van Meter, John Williams,

Whitney Tower, Robert McNair, Wayne Lukas, and others.

Mixed into this are some rather famous national sports, literary, film, and stage personalities, and a wide variety of very nice human beings, some socially prominent, some not. Some clients have become close friends with my wife and me. Others I have never laid eyes on though we may have done business for a number of years.

Frankly, Dogwood has been able to become rather selective because of the success we have enjoyed. Our clients are considerate people who understand that they are buying part of a horse. We are very grateful for their business, and we are going to try mightily to make this venture both pleasurable and profitable. But we are providing a service for the money they are investing. If they buy a share of a horse in the average reputable partnership, they will receive much more communication than they would with the average trainer. Our service includes managing the horse, providing information about him, and arranging certain amenities at the racetrack when he runs.

While I could wax enthusiastic about a number of our clients, I am going to have to single out one, who has become my very good friend. This is Paul Oreffice, former chairman of Dow Chemical, one of the world's biggest companies. This gentleman, who is very much action oriented, purchases a share in every Dogwood horse. So he owns 23.75 percent of the stable.

With a brilliant mind, and a flair for organization and for cutting through excess verbiage, he understands delegation. And if he has confidence in the ability of a certain individual, he goes with him until he has reason not to. I have always admired the fact that a strong personality of this sort has never verbally second-guessed decisions I have made concerning the management of horses. I am sure there have been times when he could have slit my throat (and I could have slit my own!), but never once has he evinced anything but complete confidence in my decisions.

I have always been very grateful for this demonstration of support.

FOREIGN DOS AND DOMESTIC DON'TS

I'll bet Dogwood has imported more racehorses than any other out-fit in history. Joe Hirsch, racing's beloved and respected journalistic dean and the closest thing we have to a historian, says not. He thinks that would be Allie Reuben (Hasty House Farm), who imported horses from South America in the 1950s and '60s with incredible regularity.

Maybe Joe's right, but from 1975 to 1992 we imported about seventy-five ready-made racehorses and put them into Dogwood partnerships. That's a gang of them!

In this chapter, we're going to deal with (1) acquiring horses by private sale (domestic and foreign) and (2) claiming horses. We've done a great deal of the first at Dogwood, but none of the second. It doesn't fit into our game plan but could be a viable option for you.

There are bloodstock agents in this country who specialize in private sales (non-auction) — and scads of them in Europe, South America, and Australasia.

At home, some agents concentrate on discovering and buying emerging stars for particularly well-heeled patrons. These are horses with the alluring aura of Triple Crown candidacy or are at least "suspects." As soon as a two-year-old wins his maiden race in smashing fashion, bloodstock agents lock their antennae on that individual, and the owner's phone starts ringing. Such prospects are unbelievably inflated. They're easier to sell than they are to buy. The closer to spring, the more astronomical the prices. For the industrious bloodstock agent, however, it's a lucrative pursuit. A successful struggle to land a $2 million colt can make his entire year. His five percent amounts to $100,000.

Other agents specialize in finding well-bred fillies whose futures are showing signs of being behind them. These are broodmare prospects for commercial breeders. Still others make a living placing horses which are tailing off, or never had much talent to begin with, on the less glamorous racing circuits. The yearling that cost $250,000 at Saratoga and never ran to his looks or pedigree may end up selling for $25,000 to a stable owner who campaigns at Thistledown in Cleveland and is now struggling to win a race open only to horses that have "never won a race other than maiden or claiming." Finding and placing these horses is grunt work and not a promising way for "the young and the restless" agent to move into the big time.

Using an agent for purchases in this country is very helpful. But for an American looking to buy a made racehorse abroad, an agent is an absolute must.

In 1975, I got a call from a well-respected agent and acquaintance in Newmarket, England (their version of Lexington, Kentucky). He told me about a very fast two-year-old filly. She had just won a prestigious filly stakes, and she could be bought. At that point, I had never bought a horse over there. This sounded promising, and there were others to look at, so I jumped on the wonderful supersonic Concorde (time being of the essence, the agent had cautioned), and I met him, Michael Motion, at Heathrow. When you are offered a horse privately, you must always determine the answer to the three-letter question:

"Putting on the dog" at Royal Ascot.

"WHY?" How come he's for sale? In England, Ireland, and France that can usually be answered quite satisfactorily, especially in the United Kingdom. The purses are rather low, and making money with a race-horse is difficult unless you knock off a real "biggie." So when a horse gets good during his two- and three-year-old seasons and has put some excess pounds in the bank, more than a few owners are tempt-ed to sell. In England, older horses have few opportunities, and the national handicapping system often saddles them with more and more weight. Also, Europeans generally stop racing in the fall and take a hiatus until spring. An English owner has a rather tempting reason to sell at the end of the season and take a nice profit. His train-er encourages it. He knows he will get a commission and the funds from the sale will be used to replenish the barn with sharp young rac-ing prospects from the yearling sales. These are logical motivations. But, believe me, fall is the only sensible time to buy a racehorse in those countries.

Anne and I had been to England several years before. We had gone to the races and spent the evening with Dick Francis, the English jump jockey who went on to become the world's most popular mys-tery writer. So we got a most alluring glimpse of English racing. If you've seen the English sporting prints of Munnings and other famous artists of the 18th, 19th, and 20th centuries, that's the way it is over there. I was smitten with the atmosphere. The English system is unlike ours. They have numerous, shorter race meetings. Three days at Newbury, or Chester, or York, or Ayr, or you name it. Each race-course (then grass only) is a gem, with every conceivable configura-tion — left-handed, right-handed, figure-eight, straightaway. The crowds are invariably well-dressed (great tweeds, hats), colorful (many of them straight out of Central Casting), and they adore and know their horses. They know their names and use them ("Ooh, just look at Ganimede! Isn't he a picture?"). When horses are in the pad-dock, the crowds are eight deep at the rail, craning to get a look. The horses are led along proudly at a sprightly clip by a lad or lass done up in his or her Sunday best. This is the same person who grooms and rides the horse back home at the trainer's "yard." The "yard" is the compound where the trainer and much of his staff live and work and where all of his horses are stabled. The horses are exercised on nearby "gallops" — large expanses of grassy flat lands or hills made into a variety of courses.

Because England and Ireland are small countries, the horses live at home and are vanned on race day (perhaps the day before) to whatever race courses are in operation. On a given day, a big-time trainer may have four in at Ascot, two at Nottingham, and three at Redcar. "Traveling head lads" go with the horses to each venue.

I bought the fast filly, Western Jewel, for 100,000 pounds (about $140,000). She was a fine sprinter. She could "scorch the earth!" But, she could scorch only that part upon which grass was growing. She came to this country and quickly proved that she was strictly turf.

Europe is a great source for U.S. racing prospects.

Couldn't stand up on the dirt! That part was OK, but she also could not run farther than five furlongs, maybe six on a good day. Sadly, in the United States we do not offer but about three or four sprint races a year on the grass. Thus, opportunities were somewhat limited. My expertise on the subject of international racing began with that lesson!

We had no choice but to run her in races of a mile or more. Compromising her career even more was that she only knew one racing tactic — going as fast as she could as far as she could. Not a bad idea at five furlongs but not very effective at a mile. She would break, zoom to the lead, go barreling into the first turn, and at this point her centrifugal force would take her to the outside fence. She would, of course, lose her lead with this antic; then she would churn furiously to the front again. But by the time the field had turned into the stretch, she would have "stopped to a walk," the rider considerately permitting her to canter past the finish line. Later she bowed a tendon and we sold her for breeding purposes.

My first trip to England told me several things. First, not many Americans were buying foreign stock, and the prices for good, solid, stakes-caliber racehorses were quite reasonable. But you needed a certain type of horse. It didn't take me long to zero in on the proper requisites for a colt or filly that should — repeat, should — do well in the States. And Michael Motion and I started going after them. I did a lot of business with British Airways and their Concorde for the next decade and a half. And then it got to where The High Street in Newmarket looked like Rodeo Drive. American buyers and the Arabs and the Japanese descended on the United Kingdom and France like a plague of locusts. For Dogwood that train had run!

I started going for middle-distance horses — seven furlongs to ten furlongs (Remember, a furlong is an eighth of a mile). I found that if a horse could get a mile in England, he could probably get a mile and an eighth going around two turns in the United States. And there is no greater indicator of bravery than a horse that runs well on the straightaway in Europe.

Imagine being a racehorse tearing down the straight Rowley Mile course at Newmarket, and another horse cruises past. You look ahead at that long, seemingly interminable stretch of green. The other horse continues to inch ahead of you, and you're giving it everything you have. What a temptation to quit! There are horses that will keep fighting to the very end. Those, my friend, are RACEHORSES, in the most wonderful sense of the word. Early in the game, I bought such a horse, and he made an indelible mark on my life and career. I think of him every day and am eternally grateful for his incredible courage and for the success he brought to our modest racing endeavor.

His name was Dominion.

On one of our early visits to England (perhaps when we bought Western Jewel), Michael took me by the yard of a highly respected trainer named Arthur Budgett. We had an appointment to see Dominion. We were shown to his stall, and in it was a wee lad holding

Dominion won five stakes and placed in four in our colors.

a rather muscular, moderately sized bay colt. He was not pretty, but he exuded class. Arthur explained that the horse might be for sale at the end of his current three-year-old campaign.

I adored him — absolutely fell in love with him. Dominion stood about 15.2 hands, was rather short-coupled, and was literally muscled to the eyebrows. He had what are called lop ears, splayed to either side. But it was his eye that took your breath away and captured the essence of his class. Believe me, his eye was the size of your fist, so luminous and expressive!

I walked up to him and put my hand flat on his shoulder so I could push my chin up against his withers and get an idea of how tall he was. While he made no perceptible protest, he did cock his head around at me, leveling his gaze as if to say, "What do you think you're doing in here!" I poked around him, picked up his feet, and examined his mouth while he suffered this indignation stoically.

To give you an idea of his physicality and personality, if Dominion had been a human being, he would have been Spencer Tracy, attractive in an aloof, homespun sort of way. We asked Arthur to let us know if he became available, and we left. Several weeks later Dominion ran in the Two Thousand Guineas, one of the world's great three-year-old classics. He was third, but he chased the great Bolkonski and Rose Bowl down that long, heartbreaking mile course in Newmarket and fought relentlessly for every inch of margin he could steal away from them.

I continued to lust after Dominion, who went on to have a very good year. In the fall he was moved to the yard of Ian Balding because his previous trainer became ill. He was sent to France and won a good race called the Prix Perth.

A week later his owner died. Michael Motion called me immediately, and I agreed to offer the widow — going through the new trainer — 90,000 pounds. Ian Balding was understandably not very enthusiastic about this offer, as he knew the horse would be going to the States. Michael — in a bold stroke of endearing genius — went straight to the widow (it was now a decent ten days after the funeral). He made the offer to her, and she accepted. I bought him and shipped him stateside, where he ran for us for the next two years. And no horse ever contributed more to the success of an outfit than did Dominion to ours.

In this country, the old boy danced every dance. He campaigned from Chicago to Miami, and from Saratoga to New Orleans. He even got on the wrong plane one day and ended up in Puerto Rico. But he didn't care. If there was a race to run, he wanted to take his place in the starting gate. He won five stakes and placed in four others in the United States. Dominion's greatest contribution to his career and Dogwood came in the very stylish Saratoga grass race, the Bernard Baruch, in 1978. One of the finest fields of turf runners in America assembled at the Spa that day. We ran an entry — two horses. Coupled with Dominion was a talented but completely goofy horse name Cinteelo.

When the break came, all eleven horses left the gate except for one. Cinteelo decided he was not in the mood and "dwelled" (wouldn't leave). I could have murdered him. But Dominion broke with running on his mind — as usual. He tucked in around fifth going into the first turn, hugged the hedge into the final turn, and angled out to launch his bid. When they turned for home and the running commenced, five of the best were spread out in a line, going head and head. In the middle was that gritty bay horse, Dominion. With his ears flat on his neck and his belly on the ground, inch by inch he fought his way through that long stretch and won by a hotly contested three-quarters of a length.

You could have heard me in Chicago. In life there are those wonderful, but infrequent, moments when you know that a mighty blow has been struck for the cause. This was one of those times. When we walked to the winner's circle through that storied box section, sanctified by such as Lillian Russell, Diamond Jim Brady, and John L. Sullivan, you could feel the thaw: "Maybe this Dogwood outfit is all right. At least they threw a hell of a horse at us today!" He was retired a couple of months later. I sold him back to England. He was bred to some of the most attractive mares in that country. And it could not have happened to a nicer guy! For five years he was a champion sire in England, and we bought a number of his sons and daughters. They were like their old man — genuine, workmanlike, tough, honest race-horses that would give you what they had whenever you asked for it.

Dominion died in 1993. Dogwood decided to honor his memory by establishing a Dogwood Dominion Award, to be presented annually to an unsung hero in racing who has made our industry a better place. Each year at a luncheon at The Reading Room in Saratoga, we present a bronze of the old horse and a check for $5,000 to some wonderful person.

Dominion would like the idea.

Two great aids help immeasurably when evaluating and buying a horse in a foreign country. One is applicable primarily in the United Kingdom — the marvelous book, *Timeform*, in which every racehorse that has started in England or Ireland is assigned a hypothetical weight. The best horse in Europe may be given 138 pounds, while the least inspiring runner may have fifty-seven pounds. It is simply the merit of the horse, expressed in pounds. Throughout the season, *Timeform* ratings are updated — with very colorful commentary — every three weeks. Further, at certain points during the season every race in the land is recreated in a chartbook. So all in all, the English provide superb tools for evaluating horses — for purchase or wager-ing, mostly the latter.

The second development has been a boon to all of racing. In 1973, the Thoroughbred Owners and Breeders Association, at the urging of European authorities, established the American Graded Stakes Committee. This committee comprises members of the Thoroughbred industry who voluntarily meet periodically to issue their collective opinion concerning the relative quality of certain

Thoroughbred races in the United States. The committee ranks eligible races as grade I, grade II, and grade III, in descending order of importance. These are stakes races; they have certain parameters that must be met before they can be considered for grading. If not worthy of a grade, a race can still be qualified as a stakes race but will be termed a listed race. Graded-stakes winners are so designated in sales catalogs, and all stakes winners are shown in bold-face, black-type capitals. Stakes-placed horses are shown in bold-face. This system is now employed all over the racing world, so one can determine that a race run in Japan with a grade II designation will be similar quality to the grade II Bel Air Handicap at Hollywood Park or the Dante Stakes at York in England. This vital system has been a godsend to the horse buyer. Here's a good example:

The British started the system of grading races prior to the Americans and called them pattern races or group races. It was badly needed in England, where every race in the entire country is referred to as a "stakes." More than one neophyte buyer was duped into paying far too much for a horse on the badly mistaken assumption he was buying a stakes winner. What he may have been buying was an animal that had just won the cheapest of cheap maiden races at an obscure racecourse in a far corner of England. Some years before this system went into effect, a charlatan bloodstock agent in Kentucky was engaged by a newcomer to racing (who had more money than sense) to take $100,000 to England and purchase a stallion prospect, a stakes-winning stallion prospect.

Off the blackguard flew to England. When he arrived, aided by associates of similar integrity, he found a rather attractive-looking, decently bred three-year-old colt with just barely enough talent to win one of England's most humble but grand-sounding races — the Royal Snailwell Maiden Stakes! This agent bought the horse easily for $10,000. He then insured him (somehow) for $100,000 and called his patron. His voice quivering with excitement, he shouted into the phone, "I got him! I got him! He's just the perfect horse, and I only had to spend $98,000! Can you believe it?" He then went on to describe the fabulous animal, painstakingly recreating his spine-tingling victory in the prestigious Royal Snailwell Maiden Stakes. The patron was quite elated and somewhat impressed that the agent had commendably stayed under the budget.

The horse was shipped back to the States. The agent pocketed about $85,000 (having certainly spread a little of it around to some confederates who played minor but essential roles in this nefarious scheme) and everyone was quite content — for the time being. However, after arriving in the United States, the horse got sick, colicked, and died. This should have been the ideal scenario. The horse would never be called upon to demonstrate what was a complete void of racing ability, the owner would get his funds back from the insurance, and the agent had made an enormous score — and could probably go back and make another one!

Oh, happy day!

Sadly for the agent, there was a slight hitch. When the insurance claim was filed, the company decided to look further into the horse's origin and the sales transaction. It did not take Sherlock Holmes to determine that the sales price had indeed been $10,000 — a good bit south of the reported price of $98,000. The insurance company saw fit to report this discrepancy to the owner and provided him with a check for $10,000, along with the suggestion that he discuss the deficit with his trusted agent. We surmise that the relationship had been seriously marred.

In these days of *Timeform* ratings and graded-stakes designations, that coup could not have been accomplished, presumably. As a member of the Graded Stakes Committee, the writer can tell you that this twelve-member group meets twice each year, and the two-day December meeting — also attended by numerous observers — is a grueling session during which every stakes race in America is examined. Decisions on upgrades and downgrades are arrived at with the aid of gigantic books of statistics, much expertise, lots of arguing, and very conscientious effort. It is an important exercise in our industry.

CRITERIA FOR BUYING

When buying a European horse, individual characteristics are important and several things must be kept in mind:

He must be genuine, perhaps not top class, but consistent with no weird wrinkles in his or her temperament. It follows that if he has shipped to a variety of racecourses in the United Kingdom and France and has competed with consistency, his temperament and disposition are good. But remember, when he leaves England and comes to the United States, he will be placed in a different environment. No longer will he be stabled in the lovely, serene, pastoral setting of the trainer's yard. He will be shipped to his new trainer's barn at Belmont Park or

Examining the goods at a racecourse in England.

Arlington Park or Santa Anita and will live at the racetrack, until that meeting is over. He will then move on to the next one. He may like this change, or he may not. It's unpredictable. The regimen is completely different. Some foreign horses love it, others miss the old ways. They all must be given several months to acclimatize.

You must select a horse with a good foot. I have found that many English and Irish horses have a flat sole, with little indentation. While this foot may present no problems to training on soft grass over there, that horse will have to train (maybe not run, but train) on the dirt tracks where the horse is stabled, and that flat sole will become sore. If he is weak in his pasterns (sort of the equivalent of a person with weak ankles), the tendency for his ankles to flex down in the grass in Europe creates no ramifications. But they will be burned severely by the sandy loam of our racetracks, and the horse simply can't tolerate this. If the foreign horse relishes racing on soft ground (turf courses

European horses often train in idyllic surroundings, unlike in America.

with a lot of give due to excessive rain), that's fine in Europe because you find a lot of it. But it is not a convenient preference over here. When a racetrack gets a lot of rain on its turf course, the race is immediately relocated to the dirt track. The racetrack must protect its turf course from being chewed up and destroyed because the meeting may last for several months.

You must not buy a pure sprinter. Other than that, I emphasize that horses change when they are imported. A front runner may indicate that he wants to come from behind or vice versa. A confirmed router (a horse that likes longer races) over there may come to the States and show speed. The grass horse in Europe may find he has a liking for the dirt in this country, but do not count on that. With a nursemaid pony to accompany the foreign horse to the post (something not permitted in Europe), you may find that the import arrives at the gate after the parade to the post much less stressed and possessing more energy to expend in the race. Do not buy certain conformation characteristics (flat feet, weak pasterns, lumbering long-bodied horses that won't negotiate our turns well). Other than that, don't have too many preconceived notions on how that horse will adapt to our ways.

And bear in mind, when discussing that horse with his English, Irish, or French trainer, these gentlemen can speak charmingly with great conviction and startling certainty about what a horse in his care will do next. Oh, it is a joy to listen to an English trainer at lunch describing a race or the characteristics of his horses! He may even disclose the identity of The Unknown Soldier!

Many are truly great horsemen, but they do have the gift of gab, and they don't know nearly as much about American racing as they think they do. They will never accept my aforementioned theory that imported horses inexplicably show characteristics here that they may never have even hinted at back in their English environment. And, as far as horses possibly being improved upon here, that is completely ludicrous in the eyes of the English trainer. The horse is simply meeting weaker American competition! What else could it be?

I loved buying horses over there and wish I could still do it. But for my operation, they simply began to cost too much. Not that I was the first human being in the horse business to buy horses in foreign countries, but in the mid-1970s, there were not many. Today there are, and the prices reflect this. With many yearling and two-year-old sales in this country, I never thought it made any sense to go across the Atlantic Ocean to buy young horses. However, the concept of going overseas to buy ready-made racehorses does make sense — for the right price. While I have laid out a lot of dos and don'ts on the selection of racing stock in foreign countries, I must admit I didn't hew to the line every time. I suppose most of us in this game have permitted our hearts to rule our heads on occasion. If our hearts were not influential factors in our make-ups, we would probably be pursuing some other enterprise.

The case of Pipedreamer comes to mind. He was one of my favorite

Pipedreamer winning the Appleton Handicap at Gulfstream Park.

horses. I saw him first at Royal Ascot, where he was one of twenty-eight horses in the Britannia Stakes. It was not an important race, but it was an assemblage of what the English call "handicappers" — allowance horses in our parlance. They are generally just a cut below stakes-caliber horses. Like a seed popping out of a grape, this tiny black horse, his tongue lolling out of the side of his mouth rather insanely, shot out of the pack about thirty yards from home and won the race by several lengths. I loved the sheer exuberance of his performance. On that trip I made a point of going to Lambourne, England, to have a look at Pipedreamer and inquire about his availability and to smoke him over physically. I learned that he would be available at an auction sale in a few months. The physical inspection did not prove to be encouraging, however.

While he was remarkably game and consistent — when kept within the confines of his capability — he was singularly unattractive and from a soundness standpoint, quite ill-suited to be a racehorse. He was a little fellow and rather frail. He might have weighed as much as 800 pounds! He made a terrible wheezing noise when he ran, and had a rather strange-looking growth on one ankle. He also had only one testicle to his name (and the prospects of using that one were not very bright) and was plagued with a heart murmur. While his demeanor would not have qualified him to be called crazy, "eccentric" would certainly have hit him right between the eyes! No one would want him!

That fall I bought him for $32,000.

Someone asked me why I would pay anything at all for such a wreck. "Because," I said, "I've seen him run. And he's a running son of a bitch!!!"

I brought him home, took him straight to the racing stable at Hialeah, and, of course, abandoned any plans to put him in a partnership. How could you offer a horse like that?

We gave him time to acclimate then decided to run him in the

Appleton Handicap at Gulfstream on opening day in early March. He had trained pretty well, and we engaged the services of the fine French rider Jean Cruguet. With a half-mile left to run, Cruguet asked him to move into contention. Wham! Suddenly Pipedreamer was six on top! And he never looked back. He cruised home with two-and-a-half lengths to spare, and what a sight he was. I can see old "Pipes" now, running with his head up in the air like a goose, roaring down that grassy stretch at Gulfstream. His long tongue was flapping in the breeze, and his eyes were about to pop out of his head. What a wonderful day! He won many races up and down the Eastern Seaboard. Naturally, right after the Appleton I couldn't NOT syndicate him. Lots of clients insisted on getting in on him. When "Pipes'" racing days were over, we were even able to find a place where he could stand at stud — Kansas! Hell, it didn't matter to Pipedreamer. Kansas — Royal Ascot — Gulfstream — they were all the same to him. He was just a little working guy — with one testicle.

Not all of our imported horses came from Europe. I have brought in many horses from Argentina and a few from Chile and New Zealand. The important thing about these countries is that they are in the Southern Hemisphere, which means their breeding season is opposite ours. Mares are bred in the fall — not spring — and babies arrive eleven months later, usually around September. This means that a colt foaled in September 1998 would actually be a year old in September 1999. Let's say he was brought to the States in January 2000. Now, he's really only sixteen months old, but in the United States he's a two-year-old! The importation of Southern Hemisphere horses makes for a handicap until the Argentine is in his three-year-old year. At that time, he's grown up physically, and the age difference is immaterial. So if you import any babies, be prepared for a long wait.

My Argentines were tough customers. They train hard down there. They are not babied, they stay lean and mean, and when they come up here — after a rather lengthy period of acclimatization — they tend to stay sound. South Americans seem almost to raise a slightly different breed. I find them to be rangier, racier-looking horses, generally possessing less elegance than their European counterparts. Perhaps their heads are a little plainer. But their hearts are plenty big. And some of the fine stars on the American racing scene have been imports from Southern Hemisphere countries. Argentines do train quite vigorously. With a man on their bare back, they come out each day and gallop at a wide-open clip for about two miles. They only wear a saddle when they breeze. Our trainers really don't make any effort to accommodate this method of training but insist, understandably, on changing them to our ways. In the first place, when the saddle goes on, the horse thinks "breeze," and they've automatically got "run" on their minds. It is very difficult to make the Argentine horses come out on the track, stand for a while, then go off on a long, slow gallop like our horses do. Maybe this is the primary reason why it takes the Southern Hemisphere horse 100 to 120 days to acclimate, while the European does so in sixty to eighty days.

One important point to make about imports: Generally speaking, you can run them once right off the airplane. For a few days after arriving in this country, the foreign horse is still operating on the feed, water, and atmosphere from home. Jet lag will take a few days (unlike we humans) to set in.

One other important point: When I bought racehorses in Europe, I envisioned a scenario where they came over here and won enough money to pay for themselves and then some. In so doing they would maybe make themselves valuable as stallions in this country, depending on their bloodlines, but certainly back home where their bloodlines would be more appreciated. On the down side, I hoped that they had done enough in Europe when I bought them to have some residual value no matter what they did here. If they were absolute flops, I wanted them to be worth fifty cents on the dollar for breeding purposes. This has always been less true of the Southern

Hemisphere horse. Because their pedigrees are more obscure and less fashionable than ours, their residual value is best considered nil in my opinion. You are strictly buying a racing animal.

Well fine, but why don't we just buy our horses in this country? We live here.

You can, especially if it's an inexpensive horse. But do keep in mind that three-letter question, "Why." How come he's for sale? The most legitimate reason is that the buyer would like to turn a profit. That we understand.

Every periodical has ads in the back, offering horses for sale. Every training barn probably has a horse or two or three for sale. People are selling weanlings, yearlings, two-year-olds, horses in training, broodmares, and stallions privately all over the country.

I think you could generalize and say that cheaper stock sells privately in relatively greater volume than costlier stock. The latter is best presented at public auction where the entire world has a chance to bid on them. The disasters are also well-suited for public auction because at least that is an avenue for getting rid of them. If you're just looking for a horse, without any grandiose expectations, then there are plenty for sale privately. You will have them inspected and vetted, and then what you see is what you get (presumably).

However, if you are looking for a heavyweight contender, if you're seeking "blue sky," then do be aware that America is a tough place to buy a good racing prospect for anything like reasonable money. That's the reason for devoting so much space to foreign horses. A lot of those good prospects are for sale for plausible reasons. Their prices are higher than they used to be — and too high for an outfit like ours that must add on a mark-up before syndicating the horse — but comparably they cost far less than you would pay in this country. It is "murder" to buy a top, proven racehorse here. There are a number of deep-pocketed players who will pay almost anything for an established premier racing prospect. If you want to play in this league, then start by getting an agent — the exalted financial neighborhood will get his or her attention.

BUYING TOOLS AND SERVICES

In addition, a variety of horse evaluation services are available, and some of them are pretty darned good. There are people who determine basically whether a prospect has the physical capabilities of being, or producing, a racehorse. A lot of physics goes into this exercise. They concentrate on analyzing the frame, and/or the gait, of the horse. They look for efficiency and economy of motion. After all, it is a question of getting from point A to point B before your competition. Believe it or not, in The Blood Horse's *The Source* 128 listings can be found under the category of Conformation Analysis!

To give you an example, there is Equix Biomechanics. They classify horses into a dozen groupings based on the horse's balance. They determine this by spending about a half-hour examining the animal and recording thirty-six angles with a measuring tape. They also do a heart scan. Scores are given in each category, and all the information is plugged into the data base at their main office.

Another leading practitioner of this art is Cecil Seaman & Company. They have the measurements of 50,000 horses, including, very significantly, some of the best racehorses that have ever lived. After taking fifteen crucial measurements, they compare that information with the successful horses in the data base. They work primarily on racing prospects and do considerable work in planning matings of stallions and mares. Believe me, Pipedreamer would have flunked any of these tests with flying colors!

What started out as resources for serious gamblers are also being used now to discover and evaluate promising horses that are beginning their careers.

One of the basics — and the one that certainly spawned a thriving cottage industry in spotting stars of tomorrow — is the Beyer Speed

Figures, developed by Andrew Beyer, racing columnist for *The Washington Post*.

You'll often hear, "What kinda Beyer did he get?" The Beyer Speed Figures are so important that now they are listed for every horse and every performance in the *Daily Racing Form* — the "bible" for the serious handicapper.

Andy Beyer, a Harvard-educated genius (my inexpert term) is an acerbic, highly energized major-league gambler who has an opinion on every aspect of Thoroughbred racing — valid, but always from the viewpoint of a gambler. While he may comment knowingly on matters having to do with the improvement of the breed, I don't think that is his fundamental motivation. Interestingly, some of the most effective people in a variety of functions in racing ARE, or started out being, gamblers. When your money is on the line, you tend to be a quick and precise study. And the intensity is there. While we don't know the specific ingredients for the Beyer secret formula, they come (oversimplified) from blending the times of the race and times of the

A completed claim slip is inserted in the box.

other races that day with the class of other horses in the race. I am sure Andy would foam at the mouth over this kindergarten explanation, but it will do for our purposes. Whether betting on or buying a racehorse, comparing the Beyer numbers is a good place to start. Much dough has changed hands over these digits. Two other important members of the "numbers industry" are Len Ragozin and Jerry Brown (Thoro-Graph). These men started out working together some years ago but split up and now compete. Unlike Beyer figures where the top performances have the highest numerical rating, both these fellows assign lower figures to the best racers. While their services are primarily for big players at the track, a number of racing stables use their data to locate keen prospects. Some of the best horses in recent years have been "discovered" by one or the other. These services will cost you plenty, but they are worth plenty…if you get the right horse!

If you want instant action, if you want to see your colors on the racetrack immediately, if you just want a horse — then you probably ought to claim one.

CLAIMING RACES

The majority of races run in this country are claiming races. It is a wonderful system for seeing to it that every horse can find a level at which he can compete. It is also one of the least understood and most underappreciated systems in any sport.

Each horse entered in a $25,000 claiming race, for instance, is subject to sale, or "claim," at the value stated ($25,000) in the conditions of the race. Claims are made in a brief window of opportunity before the race is run.

Entering horses in claiming races — and having them claimed — is a splendid way to cull stock from a racing stable that is interested in maintaining only the highest class roster. Claiming horses also is the ideal way to get into racing in a hurry. Maybe. The idea and dream behind any claim is that when you "take" the horse, your trainer (a clever devil, you are convinced) can improve on him, and soon you will have knocked out a couple of big pots, while the horse is moving up in class. Now that horse you claimed for $25,000 has won two races and put $18,000 in purse money in your racing account. And — get this — he is now running and competing terrifically in $40,000 claiming races. "Why didn't I know about this game sooner?"

The horse continues to improve because you've added blinkers, run him on the turf, changed jockeys — or some other brilliant innovation. Now he steps up into allowance company and from there graduates to stakes competition. He just needed someone to open the door to how good he could be. That's the best case scenario. Here's a moderate one:

You run him five times over the next three months, having raised him to the $35,000 claiming level. He runs fourth, fifth, sixth — right around there. You're paying to keep him, and he's not earning anything. Are we being too ambitious? Back he goes into a $25,000 claimer, and he runs second. But we need a win. He's entered in a $18,500 claimer and he does win — clears $7,000. And he is claimed. You're out, almost clean. You've had a lot of action, but other than that you haven't accomplished anything. Here's what you DON'T want:

You get that $25,000 claim back to the barn, and the trainer — whose eagle eye was a major factor in targeting the claimee — says, "Gee, this horse has a tendon that seems kind of hot. Must have rapped it in the race (uh-huh, sure — in the race!!). But I think I can hold it." Most jurisdictions have a rule that for the thirty days after a claim you must run the horse for twenty-five percent more than the value of the original claim. This is generally to slow down claims and retard any use of claiming horses for gambling coups. So our boy must run for the $32,500 claiming race we see in the condition book. We want to run him because that tendon might not last forever, and we sure as hell don't want to be training him any more that we have to.

The horse is entered in the race. He runs and bows his tendon, finishing way up the racetrack. All he got out of the race was hot and dirty and a bowed tendon. The vet checks him at the barn after the race and gloomily reports, "You'll have to turn him out for at least eight months, and then try him." The trainer and the vet know that if he was worth (sound, that is) $25,000 to begin with, he's going to be worth about half that, if he does stand training when he gets back.

The claiming game has plenty of the latter two scenarios and a few of the first scenario, but not many. This is an appropriate time to point out that, unlike purchasing at public auction or privately, the buyer is not entitled to perform any sort of veterinary exam. If you stand at the entrance to the paddock of any racetrack before a claiming race is run, you will see claiming trainers peering intently at the legs of the horses in the race. THAT is the examination, the only one. Claiming trainers and claiming owners specialize in this kind of stock. They claim a horse, hope to win several purses, and then say good-bye when some other claiming outfit takes the horse. Some employ clockers to check on the early morning training of horses and to keep their eyes and ears open for helpful comments from stable employees. This is all part of spotting what might be a smart claim.

Claiming trainers also don't make it easy. Visitors are definitely not welcome in the barn. And horses are sent over to the paddock to run, often with leg wraps, to make things difficult for spying eyes. How can you claim a racehorse? You must have an owner's license in the state in which you plan to claim, and this is not hard to obtain. You pick up the forms in the racing commission office at the racetrack. Most states now have what is called open claiming, which means you do not have to have started a horse at the meeting, or even have one stabled on the grounds. Those were previously the rules throughout the land. Now you just have to be licensed. But the practical first step is to get a claiming trainer that is geared to that phase of the game. They possess a ready-made knowledge of many of the better candidates at various claiming levels on the grounds. He will guide you, undoubtedly with great fervor, because he's interested in new clients and new horses. You might — when you feel comfortable with him or her — make him your authorized agent, so he can act in your behalf on claims. This is a good idea. You could be out of town on business when the ideal claim comes up, and you want to be able to move. Logically, you must have the funds for the claim and the sales tax, if any, in your account with the Horsemen's Bookkeeper. No IOUs in this procedure!

Claim slips are picked up in the racing office. They must be filled out accurately. You would be flabbergasted at the number of claims that are invalidated because the name of the horse was misspelled! The claims clerk can give you precise information on the claim box's location and when that claim slip has to be in there. So can your trainer. If the horse being claimed is a standout, there may be multiple claims, in which case a random selection system is used to decide the new owner. It is called a "shake" and involves just that. A container with numbered balls is shaken, and one ball is withdrawn. The number on the ball will correspond to a number on the claim slip, thus determining the new owner. If you have put in a claim, the trainer will send a groom with a halter and a shank to the winner's circle area, because if you are successful, the new horse will be led back to your trainer's barn. By the way, in practically all states he's yours when the starting gate opens. If the poor fellow has a heart attack and dies during the race, you are the "poor fellow" who owns him! The owner in whose colors the horse started is entitled to any purse money. The subject of claiming has been described as being underappreciated and misunderstood, and that's putting it mildly.

The claiming system in our country does provide a level of competition for virtually every sound horse. With claiming prices ranging from $2,500 to $200,000 at racetracks throughout America, there is a race somewhere for every horse, woeful though his talents may be. I'm amazed by the number of highly intelligent people who enter racing and are completely baffled and nettled by our system of claiming races. Here's why claiming races are good: The end use for a race-horse is to compete in races and earn money. Surely YOU want him to earn money. And, while he is just a horse, a four-legged animal, you must understand that he knows when he is overmatched and he becomes intimidated and discouraged. If a horse is asked repeatedly to compete at a level over his head, he — like a human — will become disheartened, lose interest in what he's doing, and what ability he has will dissipate. Believe me, this happens. Interestingly, a horse that has been running and losing in allowance company, can be dropped into a claiming race and win, and his self-esteem soars. Perhaps then — bolstered by his "I'm hot stuff" outlook — he can return to the allowance ranks. Because he thinks he can win, he does win. He may climb farther up the ladder. This is by no means a common synopsis, but it does happen in varying degrees. At the very least, the drop will

A successful claim will wear one of these tags after a race.

keep the racehorse from further deterioration of ability.

It is immaterial that he is sired by A.P. Indy and out of a wonderful mare that has produced stakes winners and that he sold in the Keeneland auction ring for $400,000. If he has been given every reasonable shot to develop into a racehorse, and he hasn't, something must be done. If the horse is now well into his three-year-old year, has run eight times, short and long, dirt and grass, and has not broken his maiden, clearly he is not impressed with his auspicious background. The task at hand is to get him to a level at which he can compete — and enjoy competing. Claiming races, here we come. The claiming game is fascinating with lots of psychology aimed at man and beast. Claiming is like a chess game in many ways. The fact that you didn't buy the horse to run in claiming races, don't relish putting a "tag" on him, and would be put out if someone claimed him, is not germane at this point. He is what he is. You must play the cards you're holding in your hand.

You have three choices: One, you can keep running him over his head, and soon he may be useless. Two, you can retire him, relegate him to pet status, and keep him in the backyard. Or, three, you can sensibly lower your sights and run him at a claiming level where he's competitive. When you do run a horse in a claiming race for the first time, be sure you don't waste the opportunity. Try to make it mean something. For instance, if your horse has been running in maiden allowance races and finishing nowhere, agree to run him in a claiming race. But don't promptly handcuff the horse by saying, "Sure, I'll agree to run him for $80,000." Man, those are pretty good horses. You're just going through the motions. Drop him in for $40,000. Put him where he can win.

Horses are not claimed at a feverish rate. Just enough of it goes on to keep everyone honest. Using an entirely different example than the one dealt with above, let's say you are blessed with a pretty good horse, but he's a cut below a stakes-caliber horse. You can put him in a $50,000 claimer, and you'll win by the length of the grandstand, but that horse will cool out in someone else's barn. So you don't do it. At the average racetrack on a routine day, three or four horses will be claimed.

I think the rule should be that if you're going to risk your horse in a claiming race, then make it count. Try to get the winner's share of the purse.

Our pattern tends to be this:

Our crop of two-year-olds is sent out to the races every spring. About a year later, in April, May, or June, we've got a line on them. We have given them the benefit of the doubt, with ample time for the late bloomers to begin blooming, and now it is time "to fish or cut bait" — start thinking about claiming races. However, Saratoga, with its juicy purses, is due to start in late July, so we will perhaps freshen them a bit and wait until we get to that meeting. Then that's the place to take whatever little gamble there is and run the lesser lights in claiming races. Each year at Saratoga we'll lose three or four horses for a tag, but we'll also win a few of those nice purses. Make the opportunity as beneficial as you can. You must understand this important but frustrating point: When a horse wins a $40,000 MAIDEN claiming race, this means he has beaten a bunch of horses that have never won a race. Now, there are usually "conditions" within claiming ranks. Most every race has conditions, and to be entered, horses must meet those conditions. You want to take advantage of the easiest conditions as you move forward. There's a perfect racetrack adage that covers this philosophy: "Always keep yourself in the best company, and keep your horse in the worst company."

Therefore, the ideal race is a claiming race open only to horses that are "non-winners of a race other than maiden or claiming." You've won a maiden claiming race, so you are eligible. But you are pumped. You won that last race by two lengths. "This horse is getting good now! Let's go do it again, but we'll jump up to the $50,000 level." Is that a good idea? Remember, he beat maidens and now he's going to face winners. They're bound to be much tougher. The realistic thing to do would be to enter him for $30,000. That might be too painful for you, but at least run him at the same level — $40,000. That's giving him the benefit of the doubt that he, too, is pumped and can perhaps handle these horses.

Understanding and then considering conditions is vital. If you were to run your horse — after his maiden win — in a wide-open (no restrictive conditions) $40,000 claiming race, you are sure enough asking for trouble. Some of those horses could have won ten or fifteen races. These are tough old warriors. They may have lost a step or two from age, but they come to run — every time. Higher-priced claimers are interchangeable with allowance and stakes competitors, depending on the racetrack and the season. For instance, those $40,000 claimers are borderline, or perhaps legitimate, stakes horses at Thistledown, River Downs, Hoosier Park — smaller racetracks where the purses are less attractive to the "heavy heads." A $75,000 claiming horse is close to being a stakes horse in New York in the winter. Lesser stakes races around the country attract many horses that are interchangeable within the $75,000 to $150,000 claiming ranks at Florida during January; Keeneland and Churchill Downs in spring and fall; Santa Anita, Del Mar, and Hollywood Park at their prime meetings; and at Belmont Park and Saratoga it is back to the real world! He's a $75,000 claiming horse, and he'd better be solid because that price is sometimes inflated when the meeting is teeming with good horses. At this writing, one of the greatest poster boys for claiming races recently emerged. Charismatic, 1999 Horse of the Year, three-year-old champion, winner of the Kentucky Derby and Preakness, ran in a $62,500 claiming race only a few months before achieving stardom.

Some of the great horses in the history of racing have known the ignominy of "running for a tag."

THE SELLING GAME

W hen it comes to sheer, unadulterated drama, nothing — but nothing — can touch a big-time Thoroughbred auction! Twenty-five times each hour, major theatrics play out. Dreams are dashed, thrilling victories realized, horrible decisions made, strokes of genius exhibited, financial scores achieved, and costly economic blunders committed. For some, the entire year is made or lost. Actions will change some lives. The Keeneland and Saratoga yearling sales are international "happenings." They rank along with any sports, social, cultural, or commercial event in the world in glamour, importance, and status. Some of the richest, highest-profile exemplars of clout, chutzpah, and chic — from the Arab countries, Japan, England, Ireland, France, Italy, China, South America, and elsewhere — are deposited in Lexington, Kentucky, and Saratoga Springs, New York, by an armada of private aircraft from 747s to Lear Jets.

If the racing of Thoroughbred horses is thrilling and exhilarating — and it is — then buying and selling them are just as much so. These sales are far more than venues for trading the finest young bloodstock.

They are also like international conventions, attended by every luminary, hustler, wannabe, and rubbernecker drawn to the sport and its ambiance. The big sales are places to see and be seen. Eighty percent of the human beings thronging around the barns and pavilion fall into that category. If they're doing any business, it doesn't have to do with the buying and selling of the young horses on the grounds, although most are trying to appear to be so engaged.

Very few people have been to more sales than the writer. I may not exactly rival in volume the great Maktoum family of Dubai, whose members think nothing of plunking down $40 million or $50 million at Keeneland during a couple of July days, but not many horsemen have bought as long and as steadily as I have. Dogwood probably has purchased about 900 horses at public auction since 1967. And close to $80 million has been spent for them. I've never gone to an auction in anything less than a state of excitement and anticipation.

And I've never left without being totally exhausted, relieved that it was over, and completely delighted to go home.

You are there to spend a lot of important money on young horses that will play a gigantic role in your career and business. Logistically, the inspection and reinspection of those animals, and the research and preparation for their purchase, are demanding with severe time constraints. In addition, you know practically everyone at the sale. You are constantly stopping to shake hands, be told some hot item, or answer a question about the progress of a horse you bought in the past that may provide germane guidance on one of the offerings of this sale.

It is almost like a gigantic cocktail party, but often conducted in severe summer heat in close quarters with 800-pound obstreperous animals, sometimes quite cranky from being taken out of the stalls and paraded and poked thirty or forty times a day. Most of the people at the sale really have nothing to do and are looking for companionable chatting. It is stimulating, fun — but it is not easy.

Friends, clients, or acquaintances, intrigued by the sale, often ask if they can tag along to see how yearlings at public auction are inspected and bought. The answer must be, "No." I don't know how you can look at yearlings, answer questions, introduce people, and generally engage in social intercourse, and do a decent job at any of it. Yearlings and two-year-olds are best looked at alone. This is my *modus operandi*, and I'll use the example of the Keeneland September sale.

I know that I will be trying to buy seven or eight yearlings each in the $75,000 to $250,000 range. When I receive the catalogs — five volumes with close to 4,000 horses for this sale — I will spend several nights going through the first two books, turning down the pages on those "hip numbers" I want to look at. The individuals in the sale are assigned numbers, which are plastered on their hips. The better pedigrees are positioned at the first part of the sale, so that the caliber of horses — and the prices — lessen (theoretically) through the ten days. The first two books will take me through Monday, Tuesday, and Wednesday, and if I can't find eight horses out of the 900 being offered during that time, I should have stayed home. I then turn my two books over to an assistant in my office who will prepare a chart for the inside cover of my catalog. This will give me the barn numbers and which horses in which consignments I want to see there. When I start at Keeneland's Barn One, for example, I know I will go to the Taylor Made Farm consignment and ask for hip numbers 32, 67, 86, and 98.

The only person I attend sales with is Ron Stevens, Dogwood's long-time head trainer. He and I have been together for two decades, and we are on the same wavelength. When we get to Lexington, Ron has a similar chart in his book. We agree that he will start inspecting from Barn 38 down, I will work from Barn One up, and we'll meet in the middle.

The first day we don't lay eyes on each other, but the next morning we meet early in the day. I give him my culls, and he gives me his. So now, instead of having a list of 160, we have seventy-two horses to work on. I might be crazy about some of the yearlings on that list, but I think they should be inspected by both of us. I go to the barns he has visited, and he goes where I have been. That afternoon, we meet again, and the list is whacked down to forty-five.

The next day, we revisit the short list together, and afterward the list is at thirty-eight, let's say. The horses are X-rayed and scoped before the bidding begins, but usually this is done through a convenient new service that many sales are offering — the repository. To avoid constant X-raying of ankles, knees, and hocks, and repetitive endoscopic exams — in which a tube is inserted down the young horse's airway to determine its wind soundness — these tests are done ONCE prior to the sale by the consignor, through a reliable vet. The findings are on file in the repository. This system does not suit everyone, but it saves wear and tear on the horse, especially the popular ones, and it saves you — the buyer — a lot of time. We engage our own vet to review X-rays of our short list of candidates. The list is then culled further as a result of the findings.

CONDITIONS OF SALE

The "conditions of sale" are found in the front of every sales catalog. They cover a wide variety of pertinent topics having to do with credit and payment, bidding disputes (with which I am acutely familiar), warranties concerning soundness (very important), and other "house-keeping" matters. These conditions are long, loaded heavily with ponderous legalese, and not something you'd want to curl up with in front of the fire. But if you're going to participate in an auction sale, you'd better read them, or make sure the agent and/or trainer accompanying you understands them.

Basically, any horse that is a cribber, a cryptorchid, a wobbler, twin, or has a vision defect or has undergone surgery, must be announced as such. A cribber is a horse that has the annoying habit of sucking wind, usually while biting a board. This can lead to colic, and other

Examining yearlings, hard work for man and beast.

horses can pick up this tendency. A cryptorchid, or a ridgling, is a colt whose entire testes aren't evident within the scrotum. Understandably, this is considered undesirable from a breeding standpoint. A wobbler suffers from a neurological disease caused by the compression of the spinal cord, resulting in lack of balance and coordination. You can live with the first two, but definitely not the third.

If the X-rays or endoscopic examinations in that horse's envelope indicate the animal has any discernible irregularities in his joints, the bone structure of his legs, or his air passages, and you and/or your representative have signed off on that hip number in the repository, indicating you're aware of these conditions, then you have no recourse if you buy that horse.

Any radiographs taken within twenty-four hours after the session that indicate an undisclosed problem may result in the animal's being returned to the consignor.

Disputes resulting from this situation are adjudicated by a panel of three veterinarians.

Another fact that is germane primarily to consignors, but of interest to you, demonstrates the importance of the sales company's credit check of new buyers. When the hammer comes down, it is the sales company's responsibility to collect the funds. In rare default situations, the company will seize the horses and resell them for its own account in a later sale.

These are the salient points covering the selling of horses, but they differ from sale to sale — and more than sixty horse sales transpired in America in 1999 — so read the catalog before the sale.

Back to our sale. After spending several hours back in my hotel room going over catalog notes and solidifying my thoughts, I am ready to bid on horses.

The answer to the often-asked question, "How do you know how much you should bid?" simply comes from experience. I know from previous sales results, stud fees, the stylishness of certain pedigrees, the horse's looks, and the action around the barn involving other look-ers (and who they are), about how much that horse ought to bring. Chances are it will be more than I can handle, but I want to be ready. The key to getting a good buy at a horse sale is being organized, being ready to move. Carpe Diem! Seize the day!

I remember a painful example of not being organized.

The worst thing you can have in a racehorse is a twin. Nowadays, when a mare is pregnant and the ultrasound shows two embryos, one is aborted. Back before ultrasound, the mare just went ahead and had twins. Invariably, neither twin would ever have sufficient vigor to be an effective racehorse (although females can be potent broodmares), and if a horse were to be sold at public auction, the twin status had to be revealed.

Some years ago, I attended the Nelson Bunker Hunt stable dispersal, made necessary by Bunker's dramatic but unsuccessful attempt to corner the silver market, and his resulting case of the financial "shorts."

One of the horses I saw there was a smallish, sharp-looking bay colt by the respected sire In Reality. I looked at him, thinking he was undersized, but so were some of the best progeny of that sire. He was sort of interesting.

When he was brought to the sales ring that night, I hurried up to watch him sell. On the way, someone stopped me and I became engrossed in some juicy tidbit of gossip. Suddenly, I heard the bidding start on the colt. I flew into the back of the pavilion, and much to my astonishment, the bidding had stalled at a paltry $28,000. Because I was "organized," I threw up my hand and bid $30,000. I got him! What a steal! I signed the sales slip, making the transaction official. I then strutted down the aisle to my seats, where my wife Anne was seated. She looked up at me, and pleasantly but rather quizzically observed, "I see you bought a TWIN."

"What do you mean, twin?" I shot back. "Where'd you get that idea?"

"I got it from the announcer, just as the horse walked into the ring, when he said he was obliged to warn all prospective buyers that this colt was a TWIN," Anne sweetly explained.

The blood drained from my face. I was the proud owner of a useless twin. A year later, after breaking him and just going through the motions with him at the races, I sold him for $3,500.

Pay attention to announcements at horse sales. When the sale is ready to start I take a seat among my usual reserved ones provided by Keeneland for active buyers. My credit is thankfully good, as I have been paying my invoices from Keeneland within two weeks of purchase for a long, long time.

The announcer reads out the conditions of sale; provides a list of "outs" (hip numbers that have been scratched from the sale, ostensibly because of injury); the bid spotters are in place; and the sale is on.

The announcer reads a brief description of the first horse, and hip

Prospective buyers getting one last look at Keeneland sale yearlings.

number one is led in by his somewhat nervous groom. He is turned over to one of two ringmen who alternate handling the young horses during the approximate two or two and a half minutes it takes to sell them. Horses are lined up in the chute, walking ring, or preliminary staging area behind the pavilion about fifteen at a time and then are moved forward as horses are sold. The crowds are heavy in these areas, with prospective buyers taking a last-minute look at the yearlings. Once sold, the horse is led back to his barn and stall, and the new owner, having signed a sales slip (or receipt) just after the hammer went down, arranges to transport the horse to his new home. This is repeated about 300 times a day for the next ten days. The buyers who are shopping at the top of the market do their business, then depart. They're replaced by the intermediate price shoppers. At the end of the first week, many of them now are gone, and a preponderance of white cowboy hats appears on the scene, signaling that the lesser-priced horses are coming on the auction block. Many of the trainers and owners from smaller, down-to-earth, predominantly western racing states are there to have at them.

If, while I'm waiting for my next hip, I find that I have twenty-five or thirty minutes before my horse comes into the ring, I may spend that time looking again at some horses coming up later that day or the next. Or I'll call the office, eat lunch, or walk "out back" and chew the fat with someone. We spoke earlier of signing the receipt and making the transaction official. There was an incident in my sales history when signing it did NOT make a transaction official.

In 1985, the most popular stallion in the world was Northern Dancer. His yearlings were bringing astronomical prices, averaging well over a million dollars. At a sale (which shall be nameless) I bought a lovely Northern Dancer colt for $1 million. I was overjoyed. I knew I could walk through that pavilion one time and syndicate him for probably $1.2 million, so great was the demand for Northern Dancers as racehorses, and so extraordinarily high was their residual value as breeding animals no matter what their racing record. I was also quite surprised when the auctioneer knocked him down to me because the Arabs were in an absolute feeding frenzy for sons of the great stallion.

The attendant brought me the sales slip to sign. I did. He then gave me the yellow receipt, which I stuck in my pocket while people congratulated me and the always continuous sales pavilion murmur increased markedly in volume over this surprising sale.

The next hip was in the ring when the auctioneer suddenly intoned, "Ladies and gentlemen, there has been a dispute in the bidding over the last horse, and we're going to reopen the bidding."

At this point, losing my cool (with damned good reason, I still feel), I held my receipt aloft and yelled out, "How can there be a dispute? Here's my receipt for the horse!" Now the entire pavilion was deathly silent. The announcer proceeded to read aloud a pertinent condition of sale, "the auctioneer shall have the right to adjudicate any disputes arising from the bidding."

What had happened was that the entire entourage of one of the major Arab families had "gone to sleep," perhaps expecting that it would take more time for the bidding to get to the neighborhood where they would jump in and get serious. At any rate, they got shut out, and I "bought" the horse. This was the "dispute." The bidding was indeed reopened.

The Arabs bid $1.1 million. I hit it at $1.2 million; they went up $50,000 and got the horse. Sales companies do not like to (1) leave money on the table, and of much greater importance in this case, (2) they are loathe to irritate Arab buyers. I think the auctioneer simply overreacted and went impulsively beyond the bounds of acceptable judgment.

After stalking dramatically out of the sales arena, I quickly saw that the most practical recourse was to forget it. If I sued, the horse would have been tied up legally until he died of old age, and I had little to gain by rupturing my longtime relationship with the fine sales company involved. I think its officials knew they had — in the heat of battle — acted unfairly. However, they could hardly admit this (because of legal action possibly being taken). They wrote me what was close to an apology. The press had a field day with it. I must say, I did rather enjoy that!

Oh, by the way, the horse never won a race. I also enjoyed that.

CONFORMATION

Buying yearlings is like recruiting a professional football team by looking at a bunch of ten-year-old kids. I love that analogy and have used it to death, but it is so true. If you looked at a young boy whose father is Joe Montana and mother is Chris Evert, the pedigree page would be a "ten" on a scale of one to ten. Then let's imagine his physical presentation. While he is a far cry from being mature, you can see that he will be of sufficient size to make the team. "Good shoulders, slim hips, strong legs, exudes athleticism," your notes, made while examining this child, might read. "Well-balanced, quick, lively step, strides out with purpose when asked to walk. Good carriage, straight, true action when he strides, neither slew-footed nor pigeon-toed. Good energy level.

"A countenance that is pleasing, open, direct, and bespeaks character. Looks you in the eye, and shakes hands with a firm grip. Interested and curious in the goings-on, but confident and in no way uneasy about being inspected." This is the individual you're looking for! The problem is his equine counterpart will sell for $3 million, and the Arabs will buy him! You and I will probably have to settle for a lesser prospect, and perhaps one that will have a flaw or two. It is imperative that you grasp the fact that there is no perfect horse. Even Secretariat could be called "goose-rumped." Kelso had all the charisma of a third-rate harness horse, Mr. Prospector had front legs that did not fit on just right, and Forego was too big and gross. Yet they were all remarkable, thrilling racehorses.

You want the best possible conformation you can get, of course, but there are certain flaws you can live with and certain ones you can't. However, if you get ten top horsemen together, you'll find that five of them can't abide a horse that toes in. The other five have no trouble with that, but spare them from a horse that toes out! It is not an exact science. Once you learn something about conformation — and that will not happen in a hurry if you're starting from ground zero — walk into the paddock before the running of a big stakes race and look over the field of proven, superior runners. Stand where you can observe them as they walk toward you. Take a gander at how their knees and ankles are put on. If you and your adviser had inspected them when they were ten-year-old boys and girls, you would certainly have passed on some of them. And, it is not inconceivable that the much-admired son of Joe Montana and Chris Evert would be off at some bush track trying to break his maiden. It is NOT an exact science, indeed.

In 1969, I went to the Keeneland September sale. I stopped by Barn 28 and asked to see hip number 126. This handsome brown colt looked good when he first came out. But when I asked the showman to walk him, and he came straight at me, he was clearly quite crooked in his right front ankle, winging badly in his walk. My "expert eye" told me that this was defective merchandise. I told the groom to put him up and moved on about my business.

I was in the pavilion when the colt sold that night. I remember it because when the big door to the sales ring opened and he ambled in, throwing that right leg out to the side, he was pretty easy to spot. I watched as some idiot (I thought) bought him for $1,200. Even thirty-one years ago, this was "peanuts" for a living, breathing racehorse, but someone was going to put thousands in training the badly-flawed colt. What a waste! Never thought about him again, really.

Two years later I was in Louisville for the Kentucky Derby covering the race for a chain of Southeastern newspapers. What a tremendous field it was in '71 — twenty horses. It looked like a cavalry charge as they came by the press box the first time. The race unfolded, and when the field swept through the final turn and the stretch runners began launching their bids, I saw a horse at the very back of the pack kick in with an electrifying move. Through the turn he came flying, wheeled right out in the middle of the racetrack, and his rider asked him for his life! And he gave it! As he came charging relentlessly down that long Churchill Downs stretch, collared the leaders, and stormed to the front, I noticed a very funny thing — he was tossing that old right leg out to the side!!!

Yep. That was my horse — the very one I had so smugly turned down for $1,200. His name was Canonero II. He won both the Kentucky Derby and the Preakness Stakes.

Framed and hanging in my office is that yellowed old catalog page, with the notation in the margin that reads "right front?" with a big "X" slashed across the page. On rare occasions when I might get a little high on myself, I look at it.

Yearling sales in North America are the barometer of the health of the Thoroughbred industry. If the trade at the yearling sales is brisk, that means broodmares — quite essential in the production of future yearlings — will sell well. So will weanlings (around six months old) as pinhookers shop for raw material to turn into finished products and profits during the year ahead. If yearlings sell well in the summer and fall, two-year-olds will be in big demand at the Fasig-Tipton, Ocala Breeders, Barretts, and Keeneland sales the following spring. Stud fees fluctuate in accordance with the yearling averages. So yearling sales are watched with an eagle eye. About forty-five percent of all revenue generated at Thoroughbred auctions in this country comes from yearling sales. As this is written, yearling prices have risen for seven consecutive years in North America. This is quite encouraging. But the horse market in the mid-1980s reached a zenith of silliness when one yearling brought $13.1 million, and the combined Keeneland-Saratoga sales average hit $456,902 for 468 blue-chip babies at those two summer super sales.

The bubble burst shortly after that (it almost HAD to), and sale prices bottomed out in 1992. Since then they have picked up steam annually, and in 1999 the combined Keeneland-Saratoga sales average was the third highest in history at $412,000.

The correction that began in 1992 had the effect of seriously reducing the annual foal crop. Back in 1986, a total of 51,296 registered foals were produced in North America. The foal crop in 1999 was about 36,000. This tightening of the supply was a healthy development. For many years, foreign buyers have propped up the North American horse market. In 1989, more than sixty percent of the expenditures at Keeneland and Saratoga came from foreign buyers. By 1999, that figure had dropped considerably. With a rampaging U.S. stock market, foreign expenditures were down but still healthy at close to thirty percent. Essentially, two things in addition to market conditions control the prices that yearlings (and weanlings) fetch. They are pedigree and conformation — two of the most important words in our world.

At two-year-old sales, add another ingredient: performance. If these juveniles sparkle when they breeze a fast eighth or quarter of a mile a week before the sale and again the day before the sale begins, then pedigree takes a back seat.

Some people do not agree with the logic of pushing babies to demonstrate brilliant, but rather meaningless, short bursts of speed. The writer is one of that camp; although admittedly an eighth in :10 flat will have the crowd buzzing. And fast works bring sensational prices.

PEDIGREE

A pedigree, while not infallible, is the closest possible prognosticator of character, poise, and courage — CLASS. It is that individual's family tree.

The catalog page that presents it to you is factual, but it emphasizes the achievements of the various members of the family and not necessarily any "lemons" lurking in the horse's genealogy. For instance, under the first dam you may note the only one of her sons and daughters listed is "Old So and So," a winner of $45,576. There may not have been any other foals, or she may have produced six others that went to the races and did absolutely nothing. If the latter is true, this information detracts considerably from the quality of the pedigree. And you need to know it.

A handy tool to be used along with your catalog is the *Thoroughbred Times Buyer's Guide,* which covers most sales and provides the complete produce record of the mare, the winnings of each of her foals, the sale prices of her previous offspring, and the names of the people who bought them if those horses sold at public auction. Now we're getting somewhere!

As discussed earlier, the blacker the type on the page, the more success stories in the family. Black type in all caps indicates stakes winners. Black type alone indicates stakes-placed horses.

There is quality black type, and there is cheap black type. Learn the

A view of the auction ring at Fasig-Tipton's Saratoga facilities.

difference. The appearance of G1, G2, and G3 indicates the top-three categories of stakes and gives you a good way of evaluating any stakes race in the world. If it does not have this designation but is in black type, it is a stakes race but not one of the most prestigious. An impressive-looking black page could describe the accomplishments of a family that campaigned for the most part in Western Canada. With all due respect to that fine region, it would not rank high in the echelons of racing, and the offspring of such a family would be expected to be earnest, but not sterling, competitors. The battle cry is "Look for the Gs."

We have reproduced the sales catalog pedigree pages of three different sales to demonstrate quality, or lack of it, in a pedigree.

Pedigree Number One is the page from the Keeneland Summer Sale of 1988. The horse (hip number 66) was bought by me for $300,000. We named him Summer Squall, and he won the Preakness, many other important stakes, and $1,844,282. As a very important sire, he has produced a champion (Storm Song, also campaigned by

Summer Squall, winning at Keeneland.

Property of Lane's End Farm

Hip No.		Barn
66	BAY COLT	14 & 15

Out of WEEKEND SURPRISE (7 wins, $402,892, Golden Rod S.-G3, etc.), half-sister to winners SPECTACULAR SPY ($138,335, Devon H. [L], etc.), Lassie's Lady ($46,903, 3rd Sonnenberg H. [O]), etc. Second dam LASSIE DEAR ($80,549), sister to GALLAPIAT ($106,140, in U. S.).

Foaled March 12, 1987

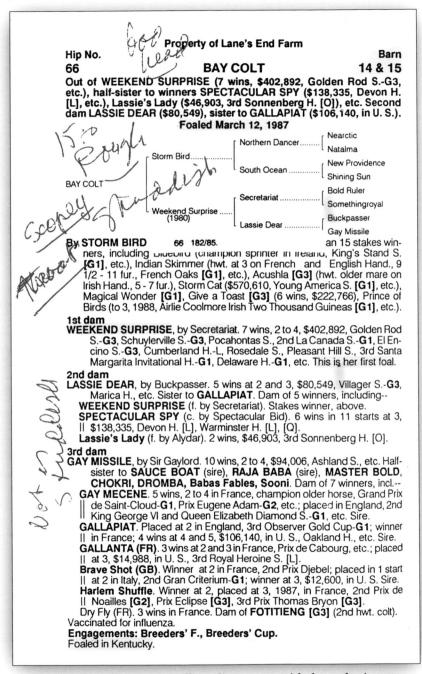

BAY COLT

- Storm Bird
  - Northern Dancer — Nearctic / Natalma
  - South Ocean — New Providence / Shining Sun
- Weekend Surprise (1980)
  - Secretariat — Bold Ruler / Somethingroyal
  - Lassie Dear — Buckpasser / Gay Missile

By STORM BIRD 66 182/85. ...an 15 stakes winners, including Bluebird (champion sprinter in Ireland, King's Stand S. [G1], etc.), Indian Skimmer (hwt. at 3 on French and English Hand., 9 1/2 - 11 fur., French Oaks [G1], etc.), Acushla [G3] (hwt. older mare on Irish Hand., 5 - 7 fur.), Storm Cat ($570,610, Young America S. [G1], etc.), Magical Wonder [G1], Give a Toast [G3] (6 wins, $222,766), Prince of Birds (to 3, 1988, Airlie Coolmore Irish Two Thousand Guineas [G1], etc.).

1st dam
WEEKEND SURPRISE, by Secretariat. 7 wins, 2 to 4, $402,892, Golden Rod S.-G3, Schuylerville S.-G3, Pocahontas S., 2nd La Canada S.-G1, El Encino S.-G3, Cumberland H.-L, Rosedale S., Pleasant Hill S., 3rd Santa Margarita Invitational H.-G1, Delaware H.-G1, etc. This is her first foal.

2nd dam
LASSIE DEAR, by Buckpasser. 5 wins at 2 and 3, $80,549, Villager S.-G3, Marica H., etc. Sister to GALLAPIAT. Dam of 5 winners, including--
WEEKEND SURPRISE (f. by Secretariat). Stakes winner, above.
SPECTACULAR SPY (c. by Spectacular Bid). 6 wins in 11 starts at 3, ‖ $138,335, Devon H. [L], Warminster H. [L], [Q].
Lassie's Lady (f. by Alydar). 2 wins, $46,903, 3rd Sonnenberg H. [O].

3rd dam
GAY MISSILE, by Sir Gaylord. 10 wins, 2 to 4, $94,006, Ashland S., etc. Half-sister to SAUCE BOAT (sire), RAJA BABA (sire), MASTER BOLD, CHOKRI, DROMBA, Babas Fables, Sooni. Dam of 7 winners, incl.--
GAY MECENE. 5 wins, 2 to 4 in France, champion older horse, Grand Prix ‖ de Saint-Cloud-G1, Prix Eugene Adam-G2, etc.; placed in England, 2nd ‖ King George VI and Queen Elizabeth Diamond S.-G1, etc. Sire.
GALLAPIAT. Placed at 2 in England, 3rd Observer Gold Cup-G1; winner ‖ in France; 4 wins at 4 and 5, $106,140, in U. S., Oakland H., etc. Sire.
GALLANTA (FR). 3 wins at 2 and 3 in France, Prix de Cabourg, etc.; placed ‖ at 3, $14,988, in U. S., 3rd Royal Heroine S. [L].
Brave Shot (GB). Winner at 2 in France, 2nd Prix Djebel; placed in 1 start ‖ at 2 in Italy, 2nd Gran Criterium-G1; winner at 3, $12,600, in U. S. Sire.
Harlem Shuffle. Winner at 2, placed at 3, 1987, in France, 2nd Prix de ‖ Noailles [G2], Prix Eclipse [G3], 3rd Prix Thomas Bryon [G3].
Dry Fly (FR). 3 wins in France. Dam of FOTITIENG [G3] (2nd hwt. colt).
Vaccinated for influenza.
Engagements: Breeders' F., Breeders' Cup.
Foaled in Kentucky.

Number One: Summer Squall's pedigree page, with the author's notes.

Dogwood) and the 1999 Horse of the Year Charismatic. The dam, Weekend Surprise, has gone on to bear the great A.P. Indy and another quality horse, Honor Grades. She was also named Broodmare of the Year.

My poor penmanship, visible on the page, indicates that he was 15 hands high, his throat or air passage was OK, he was "scopey" (had a frame that would permit him to grow into a nicely balanced horse), studdish and hard to handle ("rough"), and did not have a pretty head. I grew to adore that head, although he does have a bit of an evil eye.

I did not note, for some reason, that he was slightly pigeon-toed and his knees were offset, or that his walk was not terribly impressive. I DID comment that when I came back to see him again, he was not as studdish. The first time, I well remember, he showed in a very clear manner that he was very enthusiastic about the possibility of stud duty some day, much to the displeasure and embarrassment of his handlers.

One should note the foaling date of the colt or filly, as this is certainly an important factor in evaluating the size of the yearling. If April 15 is the median foaling date, and we're seeing these horses in July, and we earlier equated them with ten-year-old humans, then a horse foaled on January 10 is at a physical advantage and would be comparable to an eleven-year-old. Conversely, the June 7 foal has the maturity of a nine-year-old.

While we're at it, let me explain that in my opinion (and there is no scientific data to confirm this), a yearling in October is like a twelve-year-old. In January, now two, statutorily, the horse is about like a thirteen-year-old. When he goes out to the races in April, the youngster is similar in maturity to a fifteen-year-old adolescent. The maturation slows down somewhat from then on. When three-year-olds run in the Kentucky Derby the first Saturday in May, they are like college football players competing in a Bowl Game. In the fall of that year, the three-year-old could be compared to a twenty-five-year-old human. He has peaked physically but perhaps is slightly deficient in poise, seasoning, and judgment. Note that Summer Squall was the first foal out of what would become one of the greatest broodmares of her time. I like to buy first foals out of quality mares, and Weekend Surprise was certainly that. She had won several grade III stakes and had placed consistently in grade I races. She was sired by Secretariat, already established at the time as a wonderful broodmare sire. In other words, his female offspring were producing a steady stream of superior runners.

Note that the three grandsires on the maternal side were Secretariat, Buckpasser, and Sir Gaylord. You can't beat that. The entire pedigree page is riddled with high-class runners and producers of runners. The sire was Storm Bird, a son of the legendary Northern Dancer. Thus, Summer Squall (this colt) represented the highly sought after Northern Dancer-Secretariat cross. Storm Bird was one of the most expensive yearlings ever sold, and he had long since established himself as one of the world's finest and most-respected stallions. He had produced several champions.

At the bottom of the page are a few pertinent facts, the least exciting of which covers the fact that this colt had been vaccinated for influenza.

It is important to me that a horse was foaled in Kentucky, as Kentucky-breds are rewarded with very significant supplements to the purse structure in that state.

He was nominated to a Keeneland two-year-old race, the Breeders' Futurity (no real big deal), and was made eligible to the Breeders' Cup races, which is true of all self-respecting horses. Lastly, he was bred and sold by one of the most-admired breeders in the game. This was Will Farish's Lane's End Farm in Central Kentucky. One could have complete confidence in the colt's upbringing and believe any information provided about him.

Pedigree Number Two covers another horse we bought. This one was sold at the Keeneland April Two-Year-Olds in training sale, and Dogwood bought him for $180,000. He was pinhooked (bought earlier as a yearling to be resold in this sale) by Pacific Thoroughbreds (an outfit I did not know) which paid $45,000 for him for that purpose. The Summer Squall pedigree was a little more upscale than I was accustomed to buying, but this horse, already named Mythical Gem, had a pedigree right down my alley. It was quality for sure. Any horse coming from this background could jump up and be a top horse, and it would be no fluke. But it doesn't have the glitz offered by sires like Mr. Prospector, Danzig, Seattle Slew, Storm Cat, Gone West, Deputy Minister, and a few others. And prices reflect this.

The sire was Jade Hunter, who had won two graded stakes on dirt here and was a corking-good racehorse. He had at that time sired some high-class horses. The dam, Charlotte Augusta, was herself sired by a good horse, Chief's Crown, and was quite respectable as a racehorse, being stakes-placed. She had produced one previous offspring, and I had heard good things about that one's potential. But the jury was still out on Charlotte Augusta's quality as a producer.

The second dam (granddam) was an excellent, big-time stakes competitor, sired by a wonderful broodmare sire, Vaguely Noble. While they are predominantly European performers, there are some mighty fine names in the second, third, and fourth generations.

This sale produced a nice financial score for his consignor, and I was happy to provide it. One very salient reason, alluded to earlier, is that he worked an eighth of a mile on the grass the morning before the sale in the eye-popping time of ten seconds flat! This assured the consignor a happy sale.

But it was also a good buy. Mythical Gem went on to win two stakes, including the grade III Lexington Stakes at Belmont Park. Sadly, an accident terminated his racing career at a time when he would have been ranked the top three-year-old turf performer in the country.

Pedigree Number Three is an example of a mournfully GRAY (not much black) page, indicating very little of a distinguishing nature in the background of this Evansville Slew filly, presented as hip number

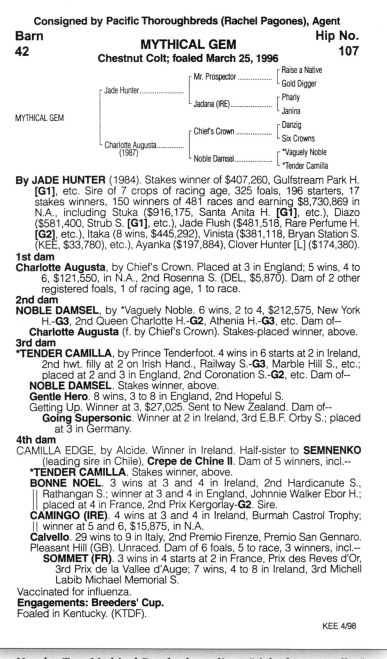

Consigned by Pacific Thoroughbreds (Rachel Pagones), Agent

Barn
42

MYTHICAL GEM
Chestnut Colt; foaled March 25, 1996

Hip No.
107

```
                                              ┌ Raise a Native
                            ┌ Mr. Prospector ─┤
              ┌ Jade Hunter ┤                 └ Gold Digger
              │             │                 ┌ Pharly
              │             └ Jadana (IRE) ────┤
MYTHICAL GEM ─┤                               └ Janina
              │                               ┌ Danzig
              │             ┌ Chief's Crown ──┤
              └ Charlotte Augusta             └ Six Crowns
                (1987)      │                 ┌ *Vaguely Noble
                            └ Noble Damsel ───┤
                                              └ *Tender Camilla
```

By JADE HUNTER (1984). Stakes winner of $407,260, Gulfstream Park H. **[G1]**, etc. Sire of 7 crops of racing age, 325 foals, 196 starters, 17 stakes winners, 150 winners of 481 races and earning $8,730,869 in N.A., including Stuka ($916,175, Santa Anita H. **[G1]**, etc.), Diazo ($581,400, Strub S. **[G1]**, etc.), Jade Flush ($481,518, Rare Perfume H. **[G2]**, etc.), Itaka (8 wins, $445,292), Vinista ($381,118, Bryan Station S. (KEE, $33,780), etc.), Ayanka ($197,884), Clover Hunter [L] ($174,380).

1st dam
Charlotte Augusta, by Chief's Crown. Placed at 3 in England; 5 wins, 4 to 6, $121,550, in N.A., 2nd Rosenna S. (DEL, $5,870). Dam of 2 other registered foals, 1 of racing age, 1 to race.

2nd dam
NOBLE DAMSEL, by *Vaguely Noble. 6 wins, 2 to 4, $212,575, New York H.-**G3**, 2nd Queen Charlotte H.-**G2**, Athenia H.-**G3**, etc. Dam of--
    Charlotte Augusta (f. by Chief's Crown). Stakes-placed winner, above.

3rd dam
*****TENDER CAMILLA**, by Prince Tenderfoot. 4 wins in 6 starts at 2 in Ireland, 2nd hwt. filly at 2 on Irish Hand., Railway S.-**G3**, Marble Hill S., etc.; placed at 2 and 3 in England, 2nd Coronation S.-**G2**, etc. Dam of--
    NOBLE DAMSEL. Stakes winner, above.
    Gentle Hero. 8 wins, 3 to 8 in England, 2nd Hopeful S.
    Getting Up. Winner at 3, $27,025. Sent to New Zealand. Dam of--
        Going Supersonic. Winner at 2 in Ireland, 3rd E.B.F. Orby S.; placed at 3 in Germany.

4th dam
CAMILLA EDGE, by Alcide. Winner in Ireland. Half-sister to **SEMNENKO** (leading sire in Chile), **Crepe de Chine II**. Dam of 5 winners, incl.--
    *****TENDER CAMILLA**. Stakes winner, above.
    BONNE NOEL. 3 wins at 3 and 4 in Ireland, 2nd Hardicanute S., || Rathangan S.; winner at 3 and 4 in England, Johnnie Walker Ebor H.; || placed at 4 in France, 2nd Prix Kergorlay-**G2**. Sire.
    CAMINGO (IRE). 4 wins at 3 and 4 in Ireland, Burmah Castrol Trophy; || winner at 5 and 6, $15,875, in N.A.
    Calvello. 29 wins to 9 in Italy, 2nd Premio Firenze, Premio San Gennaro.
    Pleasant Hill (GB). Unraced. Dam of 6 foals, 5 to race, 3 winners, incl.--
        SOMMET (FR). 3 wins in 4 starts at 2 in France, Prix des Reves d'Or, 3rd Prix de la Vallee d'Auge; 7 wins, 4 to 8 in Ireland, 3rd Michell Labib Michael Memorial S.
Vaccinated for influenza.
Engagements: Breeders' Cup.
Foaled in Kentucky. (KTDF).

KEE 4/98

Number Two: Mythical Gem had a pedigree "right down my alley."

Barn 2E

Hip No.

283

Consigned by
Mr. and Mrs. William Wofford, Agent

Bay Filly

Bay Filly . . . . April 5, 1998	Evansville Slew	Slew City Slew	Seattle Slew
			Weber City Miss
		Shape Shifter	Fappiano
			Phoebe's Donkey
	Imperial Ballade . . . . . (1994)	Imperial Falcon	Northern Dancer
			Ballade
		Bart's Song	The Bart
			Melody Queen

By **EVANSVILLE SLEW** (1992), black type winner of 5 races/7 starts, $338,040, Arlington-Washington Futurity [G2], Mathis Brothers Remington Futurity, etc. His first foals are 2-year-olds of 1999. Sire of March Magic ($97,200, 3rd Frizette S. [G1]), Erinsville (2nd Shady Well S.), Wildwood Penny (2 wins in 4 starts, $25,896).

1st dam
IMPERIAL BALLADE, by Imperial Falcon. Unplaced in 1 start. This is her first foal.

2nd dam
BART'S SONG, by The Bart. Unraced. Dam of 1 other foal to race--
    Mysecond Diamond. 20 wins, 2 to 6, 1999 in Dominican Republic.

3rd dam
MELODY QUEEN, by T. V. Commercial. 2 wins at 3, $10,152. Dam of 5 winners--
    Last Move. 13 wins, 2 to 6, $51,662.
    Il Ira. 3 wins at 3 in France.
    Vaguely Lady. Winner at 2 and 3, $11,632.
    Bay Rapid Transit. Winner at 3, $7,560.
    Tar Who. Winner at 3.
    Musical Spruce. Placed at 2.

4th dam
Menelodie, by *Menetrier. 4 wins at 2 and 3, 2nd Woodbine Oaks, Maple
    Leaf S. Dam of 9 other foals, 8 winners--
    PHELODIE. 12 wins, 2 to 7, $82,711, Quebec Derby S., Achievement H.,
    ‖ 2nd Breeders' S., Durham Cup H., Carleton S., 3rd Canadian Maturity S.,
    ‖ Connaught Cup H., Marine S., Toronto Cup H., Display S., Canadian H.
    Artilleryman. Winner at 2, 3rd Cup and Saucer S.
    Celesta. 4 wins at 3 and 4, 3rd Bison City S. Dam of 1 foal--
    ‖ Tudesta. 5 wins at 3 and 4, $26,152. To Japan. Dam of **SILK GRAYISH**
    ‖ (4 wins in Japan, Fukushima Kinen).
    Barley Sugar. 3 wins at 2 and 3, 2nd Plate Trial.
    Aeromaster. 13 wins, 2 to 7, $60,686.
    Menelu. 9 wins, 2 to 6, $32,055. Dam of 3 foals, 2 to race, both winners--
    ‖ Kara's Mene. 4 wins, 2 to 5, $31,357.
    ‖ Vodika's Mene. Winner at 3, $5,435. Producer.
    Koura. 7 wins, 2 to 5, $17,550.
    Citatius. 3 wins at 2 and 3.

Eligible for KTDF.

10/99

Number Three: An example of a pedigree with a scarcity of "black type."

283 at the Fasig-Tipton December Mixed Sale in Lexington.

With apologies to the seller and buyer (I hope they're the only two people in America who don't buy this book), there's just not much here, and nothing that would give you any confidence that this would be a quality racehorse. While the sire is respected, there are plenty like him, and the winners on the maternal side either won cheap races in this country or races in cheap racing countries.

Most of us who have been at this for years and have seen thousands of specimens of the breed, know what the ideal Thoroughbred horse should look like. We know good conformation — or the lack of it.

There are men and women in racing who have an eye for a horse, but then there are those who have a brilliant flair. Bear in mind that the ones deserving the most credit are those with limited funds who must find diamonds in the rough. Shoppers with deep, deep pockets buy wonderful-looking horses, but obviously the million-dollar babies tend to be pretty easy on the eye.

The most praiseworthy buyer during my time in the game was a rather portly Englishman named George Blackwell. A resident of Martinique in the Caribbean, George would journey up to the States only when an important auction was gearing up. For some days in advance he would mosey (the ideal word for George) about the sale grounds preparing himself to fill orders from a variety of clients. Clad in a Hawaiian shirt, employing the brightest hues, skillfully coordinated with a particularly vivid Scotch tartan introduced on some rather voluminous walking shorts, George would be comfortably shod in sandals and black silk socks. He topped this off with a rather disreputable-looking golf hat, and he smoked a Sherlock Holmes pipe. He never got in a hurry. He moved at a steady day-long pace, languidly looking at yearlings and amiably chatting with passersby. But when he departed for Martinique, George had usually bought some stars of tomorrow, a lot of them in the $40,000-$70,000 range.

Demi O'Byrne, an Irish vet, also is a wonderful judge of a horse, and so, of course, is Wayne Lukas. Veteran trainer and manager Johnny Nerud has a marvelous eye. The McKathan brothers from Ocala spot some wonderful horses for the clients of Bob Baffert, currently the poster boy of hot horse trainers. And there are others.

But nobody, but nobody, has ever had it all figured out. That's what makes the game so intriguing. If the trainer who breaks the horses, or the racetrack trainer, or the exercise rider, or the groom knew which ones would be good horses (or which ones to bet on), they would be running the game. It's amazing, though, that a lot of successful people — in other fields of endeavor, that is — don't grasp this fact.

Look at the legs from all angles.

We'll have people come to Dogwood to look over the young horses we're offering in partnerships, and after they've seen the horses gallop, that person, playing all the angles, will surreptitiously slip over to the riders to get "inside information."

When inspecting a horse at an auction barn, or anywhere, you fall into a certain procedure, or rhythm.

You arrive at the barn and go to the consignment where there will be a greeter of some sort. He or she is usually as busy as a one-armed paperhanger, but won't act like it. You get a card with a list of its hip numbers, check the ones you want to see, and sign your name (for their records in evaluating the number of "looks" each horse is getting). Then you go find an empty spot on one of the walking rings and wait for the horses to come out. Consignors generally do a remarkable job. Ten prospective buyers may be at that barn at that point. The person, or persons, handling all those cards will make sure you see a steady flow of the horses on your list. As soon as you have seen one horse, and thank the showman, another one should be on the way. Showing these horses at a sale is truly a fine art, and many consignors do it incredibly well. By the way, be careful at these sale barns. A lot is going on, and it would be easy to get hurt.

When the horse comes out, I first stand ten to fifteen feet from his profile and put a lot of emphasis on the first overall impression. This viewing gives you your initial sense of the horse's quality. I walk up to him, measure him by putting my chin to his withers, and then feel his throat to determine if the air passage is roomy or constricted. I look under him to check on any surprising omissions or irregularities in his genitalia (one testicle, maybe?), although this will be covered verbally by the showman, or should be.

You observe the shoulder and the hip. The former should be deep, flat, and set

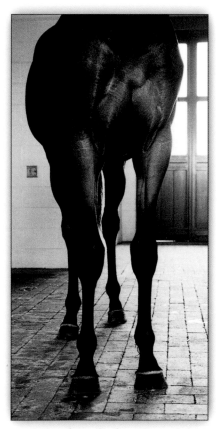

A view from the front is crucial.

on at a forty-five degree angle. The hip must have an adequate distance (the longer the better) from the point of the hip back to the end of it. I love it when both of these features are right! Then look at the colt or filly from the front end. This is crucial because you will see if the knees are fitted onto the cannon bone properly and if there are deviations from the ankles down. Usually something comes to your attention. (During all of this, I am writing notes in my margin. I also write insignificant points that will help me remember that animal vividly when I am back in the hotel. For instance, "warts on nose," "pear-shaped star.")

Standing at a forty-five-degree angle, I look at the front end to check for a major flaw that must be avoided: "calf knees." Simplified, this would mean that the knees exhibit a convex appearance. Observe how a cow stands with its knees sprung back, and you'll get the picture. This is a flaw that leads to trouble, often bowed tendons, chipped knees — nothing good. Now I move back to the hind end to look at the other profile of the yearling. The hocks are examined thoroughly. They should come down as if put on with the aid of a plumb line. You don't want them behind him, or "out in the country" as the English say. You move directly behind the horse now and look at the musculature of his hips, gaskins (that area between the hips and hocks), and ascertain that he is not "cow-hocked" (his hocks come too close together). The poor bovine is hardly flattered with all of these odious comparisons!

Next we walk the horse. A nod to the showman and off he should go at a brisk pace. This is very important because it is a precursor of what the horse's gait will be like and is the only demonstration of athleticism in an unbroken yearling. The saying goes that the ideal filly has the head of an angel and the ass of a "wash woman." That occupational term will certainly indicate that it was said a long time ago!

You want to see a swinging, cocky walk with some attitude about it. You look for energy, enthusiasm, and sometimes around 4 p.m. on a July day, you might not see it, and you must make allowances. Another important factor is the over-stride of the yearling. In a perfect world, the print of his back foot will come down from six to twelve inches in front of his front hoof print. The procedure is to stand in front of the horse and have him walk directly toward you — back and forth several times. This will show you how he tracks. Does he paddle (like Canonero when he won the Derby!), or does he walk so close that he almost interferes with himself. The walk is plenty important, and more so at a yearling sale than at a two-year-old sale where you see the horses gallop and breeze. The feet of the horse must be checked. You do not want a big, flat pancake foot (good for turf, some say) nor do you want a contracted "mule" foot or a club foot that is set on like a box and does not offer the desired forty-five degree angle.

A horseman can pick up the yearling's foot and quickly see any "corrections." This means that a farrier has made the foot uneven in one portion to try to overcome the obvious tendency to toe in or toe out in one or both of his front limbs. I would much rather go with the horse as God made him, but many consignors will present their horses with corrections in their feet.

There are certain tips, rules of the road, and points of etiquette that are good to know.

Consignors prefer that buyers not look at horses simultaneously, and so should you. So, if a buyer or party of buyers is looking at a horse, don't intrude. Give your card to the consignor, and that horse will be back out for you in due course.

If you don't like a horse, at least go through the motions of completing the examination, albeit quickly. If you see a horrible problem keep it to yourself. No pointing at a crooked knee while guffawing loudly to your companion or shaking your head knowingly while the horse is being walked toward you.

Unless it is your closest friend, never ask another buyer what he thinks of a horse. That's like asking a business competitor to share market research with you. It is clearly none of your business.

I think it is a very acceptable and intelligent practice to go up to a consignor and say, "I'm looking for a nice filly, but I can't spend over $100,000. What do you think I should see?" He'll run down his list and pick out three or four that should fall into the bracket. And, he'll appreciate not having to drag out the Mr. Prospector and Danzig fillies that he knows have reserves on them that are five times your budget.

Asking a consignor about a reserve is practical and perfectly reasonable. (The reserve is the minimum price at which a consignor will sell a horse at auction.) If he knows you or if he thinks you are a serious buyer, he'll probably tell you, if, indeed, it has been established at that point. Now, he may not want to etch it in stone, but the "code" clause might be, "Oh, I'd think he would bring around $50,000." But chances are he will be very specific.

And don't be upset about reserves. If you were selling a decent horse, you would certainly make sure he brought a certain amount or you wouldn't sell him. When I go into a sales pavilion, I know about what I am willing to pay for a horse and about what he should bring. I know the seller has put a reserve on him. Either he has arranged that through the auction company, in which case it will simply "manufacture" bids up to that point; or he has arranged with one of two associates to bid on the horse ("Bill, make someone pay fifty for this colt, will you?"). Or if he doesn't worry about being subtle, he may just bid on him himself. Then he can be flexible, taking him higher than he planned if the bidding is brisk (and he's got the guts!), or lowering his sights if it's sluggish.

I have heard people say, "Mr. Johnson quit bidding and stormed out of the pavilion when he saw Old Man Simmons (the owner) bidding him up." That's childish! Bid up to what you think the horse is worth and then quit. It is very simple.

Keep in mind that a lot of horses that did not meet their reserves are later sold privately before they leave the sale grounds and often for prices below the reserve that was originally set. So, if you had interest in a horse, and the sales results sheet lists him as R.N.A. (reserve not attained), go by the barn and inquire. A bargain may be waiting. Sometimes consignors, emboldened by pre-sale interest, set unrealistic reserves, and in the cold, gray dawn of reality they are willing to set a price that will move the horse.

Thoroughbred auctions have changed over the years. First, as a buyer, I want all the protection I can get. However, I do think the pendulum has perhaps swung too far back in the direction of the buyer, and it sometimes strikes me that the sales companies and their consignors have to provide an excessive amount of protection and warranties concerning soundness. Ours is inherently a risky business and removing all the pitfalls along the way is too much to ask. Thoroughbred market breeders have numerous hurdles to overcome,

Most yearlings enter the ring with a "reserve" price.

and getting a crop of foals to the yearling sales a year and a half later is tough sledding. Young horses get hurt and can die, or they don't evolve into the sort of animal that has buyers clamoring.

The sales companies do a fabulous job, considering the "organized chaos" of the auction scene.

The horse business, I know for a fact, has some crooks in it, but no more than any other business, and, considering the product involved, a surprisingly low number. And this wonderful business is chock full of people on whose word you can stake your life — more than a lot of other fields of endeavor, I believe. One unfortunate practice that exists in the marketing of racehorses — and, regrettably, you should be made aware of it — is the hidden commission in the sale of horses. This shenanigan has existed to a minor extent for a long time and will probably never be stamped out.

An agent or a trainer has you for a client. You have committed to bidding on hip number 342, and you are willing to go to $100,000. In the case of the agent, he is going to receive a five percent commission on anything you buy. The trainer may be charging you a commission, but probably not. His incentive is that he's going to get some nice horses to train. But either one could take the position that a little more gravy wouldn't hurt.

So, knowing of your plans, quietly he or she goes to the consignor and says, "I'll go a hundred grand on your horse, for my man, but I want ten percent."

Or, another approach: "Would you sell me this horse right now — before the sale — for $75,000? If you will, then I still want you to run him through the sale for me but in your name, of course."

If either deal is struck, the agent or trainer then sees to it that the bidding reaches $100,000. If his client is outbid and the horse finally sells for $125,000 to someone else, then so much the better!

Not much of this goes on, and not many consignors would go along with such an arrangement. But it should be mentioned.

Years ago, it was the kiss of death for market breeders to race a string of horses on the very logical presumption that they might want to keep the good ones and sell the rest. Then a few breeders started getting by with it, rationalizing that it made perfectly good sense for them to put a few fillies (future broodmares) in training. Nowadays, no one gives a thought to buying a yearling or two-year-old from a farm that also maintains a major racing stable. When you think about it, it is strange that they can get by with this. However, we won't lose any sleep over it. We will just trust ourselves to evaluate properly what they do show us and not fret about what we might not have seen.

In the 1960s, '70s, and into the '80s, sales yearlings (there weren't many two-year-old sales then) were sent into the auction ring in sloppy, fat condition, the theory probably being that all that avoirdupois hid a few conformation flaws, and indicated a thriving young animal. Happily, the sales horses of today are in better condition through better feeding and much more exercise. We buyers are much better off because we don't have to spend four months getting all the lard off those babies.

No matter how well-bred or conformed, most yearlings don't succeed as racehorses.

Some agents like to look at yearlings on the farms before the sale — a month or two before. I don't. I would rather concentrate my looking within a three- or four-day period prior to the sale of the horse. I think the eye becomes more sharpened, and there's more basis for comparison. Also, I rather like buying two-year-olds from pinhookers. They are good horsemen, invariably; they select good horses, and most of them bring the colts and fillies to the sale in top condition. Lamentably, they ARE going to make sure their two-year-olds work fast in the preview shows, so I think a thorough vet check before the sale, and after their last work, is very much in order. Pinhookers have taken the risks, put the work in, and they're entitled to a decent profit. I know how much I'm willing to pay for the horse, and I like knowing there's a legitimate reason for selling the animal: profit. Buying from them probably makes more sense than buying from the farm that also races its own stock.

Many diverse theories, techniques, procedures, tools, skills, and outright voodoo-isms go into the quest for young Thoroughbred horses. But what the whole rigmarole boils down to was once explained to me in indelible fashion by one of the greatest race riders who ever lived. The story starts with my purchase in the mid-eighties of a very expensive yearling colt. At the Keeneland July sale, I purchased for $230,000 a big, handsome son of Seattle Slew and the fine stakes-producing broodmare Miss Suzaki. What a superb prospect he was!

Back in Aiken, we developed him in the most patient, conservative manner. We really took more than a year to get him ready to run.

But in the fall of 1984, this colt, Slewzuki, was sent to California to the fine trainer John Russell. He had trained quite nicely, and we had picked out a race for him at Hollywood Park. Of course, we had secured the services of the finest rider in that or any other jockey colony: Bill Shoemaker. Shoe!

To say there was a great deal of pressure attending this colt's debut is a masterpiece of understatement. The other partners were excited; I was definitely excited, and, of course, I was going to California to see the colt run.

The day arrived. He was in the sixth race. I came in the night before and watched him have an easy gallop that morning (just to take the edge off). This colt was as sharp as "jailhouse coffee!" After the fifth race, I rushed to the paddock. The colt came in looking an absolute picture. I could not have been prouder. John Russell put the tack on him and he and the other two-year-olds went out on the walking ring. The riders came out. Shoemaker, befittingly dazzling in a brand new set of Dogwood colors, walked over to John and me.

It should be pointed out here that Shoemaker was known to be rather laconic. They did not call him "Silent Shoe" for nothing. The trainer and I greeted Bill, shook hands with him, and he favored us with a barely audible murmur (you might call it).

Now, I know better than this. But I did feel that it was necessary to impart to Bill that this was not just any old race, but it was the debut of what should become one of the true legends of the Turf. This was important! So I said, "Well! Bill, this is a colt by Seattle Slew. I got him for $230,000 last summer at the Keeneland sale, and we have really taken our time with him."

Shoemaker looked up at me and replied, "Oh."

I pushed on, "Bill, he's out of a wonderful producing broodmare named Miss Suzaki. She's had two stakes winners. Never thrown a blank!"

"Hmm," Shoemaker observed.

Now I was becoming desperate. Somehow I felt I had not yet ignited the fire, so I became more aggressive in my approach.

"Just look at that colt, Bill! Doesn't he look like a hell of a horse?"

Shoemaker cocked his head over to the right, glanced at the colt, then looked back at me, grinned almost imperceptibly, and said, "Well, now, if this big son of a bitch can just RUN a little bit, we ought to be all right, shouldn't we?"

I'm afraid the son of a bitch couldn't.

A LIFE ONLY A TRAINER COULD LOVE

Why would any human being possessed of all his faculties elect to become a Thoroughbred horse trainer? This key role in our business is surely the most outrageously demanding. There can be only one answer: The love of racehorses and horse racing.

Why else would a person consider a business day that starts at 4:30 a.m. and ends with a visit to the barn after dinner? Ends, that is, if all goes well and the night watchman doesn't call at midnight with news of a sick horse.

Why would you put up with a life that permits no days off? (And as far as vacation plans are concerned, you might as well contemplate a trip to the moon.) Or a business in which you deal with disappointing news eighty percent of the time? Where you have no contracts? A million second-guessers? Where egos are often mammoth and emotions hover at the boiling point? I could go on and on.

I think the nature of the horse business and my role in it puts me in a unique position to understand and empathize with both the owner and the trainer in what is definitely a natural, ingrained, inevitable, and adversarial relationship. Or at least it is one that — without complete understanding of each other and careful planning — is potentially explosive.

The attitude of the average Thoroughbred horse trainer has changed markedly in the past two decades. This probably has coincided with the decline of the foal crop and a slight shortage of racehorses, making some trainers somewhat more communicative and public-relations conscious.

In the old days, the philosophy of many public horse trainers was to treat owners as if they were mushrooms — "Keep 'em in the dark, and feed 'em plenty of manure!"

Both racetracks and horse trainers are much more obliging and nurturing to owners than once was the case, and this is a laudable trend.

You should look on the trainer you hire as you would a chartered air pilot. If you want the destination to be Pittsburgh and he's headed for Toronto, then you'd better quickly bring this to his attention.

However, if you are in full accord on where you're headed, then leave him alone and let him fly the airplane. He doesn't need any suggestions. But it is not unreasonable for you to expect accurate and fairly frequent reports from him on your progress and an estimated time of arrival.

When you select a trainer, determine first whether he knows how to train racehorses. How long has he trained? What good horses has he developed? If he's a relatively new trainer, then find out where he has been (Did he come up under a fine trainer of trainers?), and be convinced of why he should be a good trainer.

If you've been going to the races and are impressed by a certain trainer, go by the racing secretary's office, get his barn location, and go see him. Or call him up. Obviously, the more people you know in racing the better, because you certainly want references.

You might want to check on his statistics with the *Daily Racing*

Form, Bloodstock Research, or The Jockey Club Information Systems. Find out what his win and in-the-money percentages are.

Determine whether you like the guy. Is the chemistry good between you? It needs to be, because if he annoys you to begin with, when that horse of yours finishes dead last, you're going to detest that S.O.B.!

Find out what geographic racing circuit he follows. Is that where you want to race? If you already have horses, does your stock fit in that league?

The next question: Does he want YOU as a client? Believe me, a lot will depend on the horse or horses you plan to send. If it's a stakes horse: "Yes sir, we'll put him right next to the tack room."

If the animal in question is still a maiden after running fourteen times at Charles Town, then stall space availability may be standing in the way of this relationship.

Next, what is the financial arrangement?

Here's how trainers work:

They get a per diem of anywhere from $35 to $100, depending on the locale of the track and its purse structure. If he's training at a very small track, the rate will be cheap (and deserves to be). If we're looking at one of the most fashionable trainers at Belmont Park or Santa Anita or Keeneland, then we are shopping at the top end of the scale.

This per diem compensates the trainer for the care of the horse — his training, feed and shelter, and some very basic veterinary supplies. You will be billed separately for transportation, shoeing, dentistry, vet work (a horrendous item), and special equipment such as blinkers.

Nowadays, the trainer will probably pay for phone calls (he won't call collect as was the practice in days of yore!); but then, improved communications notwithstanding, YOU will initiate most of the phone calls.

Theoretically the per diem covers the trainer's basic expenses. And with one groom for three horses (four or five at the smaller tracks and the bush tracks), hot walkers, exercise riders, foremen, assistant trainers, and secretaries (just the really big ones), the payroll is plenty big. There are feed on top of that, and equipment such as saddles, bridles, blankets, coolers, etc.

The trainer's profit — if there is one — comes from ten percent of the gross earnings of the horses in his care. If your horse runs fourth and earns $900, the trainer will have an item of $90 on his next bill. This is where the "goody" is, and that is why he loves to have those stakes horses in his barn. And, it is also why he's not interested in training an animal just for the per diem itself. Don't ever think that is an incentive.

How does the trainer figure in the sale of horses or the retirement of a successful horse? There is no arrangement etched in stone, but here's a guideline of what we do, and I think it is pretty fair and sensible:

If the trainer finds a buyer for a horse, and the price is significant (not a disaster, that is), then five percent commission is fair. He's been getting ten percent off the top, so I don't think more than five is necessary. If you sell the horse and the trainer has no role in the transaction, then the trainer is not entitled to anything, unless he really developed him into a valuable horse. If you sell the horse at a "bargain basement" price, then no compensation should be necessary.

Suppose the trainer took a two-year-old from you and made him into a stakes-winning horse that is now headed for stud duty. I think the fair arrangement is a lifetime breeding right. No expenses in connection with it, and he can get the farm to sell the season every year. If the horse is going to stand for a $10,000 stud fee, then in a perfect world with a mare getting in foal and delivering every year, this is worth ten grand annually. Very nice.

Now, if the horse is going to Japan, Australia, or any foreign soil, then the logistics and the value of the breeding right are complicated and settling some cash on him would be better.

If the trainer acts as agent and performs agent duties at a public auction, then he is entitled to five percent commission.

There's a wrinkle in every situation, so it is simply a matter of common sense from here on in.

An interesting mathematical inequity on standard trainer commissions is this one: If you pay $3,000 to run in a stakes race ($1,500 for nomination and the same fee to start), and your horse runs third, and picks up $20,000, you will pay the ten percent on $20,000 and not $17,000, the true amount you netted from the racetrack. I've never argued about it, nor have I heard of anyone else bucking this practice.

Most trainers, I am sure, pay bonuses to certain staff members, and this is keyed to winning days or monthly or annual earnings.

Dogwood's practice is to give two percent of any winning purse to the trainer for "barn stakes," and this is spread around by the trainer to the appropriate spots.

I love the grooms and the little guys in racing and know as many of them by name as any person around, but I do not make it a practice to start tipping and "taking care of" certain barn employees. An injustice will inevitably be committed. The trainer is in the best position to know where to put it.

The groom is the forgotten man (or woman) in racing, in my opinion. Photographs of winning horses are seen in the press with identification of the owner, trainer, jockey, presenter of the trophy, but NEVER is the groom identified.

Any avid racing fan can probably tell you that Secretariat's great groom was Eddie Sweat. But who can tell you who rubbed Affirmed, Seattle Slew, Cigar, Kelso, Citation, Charismatic?

The groom is the horse's closest friend. But he is not a glamorous figure in the big scheme of things, and we don't pay much attention to him.

He works difficult hours, often has unspeakable living conditions, doesn't get paid too well, and gets little or no recognition. One contributing factor to the last point is that many grooms can barely speak

English (it is almost a modern-day requisite that most barn foremen be able to speak Spanish), and certainly this retards conversational banter between owners and grooms. If and when you do own race-horses, remember to speak to the groom and pat him or her on the back. Grooms are important in developing the winning equation.

They do what they do for the same reason as the rest of us: They love horses. You may not see a lot of cooing and kissing in the stall, but most have a great affinity for the animal.

When the trainer, his assistant, or foreman, puts on his "personnel director" hat, he is faced with a daunting task. Finding good help on the racetrack in this day — when other job opportunities are in great abundance — is sheer hell.

Drive in the stable gate of any racetrack about dawn, and you'll hear the stable gate public address system blaring out, "Any hot walk-er looking for work should go to Barn 14," or "Any outfit in need of a groom please come to the stable gate."

At the very bottom of the employment chain of command is the

Grooms and hot walkers are the "forgotten" people of racing.

"hot walker." His job is to hold the horse while the groom gives him his post-exercise bath. He then walks the horse around the aisle of the barn or on an outside walking ring until the animal has cooled. After delivering him back to the groom, the hot walker does it again with another horse. This goes on from the crack of day until around 10 a.m. when training has been completed. The old racetrack joke about indoctrinating new hot walkers is, "Keep turning left."

He may be assigned to go over to the paddock in the afternoon to "run a horse." If you see a rather forlorn-looking character with a bucket, a blanket, and maybe a set of blinkers, trudging along behind the groom and the horse, that will be the hot walker.

It doesn't require a lot of skill, but it is pretty important that he hang on to the horse. And on cold days, with a half-ton of romping, stomping meat on a shank, this can be challenging to say the least.

Women began coming on the racetrack several decades back, and this trend was a godsend. Many of the top exercise riders today are female, and many very high-class grooms are women.

While some of the major racing stables in the country have women as assistant trainers, there are not many high-profile female trainers in this game. Maybe there should be more, but there are not.

Jenine Sahadi in California is a substantial trainer on the West Coast scene. She is a splendid horsewoman to begin with, but she also has a strong personality, a gift for gab, and good connections. In the East, Linda Rice, a young woman with a likable, confident way about her, and hailing from a family of respected horsemen, has made a bit of a splash. There are many other fine women trainers, but the distaffers have not made the inroads into the training hierarchy that they deserve.

Another boon to life on the racetrack has been Hispanics. Most of our grooms in Aiken are Mexican. Our trainer and assistant trainer, Ron Stevens and Brad Stauffer, swear by them. And so do I. Most of them have migrated to Aiken in family groups. They work well together, pitch in for one another, and they have a flair for living with and communicating with horses. This employment trend is being seen all over North America.

But back to the head man — the trainer. How does one get to be a trainer? Trainers come from every walk of life and every conceivable background. A few are from affluent backgrounds, and they gravitated to racing through riding, showing, or because their family was involved. Many trainers are the sons or daughters of trainers, and never considered doing anything else.

Most of them have served as grooms and hot walkers at some point and have worked up from those ranks. Others were essentially gamblers. Some were jockeys, jock's agents, or what-have-you. And this is one of the great charms of racing. All men are equal on the Turf, or UNDER it!

What background supplies the best trainers? This is a dangerous subject (not unlike others I have dealt with!), and a few people could get their noses out of joint with my answers, which — let me carefully stress — are generalized.

In my opinion, an uncanny number of steeplechase riders become superb flat trainers. Flat-track jockeys don't enjoy automatic success, nor do as many pursue training careers as you would think. Veterinarians — who are asked all day long what to do about unsuccessful racehorses and provide expensive answers — rarely make good horse trainers, although one of America's finest practitioners of the training profession came from the vet ranks. That is John Kimmel, who has had sparkling success in the East.

To be a successful trainer, you probably should have started from the ground up — literally the horse's underpinning, which is really what it's all about. Keeping a horse sound and happy and competing in the right spots — those are vital keys to success in training. But attention to detail needs to be mixed into that equation, and maybe double that potion while you're at it.

People in the steeplechase game are unwaveringly fanatical horse nuts. If they weren't, they wouldn't pursue such an unreachable Holy Grail as supporting oneself — while trying to stay in one piece — by winning races over jumps. Steeplechase riders are gritty, determined types who adore what they are doing, and they live, work, and play hard in their pursuit of it. Not only do they ride the horses, but they work around the horses before and after they get on them. They KNOW horses — legs, ailments, personalities.

In steeplechasing, the purses are relatively low, the pool of potential clients is small, the stock is hardy but injury-prone, and the outfits must ship each week to a different racing venue.

If horse racing is a demanding sport and way of life for all of the rest of us, it is excruciatingly tough for the jumping fraternity. When they decide to train flat horses rather than jumpers — if they do indeed opt for the route that at least gives them a fighting chance at economic survival — the spirit is there and the practical knowledge of the animal is there.

Something else is there. The hustle. These former riders, when hungry and scuffling to promote decent rides in steeplechasing, have had to become past masters at ingratiating themselves with owners. No matter how shy and retiring that kid may have been, he has made himself ooze charm when dealing with owners before and after races. That is a pretty important arrow to have in your quiver. Combine that with know-how and desire and you've got a winning combination.

These fine Thoroughbred trainers came — broken bones and all — from the ranks of steeplechase riders: Scotty Schulhofer, Tommy Skiffington, Leo O'Brien, Jimmy Murphy, Billy Turner, Barclay Tagg, Jonathan Sheppard, Sidney Watters Jr., Mike Freeman, Charlie Peoples, and Michael Dickinson. And there are plenty of others.

Flat jockeys ride the horses in the afternoons, and they work them in the mornings, but they are not called on to toil "under" a horse. Because they are small, the accent is on getting them up on horses' backs right from the start. As absolutely crucial as that vantage point is, it doesn't prepare them as well for a training career.

Why don't vets make absolutely infallible horse trainers, when they decide to depart from their very demanding but often exceedingly lucrative professions? I do not know. But I don't think the ones who have entered the ranks of racehorse conditioners have exactly "broken up the game." Maybe they employ too much theory and academics. I really don't know.

While the attitude of a few trainers toward owners could still improve, trainers today are much more cognizant of the need to establish a reasonable business relationship. In other words, the inmates are no longer running the asylum!

Here's why the relationship is fraught with opportunities to fall out: The owner has paid money to own this horse. He has high hopes for him. Racehorse ownership is a highly charged emotional trip. The owner's adrenaline is flowing, his emotions are stretched tautly, and he is hungering for action. The truth is he is DYING to talk about the horse, even when there is very little to say.

On the other hand, the trainer has the horse in his care twenty-four hours a day. He suffers and bleeds through all the scary episodes which the owner — thank God! — knows nothing about (When the colt got loose from the hot walker the other morning and galloped for a quarter-mile down the expressway near the track, the boys rounded him up and got him back to the barn, and he's none the worse for wear. Is there any need to burden the nervous owner with these details? One doesn't think so!) The trainer spends much of his time struggling with the horse, and he gets damned tired of discussing elementary aspects of his condition. He suffers suggestions from the owner, most of which he has long since thought of and discarded.

And believe this: When a horse becomes a star, his owner, no matter how meager his experience, overnight becomes an expert. The trainer, understandably, thinks — and often comes close to saying —

"Why don't you just shut up and let me train this horse?"

But the inescapable fact remains: The man or woman does indeed own this horse, pays the trainer for his services, and is entitled to information and common business courtesies. That should go with the territory.

A motivating factor in getting involved in the ownership of a good racehorse is recognition. When a horse wins a big race, the owner is understandably bursting with pride, and his name and connection with that horse should be made known.

Anyone who tells you he doesn't like to see his name or picture in the paper is either a spy, a criminal, or is lying, in my opinion. We all adore it! The racing press can be a trifle sloppy about printing owners' names, but the trainer can help with this, and the sharper, smarter ones do ("I'm not sure what our next race will be until Mr. Zilch and I get a chance to talk it over.").

Most of us have strong egos (the writer certainly does), and I will tell you that trainers are no exception. A good trainer probably ought to be a trifle on the independent side; he should have confidence and not brook a lot of interference. But again, he should see to it as much as possible that you, as the owner, get some recognition when those infrequent big-moment opportunities come.

Much of running a racing stable has to do with dealing with trainers, and, therefore, I can supply some hints, suggestions, and dos and don'ts in connection with understanding your trainer.

The condition book is a small and vital publication put out every two or three weeks by the racing secretary at your racetrack. In it is a description of every race offered there for the period covered. The "conditions" are detailed, tricky, and often difficult to grasp ("for four-year-olds and up, non-winners of $26,800 twice, at a mile or over on the turf, since August 14"). If you are new at it, you're going to have a lot of trouble. And your trainer is an old hand at understanding the nuances and hidden impact of some of the conditions and will be adroit at avoiding booby traps. The race partially described above might have been written expressly to provide Cigar with a prep race! God forbid that we be in the same race!

If your nice colt has broken his maiden and won another race ("non-winners of a race other than maiden or claiming"), and you are now eligible for "non-winners of two races other than maiden or claiming," then you surely don't want any part of the booby trap race, and your trainer knows that. Oh boy, does he know it!

Certainly you should have a condition book, but be aware that the trainer is on the scene dealing daily with the racing secretary, asking for "extras" — races not found in the condition book that may be perfect for your horse — and he KNOWS the book.

When I have my daily — thorough but brief — conversation with trainers, I have gone over the book and may ask, "Todd, how about that non-winners of two lifetime for Canfield on the twenty-third? Does that make any sense?"

Typically, he might answer, "Well, there's going to be the same race in the next book. It's on the twenty-eighth, and I think the seven furlongs will suit him better than the six. How about that one?"

Sure, of course. And the fact that I would have been in town for the first race but can't for the second must not be cranked in the equation, if you want to win horse races.

So have a condition book, but don't have too much confidence in your interpretation of it early in the game. The trainer knows it like the palm of his hand.

Trainers tend to strike up an affinity with certain riders and may develop an informal first-call relationship. The rider — hopefully one who is riding with a hot hand — will tend to come by the barn early each day. He will get on certain horses, maybe working one out of the gate in preparation for an upcoming race. The jock will be accompanied by his agent — an important man (women are scarce as hen's teeth in this vocation!) — who will then go over the book with the trainer, comment on what other to-be-avoided-if-possible horses might be headed for the same race, and then write down his "calls"(commitments). These are then honored religiously. Although sometimes if the agent (who always speaks in the first person singular pronoun) is riding a longshot for Trainer Brown and is asked to ride a 2-5 shot for Trainer Jones, he may go to Brown and ask if he will let him out of his commitment. And Brown will probably go along with it. A lot of practical give and take goes on at the racetrack. A commendable amount of it.

Loud and clear, it should be inserted right here while discoursing on trainers and jockeys that both professions get blamed far too often for the unsuccessful performance of horses. The more ignorant or unsophisticated the owner, the quicker blame will be attributed to a poor ride or a stupid mistake by the trainer ("What did he want to put those damned blinkers on for?"). Often that flame will have been fanned vigorously by the carping of a buddy who goes to the races, is a serious handicapper, and, of course, bet on the horse.

Usually, the problem with a horse is that he cannot run fast enough. Only God knows why, so maybe He should bear the responsibility.

Try to be open-minded when your trainer suggests gelding the horse or running him in a claiming race. Neither is appealing to the new owner, but the longer you stay around, the more you will appreciate them both. The trainer's tried and true motto is "Run 'em where they belong!" and that's what claiming races make possible.

And I don't think you should get your feelings hurt if the trainer runs an entry. If your horse is looking for a $50,000 maiden race, and the trainer has another owner's horse in the barn that is ready to run and fits the same race, I think it's unreasonable for one owner to beef about being part of the entry. It would hardly be fair for the trainer to announce to you that your horse can't run because Mr. So and So's colt is going to run. Or vice versa. So he enters them both and each horse will take his best shot. If your horse is good enough he'll beat the other one. If he's not, he won't. The jockey situation could get thorny, but the politically correct solution is to let the stable jockey choose his mount. Otherwise, the trainer should try to line up two riders of equal ability and if he's smart, he'll get both owners to "sign off" on the choices. Running entries that involve different owners is a "sticky wicket" for trainers. Some owners go berserk at the very idea.

How do you start being a horse trainer? Well, you just say that you are! Simple! But there are a few other details. You've got to have the horses to train and a place to put them. You must pass a written and verbal test before you can get a license, the severity of which is not a formidable stumbling block.

Many successful training careers were launched when one of the clients with horses in a particular barn took a shine to a bright, young assistant trainer while simultaneously becoming disenchanted with the head trainer.

"How'd you like to take my six horses and start your own training barn? Hell, you're doing all the work around here anyway!" It's called being in the right place at the right time. A more harmonious way is when the head trainer, out of benevolence and the realization that his assistant wants to test his own wings, suggests the time is coming when his trusty aide might launch his training career. The trainer helps his assistant get started, perhaps on another less demanding circuit, with some stock in the barn that is finding it too difficult at Gulfstream Park or Santa Anita.

Others simply stick around until the head man wants to quit, and then try to inherit the horses. Trouble is, horse racing — tough and demanding as it is — gets into your blood and not many EVER want to quit. And that speaks volumes for the charm of our sport and industry.

Now he's got the horses, how about a place to put them? The race-track provides the stalls. Maybe!

The average racetrack is on enough land to accommodate about

1,200 horses in stalls. The racing secretary's job is to put on the show — attract horses to run in the races, entice customers to come and bet their money (from whence comes the purses to get the horses), and so forth and so on.

He, therefore, allots stalls to trainers who have balanced strings of horses that will compete with reasonable frequency in the races in his condition book. The more fire power the trainer has the more stalls he is assigned. Racing secretaries adore the Wayne Lukases, Billy Motts, Bobby Barnetts, Todd Pletchers, Roger Attfields, Bob Bafferts — men who have big strings of horses and will customarily run three or four horses a day and who also have in their barns some of the marquee performers that will bring people to the racetracks.

When the unknown young fellow, his hat in his hand, comes in, introduces himself, and tremulously points out that he wishes to race at Churchill Downs this spring and would need ten stalls (if he hopes to get six he asks for ten), he may well get a big fish eye from the perpetually harassed racing secretary.

He might instead wish to look into the facilities at a nearby training center. For instance, many of the trainers racing in South Florida in the winter opt to stable at Payson Park or Palm Beach Downs or some other training center within fifty miles of the racetrack. Most of these trainers actually prefer the tranquillity of the setting, but others are there because they were not allotted stalls at Gulfstream. They have to pay for the stalls and that is not as economically pleasing as getting them gratis from the racing secretary, but what is the trainer going to do? He's probably going to adjust this into his per diem, and you'll end up paying for them.

No trainer in history has changed the course and the customs of American racing as has an ex-high school basketball coach from Antigo, Wisconsin, named D. Wayne Lukas. Many of the practices, procedures, and beliefs of today have been fashioned by him and his extraordinary success. Born with a raging fire in his belly and a keen understanding and appreciation for style and showmanship, this young man was soon consumed by his part-time avocation of breaking and trading horses. He gravitated to training Quarter Horses at small racetracks in the Southwest. That Lukas was a gifted horseman soon established itself, and he quickly began dominating the Quarter Horse sport. With one or two important Thoroughbred clients behind him, he was able to cajole the racing secretary at Santa Anita into giving him some stalls, and he was off and running. He never looked back, "widening out his lead at every pole."

In addition to his superhuman drive, Lukas brought to racing three things: (1) superb, inherent understanding of horses, (2) a flair for rhetoric, pizzazz, and drama, and (3) realization that prospective clients might react favorably to a little salesmanship and the niceties of commercial intercourse, as practiced in most other fields. His trendsetter ways stuck in the craw of a few of his competitors and some segments of the racing public.

After a quarter of a century on the Thoroughbred racing stage, Lukas has trained twenty Eclipse Award winners, won fifteen Breeders' Cup races, thirteen Triple Crown races (six in a row), four Kentucky Derbys, and his horses have won more than $200 million.

If the name of the game is to win horse races and amass significant earnings in the process, then Wayne Lukas is the most successful Thoroughbred horse trainer in the history of the American Turf. If, indeed, that is how you keep score, then unequivocally he is the best. Perhaps not the most popular, but the best.

For some reason, some hard-to-explain customs, attitudes, and posturing have always existed among a portion of the horse-training fraternity. For example: Let's say a trainer, not enjoying much success at the moment, was given a surprising and much-needed opportunity to train a highly desirable, money-earning horse. It is the horse trainer's code that he must avoid demonstrating the gratitude and enthusiasm he must feel and instead nonchalantly respond,

"Well, I'll be glad to help you out."

An indication that a trainer is absolutely desperate for horses is when he phones you with the old ploy, "Deadline for stall applications at the racetrack is Friday, and I wanted to make sure you didn't get shut out." Rarely can a trainer bring himself to say to a prospective client: "I would love to train some horses for you and would appreciate your business." "Asking for the business" is done in almost every other form of commerce in our land. Why would this principle be considered taboo by horse trainers?

Well, it wasn't by Lukas. He got the clients; he got the horses. He knew what to do with them when he got them, and he won $200 million in the process. Some of the other fellows actually began to express enthusiasm when they had an opportunity to train horses for people. It worked wonders.

Lukas was the first to beautify his barns at various racetracks. Right after his outfit shipped in and the horses were unloaded and bedded down, workers would begin laying down turf and planting flowers. Baskets of pansies and other bright posies hung all the way down the eaves of the barn. Rules, motivational slogans, and mottoes were displayed in tack rooms. The shed rows were spotless, his employees were neatly dressed and courteous, and his horses were languishing in straw so deep their ears were barely visible! If you were an owner, the overall presentation knocked your socks off!

The traditional big name private and public trainers up until that time took the position that thirty or forty horses were about all they could "say grace over." Wayne soon had more than 100.

He was the first trainer to emulate Muhammed Ali's celebrated credo of "float like a butterfly and sting like a bee!" He opened up divisions at various racetracks. He might have forty at Belmont, another thirty at Churchill Downs, and forty back home at Santa Anita, all under top-notch young assistant trainers — one predominant key to his success.

He considers no stakes engagement anywhere in this country to be off limits. He will pop a good horse onto an airplane, and suddenly the colt that had galloped at Santa Anita on Friday is in New Orleans on Saturday morning ready to run in the Louisiana Derby. And he wins races.

One hears at the betting windows from knowledgeable gamblers this lilting phrase of support: "D. Wayne off the plane!"

His critics claim his success comes from the fact that he is a skilled "promoter." Promoter he is, but he's also a gifted horseman. After he won the Derby in 1988 with the great filly Winning Colors, she went on to Baltimore to run in the Preakness. I was in the paddock (set up outside for that day on the grassy turf course) when the big gray filly came in to be saddled, and she was plenty wound up. She had a person on a shank on either side of her, and she was about to go into orbit! She could have left her race right there.

Lukas simply walked up to her, murmured something in her ear, patted her on the neck, waved off the two attendants, took the shank himself, and within a minute she had dropped her head and was grazing!

One significant factor in his success, considering that he is operating on several fronts, has been his ability to recruit, train,

D. Wayne Lukas, a modern master.

and motivate outstanding young men. He teaches them horseman-ship and is doggedly dedicated to doing things "the proper way." Those who do not have it to begin with, soon develop the Wayne Lukas brand of *savoir faire*.

Mark Hennig, Todd Pletcher, Bobby Barnett, Randy Bradshaw, Kiaran McLaughlin, Dallas Stewart, and Jeff Lukas would all rank among the top thirty horse trainers in America. They are alumni of D. Wayne Lukas University. When the dean was inducted into the National Museum of Racing Hall of Fame in 1999, six of these out-standing young men made the presentation, and Mark Hennig told a story illustrating his mentor's devotion to style and class.

Hennig was in charge of a division of Lukas horses at Monmouth Park and had saddled three horses one afternoon. One had won an allowance race, another had won an important stakes, and the third had just been second in a maiden race. Quite a day!

Wayne, who had his hands full at Belmont Park that same day, called down to the Monmouth barn in the late afternoon to see how things had gone. Mark came on the phone and excitedly exclaimed, "Wayne, we done good! We won the____"

Lukas, with a cold edge to his voice, interrupted, "You what?"

Mark repeated, "Man, we done good! In the stake race…"

Lukas, his voice rising now, "Don't you EVER USE THAT KIND OF GRAMMAR! Suppose you were talking to one of our clients? WE DID WELL. Not 'We done good!' Got that? Now, tell me how we ran today."

Mark Hennig — grinning from ear to ear — concluded his remarks at his old boss' induction ceremony by saying, "Wayne, YOU DONE GOOD!"

I would like to make several points concerning deportment of the model owner that will contribute to a happy relationship with one's trainer.

Trainers have strange and demanding hours. They get up early, try to take naps, and generally retire early. Therefore, there are good times to call trainers on the phone, and there are definitely bad times. I think the ideal time to phone is after training hours. If you'll give him until 10:30 a.m., he will have trained your horse and all the others, made his entries, dealt with jock's agents and veterinarians who will have looked in on various horses, and he'll still be an hour or two before going home and getting ready to run some horses that afternoon.

I feel strongly that I am entitled to know everything about my horses, but the other horses in the barn and their plans are not any of my business. I don't interrogate the poor guy about plans for someone else's horse, no matter how glamorous and interesting.

Trainers receiving horses from other trainers or farms are not inclined to be lavish in their praise of the condition of that animal, so don't worry too much about the initial report on a horse that has just shipped in. Most likely, the trainer will have "straightened that out" within two or three days.

Also, trainers — probably in the interest of conservatism — tend not to take the word of other trainers as to how far along a horse might be in his training. I am resigned to this situation, and so should you be. It is a waste of time to get a two-year-old up to working five-eighths of a mile out of the gate at the farm, ship him to the races, and expect him to run within a couple of weeks.

Chances are you will read in the *Daily Racing Form* two weeks after the colt arrived that he has worked three eighths in :39! The intelligent thing is to understand this and let the trainer have the six to ten weeks he is inevitably going to take to put his stamp on the animal.

In a thoughtful article entitled "Trainers are from Mars," Don Clippinger, managing editor of *Thoroughbred Times*, states, "Of all the difficult questions facing the Thoroughbred industry, the relationship between owner and trainer is perhaps the most crucial to the sport's success. In short, they make the game go. The owner provides capital and raw material, and the trainer provides the expertise to develop the finished product."

Some of my greatest friends are trainers, and I tackled this subject with fear and trepidation. Hopefully, I have struck some beneficial blows on behalf of the trainer — whose life is wonderful, but not easy! I hope I have encouraged those who needed it to continue accelerating the trend toward wide open communications and consideration for the owner.

As stated earlier, when one uses specific names in dealing with this subject, the opportunities for hurt feelings and bruised egos are limitless.

While I happen to like him, and he likes me (or he wouldn't have written the foreword to this book), I devoted considerable space to Wayne Lukas for two absolutely legitimate reasons. And I want to reiterate them.

By the only clearly defined method of keeping score, he has been thus far the most successful horse trainer in history. Further, he has

Lukas and one of his proteges, Todd Pletcher, who now trains for Dogwood.

been revolutionary as a trendsetter and has changed the complexion of the sport, whether or not those changes have been universally popular.

Discussing great horse trainers is like debating the best racehorses, the finest quarterbacks, or the most gifted shortstops. Or religion. Or politics. It is fruitless.

But how can you write a chapter on the subject of current day Thoroughbred horse trainers and not mention some of the shining stars of the last decade of the 20th Century — Bob Baffert, MacKenzie Miller, Elliott Walden, Nick Zito, Scotty Schulhofer, Carl Nafzger, Bill Mott, Shug McGaughey, Ron McAnally, Richard Mandella, John Kimmel, LeRoy Jolley, Allen Jerkens, Jimmy Croll, Bobby Frankel, P. G. Johnson, Sonny Hine, Jack Van Berg (I dare not stop, but I will!).

Our business has a natural ebb and flow of owners and their trainers. When things don't work out as you wish them to and think they should, and a lot of money is invested in the venture, you try different approaches. I am one who has tried those different approaches and will continue to do so. One must give a trainer a chance to "work his magic." When it is clear that the magic is not doing the trick (again, probably because the horse can't run fast enough!), then the trainer himself will often suggest a change.

Dogwood carries about sixty horses on its roster. We add a combined new crop of about twenty-eight yearlings and two-year-olds each year. What with culls and retirements, this keeps the complement fairly constant. For this reason, having less that three trainers is not practical. In mid-summer it would not be unusual for us to have eighteen two-year-olds looking for maiden races. If they are spread out over three racetracks, it does wonders for the logistics of getting them in races. A Dogwood horse that does not seem to be reaching his hoped-for potential (one more time: probably because the horse can't run fast enough!) can be moved around from Baltimore to New York or Louisville.

At this writing, we have divisions with three outstanding young trainers. These men, any one of whom is a candidate for Hall of Fame honors someday, are Todd Pletcher, Dallas Stewart, and Graham Motion, in order of longevity.

Pletcher, deserving the designation as our number one man, has our New York division, which campaigns in Florida in the winter; Stewart headquarters in Kentucky basically and goes to New Orleans for winter racing. Graham Motion is based in Delaware with a draft of horses that "floats" (goes to Saratoga, Keeneland, or Florida).

I will refrain, for a variety of good reasons, from extolling their myriad virtues. My reference to their Hall of Fame potential speaks volumes about what I think of them. I hope when I retire from racing at age 100, this trio of splendid young men will still be training stakes winners for Dogwood. But knowing the capriciousness of racing, by the time you read this, they may have been replaced by a trio of octogenarians, or they may have fired me. I hope not. I think not.

But owner-trainer relationships DO change and cease to be viable — and often for reasons that have absolutely nothing to do with dissatisfaction.

In our almost thirty-year history, there are trainers with whom we are not currently associated (other than through friendship) who played major roles in our success. They are Angel Penna Sr., Steve DiMauro, Frank Alexander, Nick Zito, Jimmy Iselin, Neil Howard, Leo O'Brien, Bill Curtis, and Niall O'Callaghan (now back with us with a string at Arlington Park in Chicago). I'm indebted to all of them, and others.

We have always kept a few steeplechase horses. We started doing this almost eighteen years ago, and one man has trained them. He is Charlie Fenwick, who developed Inlander into a North American champion, one of our two Eclipse Award winners.

In the style of Bill Shoemaker's easily understood comment to me about racehorses, covered in the previous chapter, here is one final truism about trainers:

If you are winning a lot of races, you'll idolize your trainer. "He is an indisputable genius!"

But if those horses start running badly, and all they're getting is hot and dirty, you may well decide, "He couldn't train a dog to eat meat," and fire him.

The next thing you'll know, he'll train a Kentucky Derby winner for someone else.

NOT AN EXACT SCIENCE!

Spring is a glorious time of the year, but in the Thoroughbred world it is sheer magic.

The foals are arriving, the yearlings are cavorting, and the two-year-olds are heading to the races to begin their careers. Older horses that have been vacationing in winter quarters are going back to the wars — and the Triple Crown Campaign is raging. What could be a better time? The previous September the yearlings went under tack, throughout the fall they learned their lessons and got muscled and fit, and since February the now two-year-olds have been doing some speed work and learning about the starting gate.

In mid-March, the Aiken Trials take place. This delightful racing exhibition — a day to give bright and forward two-year-olds some experience — has gone on for fifty years. The charity event attracts about 5,000 people to our training track. We have six or seven races — half-miles for the older horses, quarter-miles for the babies. The riders are Aiken exercise riders (some of whom are jockeys at the smaller tracks up North in the summer). And we only run the super-precocious in these exhibition races. We all say, "It doesn't matter if you win. It's just a lot of fun."

Like hell it doesn't matter!

I will say that victory — or the absence of it — with the two-year-olds is certainly not meaningful. The best horse Dogwood ever had — Summer Squall — ran third in the Aiken Trials, and then went undefeated for the entire year! His daughter, a North American champion, was second in the Trials.

At Dogwood, we break camp with our two-year-olds on April 1. Participants in the Trials are usually shipped to Keeneland in Lexington for a start during its prestigious April meet. When they get to Kentucky, and the starter springs the latch, those two-year-olds will leave the gate like their tails are on fire!

This is the time of year that you're getting ready to ship that colt you bought last fall to the races. The racetrack trainer you selected has checked in with the training farm during the winter to monitor progress, and, Lord knows, so have you. The trainer has completed the winter racing campaign and is ensconced at Belmont Park (Pimlico, Churchill Downs, Woodbine, Santa Anita, Calder — you name it), and he or she is ready to receive the young horses.

When should you plan to race your colt? It depends entirely on him. He will tell you.

This is a good time to discuss juvenile racing, a subject on which everyone is an expert, especially a surprising number of people who have horses in other completely unrelated disciplines — dressage, fox hunting, show jumping. Unsolicited and unqualified criticisms of two-year-old racing tend to strike a nerve with me, as you can tell.

Lest you fall prey to the wealth of misinformation concerning the "horrors" of two-year-old racing, let me answer the question of whether it is all right.

It is. For certain horses, that is. If a colt or filly is precocious physically and mentally, he or she should be raced as a two-year-old. We X-ray the knees of all our young horses to determine their maturity and closely monitor their mental and physical development. We have some horses that should not race until they are three, and they won't. However, it is ridiculous to conclude that no horse should race when he is two.

Since the early days of the sport, two-year-olds have raced, and most have loved it. Man o' War ran four times in seventeen days as a two-year-old! Seabiscuit ran thirty-five times (a trifle on the excessive side I will admit). Most of the great horses in history raced as two-year-olds, and it is rare when a Derby candidate did not campaign at two.

The point is this: A two-year-old racehorse is comparable to a high school athlete, as we pointed out earlier in the book. Any physical education coach would tell you that an athlete should begin his or her sport at an early age, and the same is true of an equine competitor. Bone and muscle develop as a result of early athletic endeavor, and mental and physical skills are acquired quickest at a young age.

If you were developing a fourteen-year-old potentially great female

Summer Squall ran third in the Aiken Trials, then was undefeated at two.

tennis player, it would be stupid to have her wait until she was twenty to begin tournament play. If she is going to achieve stardom, she should start with appropriate tournaments at fourteen, although her emotional and mental reactions should be monitored carefully.

Then which horses should not run early?

A nervous, excitable filly that would require considerable time to mature and settle down. The excitement of a race could cause her to blow her mind. She — and all horses — should enjoy their first racing experience. Wait until she mellows out a little.

Horses with physical weaknesses must proceed cautiously. Putting stress on that weakness could be the end of the horse's career. Their knees must be "closed," meaning that the growth plates should be matured and filled in with cartilage to protect the joint from the impact of running. Big, growthy, coarse horses should be given a conservative amount of time for their bones to mature fully to carry their weight. Also, this type of heavy horse tends to be ungainly and poorly coordinated until it has grown into its frame and completely filled out. Typically, in a crop of twenty-eight two-year-olds, I would say that we would run three in April, another three in May, three in June, four in July, and five in August. A few more will run in the fall, and the rest — about twenty-five percent — will run as three-year-olds.

The people on the farm where your baby has been training will have given you an idea on just how mature they think he is. Your racetrack trainer will certainly have an opinion, but give him two or three weeks with the horse before you try to pin him down.

When your colt arrives at Belmont Park, let's say, he is going to be like a country bumpkin in the middle of Manhattan. For a few days he's going to walk around with his mouth open, staring at the bustling crowds and tall buildings. This youngster is going to take about a week to quit gawking at all the strange sights.

Your trainer will make up a "set" of two-year-olds, usually three to five youngsters, that will work out together accompanied probably by the trainer on the stable pony (the nursemaid). The first day they'll walk up to the racetrack and jog around once, maybe breaking into a gentle canter if all is proceeding smoothly. Then back to the barn. Not very exciting. But this is not the time for excitement.

Your horse will have a training companion that is at the same stage of development.

The first few days are spent getting the young horse used to "big-city life." As the charges settle in, the tempo increases, and soon the new-comers are galloping a mile and a half. A week of this, and it is time for the first breeze. Your colt may go three-eighths, by himself or perhaps with his workmate. This is an easy work, not designed to break any clocks!

If your horse has done a lot of gate work, and if the training chart sent up from the farm says he is ready to "break," then soon the train-er will ask him to walk in the gate alongside others in the set, "lock him up" (shut the front and back doors), and then let him gallop out

Dogwood horses grouped in "sets" for training.

easily with the doors open. No slamming doors, ringing bells, or other hooplah. This exercise will tell the trainer if he agrees with the training center's assessment.

From there, the breezes get more serious and the gate work intensifies. After another month, the colt has worked several half miles, and now he works out of the gate five eighths of a mile. He breaks sharply, and the starter — a vital cog in this starting gate schooling — issues the trainer a gate card for your horse. As far as he's concerned, the horse can start. Without that card he cannot.

Now it is almost June. You and the trainer have talked a couple of times a week. He tells you, "He seems OK" — not an overwhelming accolade, but be happy to settle for it. Remember that trainers do not speak in superlatives, and for a very good reason. They would rather you be pleasantly surprised with a decent performance than crushed by a poor one. Then, too, it's part of the matter-of-factness that goes with being a professional in almost any field.

Understanding "trainerspeak" is very essential. And understatement is where it starts.

In all of history there are perhaps two "great" horses. Man o' War and Secretariat. Citation, Kelso, Dr. Fager, Nashua, Cigar, Seattle Slew — those immortals — are "good" or "nice" horses. Beneath that mighty echelon come those wonderful campaigners referred to as "useful" — horses that might have won a million dollars! Then come such dynamic descriptive designations as "honest" or "genuine" or "talented." The rest of the breed hardly merits a label. Maybe a "He's all right."

If your trainer ever lets it drop that "this colt might be able to run a little bit," then you can go the bank! That means you are the owner of a double-barreled, triple-jointed, silver-plated running son of a bitch!

A few comments — and this is just scratching the surface — on "walking the walk and talking the talk."

If a horse trains terrifically, he did not train "well." He trained "good" or he worked "good" — the protestations of Wayne Lukas to his young, enthusiastic, but ungrammatical assistant notwithstanding. If a horse goes to the racetrack, he "trains" or "gallops." Unless, of course, he "breezes," in which case, he "works." Works or breezes are speed drills.

When a horse is victorious in a race, old-timers still say, "he win." Not "won." As in, "The boy asked her at the half-mile pole and she went on and win by the length of the grandstand!"

When a horse goes onto the racetrack, he will "jog" not trot, "gallop" not canter. To "run" is to compete in a race. If he "tack-walks" that means he walks around the aisle of the barn with a rider up. This is sometimes the training procedure when light exercise is requested for several days following a race.

Horses on the racetrack gallop or breeze "the right way," meaning counter-clockwise. Horses coming on the racetrack always jog for a distance while they get warmed up, and this — in accordance with the strict "rules of the road" — is done "the wrong way," or clockwise.

A claiming race is referred to as a "tag." A whip is a "stick," as in "he's a good stick horse" (responds to it). A "furlong" is an eighth of a mile, and it is NOT a "furlough."

A female is a "filly" until she gets to be five years of age. Then she's a "mare." A "colt" becomes a "horse" when he's five. If he is a breeding animal, he is a "stallion" or a "stud." A horse is "sired by" a male and "out of" a female (the "dam").

"My colt is out of Secretariat." NO WAY!

And surely the most ghastly faux pas is to see some big, strapping bruiser of a stud horse come out exuding masculinity, and a wretched bystander exclaims, "Isn't SHE pretty!"

Horse people talk in sort of a strange verbal shorthand in which, amazingly, everything is understood without using a horse's name. My wife has always laughed at the way a typical conversation might go between Ron Stevens, our longtime "farm" trainer, and me. With a roster of sixty horses, neither she nor anyone else would have the vaguest idea what animals were being discussed.

Me: "You want to go ahead and work that colt Saturday?"

Ron: "Yeah, I think he's ready for an easy three-eighths."

Me: "How's that filly?"

Ron: "She trained much better yesterday. What are you going to do about the horse in Maryland?"

Me: "I'm going to bring him home."

What's not to follow?

Training a barn full of horses at the racetrack is an exercise in precision and organization. Training starts at dawn, or before, in order to get the horses out and exercised before the track closes at about 10 a.m. so that it can be renovated and prepared for the afternoon's racing.

The trainer, or assistant trainer, makes up his "set chart" indicating which horses will go in which groups or sets, roughly on half-hours. This depends on grooms, who cannot prepare two of their horses for

Young horses finish a "breeze" at the Keeneland training track.

the same set, or maybe the availability of a jockey who may be coming by at 8:15 to work a horse he is going to ride later in the week. If you have arranged with your trainer to hold your horse for the 7:45 set, get there at 7:30. Do not even think of being late. The trainer should, and will, go on without you.

I'm amazed by the number of neophytes who think training racehorses at a major racetrack is simply an informal morning of storytelling, amiable chatting, and leisurely horseback riding, with a sports ensemble fashion show thrown in! Things are cracking at a racehorse training barn!

More on preparations for your first start:

Do you have insurance on your horse? Have you sent your certificate of foal registration to the trainer? Surely, you've got your colors (silks). How about your license? Do you want to run in a stable name, and have you made those arrangements? Credentials? You probably named him right after you got him!

The trainer would have given you guidance on all these projects and held your hand in getting them crossed off the list.

Insurance has a lot to do with your personal business philosophy about protection of this sort. At Dogwood, with four people involved with us in each horse, we would not think of insuring the horse for anything less than full mortality. Although if one of the partners is anti-insurance or owns several multiple interests and wishes to self-insure, then he can certainly opt out.

INSURANCE

We automatically insure every horse we buy — at the fall of the hammer. If we bought a colt at auction for $100,000, the moment the gavel comes down, his life is insured for that amount by Old Colony Insurance Service with whom we've done business for twenty-five years. Several months later, when that horse is syndicated at a marked-up price, the amount of the insurance is increased accordingly.

Should the horse begin doing some big numbers, we increase the insurance. By the same token, should he be gelded, run in a claiming race, or simply indicate that he's not much horse, then his insurance would be adjusted downward. In the case of a claiming race, the claiming amount would dictate exactly what he could be insured for. All requests for life insurance are subject to the approval of the insurance company.

Chances are when you bought your horse, you insured him for what you paid for him. You probably should have insured him when you bought him because the early days of training are just as risky as racing.

And, by the way, there's no such thing as insurance for unsoundness. Full mortality covers death for any reason or euthanasia for humane reasons.

Here are the kinds of basic insurance policies available to you through most good insurance agents (and you should be comfortable at this point that you selected a reputable agent and that he represents financially secure insurance companies.): full mortality — covering all risks; fall of the hammer — covers your purchases at any major sale in the amount of the purchase; limited perils — fire, lightning, transit, and windstorm only; prospective foal — to guarantee that a broodmare will deliver a live foal; barrenness — to guarantee the mare will get in foal and produce a live foal; guaranteed fertility — available to new stallions in service for the first year; stallion availability — to indemnify the assured in the event of a stallion's failing to complete two services of the mare.

Now, a word on liability and worker's compensation insurance. A lot of people running horses are under the illusion that their homeowners' policy embraces the horses. In most cases, it doesn't.

Once you enter the horse industry as an owner, your liability insurance should be closely evaluated to protect your interest as an owner of racing or breeding animals. An owner's liability policy is designed to protect you against legal claims for bodily injury and/or property damage to third parties. In addition to an owner's liability policy, you should secure documentation from the trainer who has your race-horses, or the farm that has your breeding stock.

Get some sort of assurance from your trainer that he has liability and worker's compensation for his or her employees. The same from the farm, if you have breeding animals.

REGISTRATION PAPERS

A horse cannot start, nor do anything else, without the certificate of foal registration. When you bought the horse privately or purchased and paid for the horse at public auction, you should have been issued this certificate — like the title for your automobile. It would be signed by the previous owner. This certificate should have accompanied the horse when he was sent to the trainer, and it is kept in the trainer's envelope in the racing secretary's office.

On it is a detailed — oh, man, is it detailed! — description of the animal, right down to "whorls" of hair on his body. Shortly before the colt is ready to start, the horse identifier at the track will come by with this document, inspect the horse, and satisfy himself that this is the right horse. He then tattoos the horse's registration number on his upper lip. This is one of many jobs on the racetrack that is not easy! Nor is lifting the horse's lip and reading the number when he comes in the paddock to be saddled for his race, breathing fire and brim-stone and walking on his hind legs!

Many racetracks record the date on which the certificate of foal reg-istration was filed in the secretary's office and use this to prioritize the order of acceptance for horses entering a race. If seventeen horses entered the two-year-old maiden race you are going for, then only twelve can start. They would be taken on the basis of the date system.

Racetracks that don't use this system use the "star" system. The sev-enteen names are put in the entry box, drawn out at random, and the five that did not get in are given "stars" and next time they will get preferential treatment. In Florida in the winter, a maiden may need two, three, or four stars to be assured of getting in next time. Knowing this, a trainer can enter a horse earlier than he wishes to run in order to build up enough stars.

CHOOSING YOUR COLORS

One of the many, many fun things in racing is designing your silks, or racing colors. These are very personal and should be a source of great pride during your racing career. The amount of pride will be in direct proportion to how fast the horses run!

You should design your colors — selecting the brighter hues — and turn the design over to the local silks-maker near or on the racetrack. In a week or so, you'll have your colors, having spent about $90 for a basic, straightforward design. You can use them anywhere in North America EXCEPT New York and Ontario.

If you have any idea that you might run in New York — and we all

Racing silks are very personal and should be a source of pride.

aspire to some of those big races — then you really ought to have your colors registered with The Jockey Club (under whose rules and jurisdiction New York races). They have thirty-eight jacket and eighteen sleeve designs, and your design must fall within those pattern parameters. The Jockey Club has registered 28,000 sets of colors. Once registered no other owner can use those silks in New York. You will keep this "patent" current by renewing it each year for a small fee.

In any other state, you can just haul off and say these are my colors — and they are!

In 1988, aerodynamic silks were introduced, creating an immediate flurry of interest. Ostensibly they would cut down on wind resistance and make the horse get to the wire a little sooner. Who is to say that they do or don't. Many use these skin-tight colors. I happen to prefer the traditional look of the nylon colors.

The colors, once made, are turned over to your trainer, who will probably keep them in the trunk of his car for about a month. If he has a flat tire, he'll find them and remember to turn them into the Colors Room adjacent to the Jock's Room at the racetrack. That poor custodian has the awesome task of having the right silks out and ready for the jockey's quick change before each race.

We keep several sets in the room at tracks where we are competing. One brand new gleaming satin set is our "stakes colors." They're sharp looking but hotter than hell, and the riders try to get out of using them in big summertime races. We keep another OK set, and then we have mud colors, slightly faded but just fine for a horrible mud-splattering day. Usually the mud silks go on for the stakes, and the satin beauties are seen when the hurricane is raging!

The jockeys keep an assortment of colored helmet covers (caps) that they use with your colors. The cap provided by the maker of the silks is promptly lost and usually ends up on the head of some exercise rider. Our colors call for a yellow cap, and nothing drives me further up the wall than when the rider strides out with a nice green cap, his valet having decided that this color was even more aesthetically pleasing than the yellow one! If our colors call for a yellow cap, then I want a yellow cap! We won one of America's biggest races — the Super Derby — with a horse named Wallenda, who roared up in the last stride to win a four-horse photo. He was on the outside. Guess what color cap the rider wasn't sporting? Right! But we didn't refuse the $600,000 first-place money!

OWNER'S LICENSE

The trainer should have dispatched you early on in the direction of the racetrack's licensing office, or he should have mailed you the license forms. You'll have to get a license, as does the jockey, trainer, and every person who has any job on the racetrack. Unfortunately, this usually requires fingerprints, which are not fun to come by. You can either have them done at the racetrack, or go to the police department in your town, or to a bona fide security office. They will fingerprint you, using the form you were given at the racetrack.

There is constant conversation — and it has neither abated nor come to fruition — about uniform licensing (one license for all racing jurisdictions in America). How divine it would be! Think about it. In a year you might race in Florida, Maryland, Pennsylvania, and New York with one horse. That entails more fingerprinting and paperwork than you bargained for.

When you are licensed, your trainer will turn into the credentials department his "badge list," those owners in his stable who should be issued credentials that will get you into the horseman's parking lot at the racetrack. Remind him about your badges. Securing and distributing these will not be the highest item on his priority list.

NAMING YOUR HORSE

Most people do two things very quickly after buying their first horse — design their colors and name their horse.

Naming them is fun but not very easy. First, about 40,000 horses are named each year, and you cannot use a name that has been in existence for the past five years. You'd be surprised at how many are unavailable. The name must fit into eighteen characters. It must not be commercial. It doesn't want to be obscene, and you'd be surprised at the number of people who absolutely delight in trying to slip past The Jockey Club registrar a suggestive or downright filthy name — in our language, or if that won't work, some other language.

The names of famous horses have been retired permanently, and can never be used. The names of famous people cannot be used without their permission.

When horses get good, the name seems to get good, even when it isn't. One of the great middle-distance horses of his day was Bally Ache. Another fine racehorse was Oink. They're both horrible names but because of the luster of the horses they were looked on with great affection and favor.

Dashing names of importance were Cavalcade, Citation, Assault, Warfare, Nijinsky, Man o' War, and Discovery. Secretariat was a good name, but the horse himself made it magnificent.

Work hard at giving your horse a good name. It is important. And we may have too many noble horses around that are carrying silly names. Having a name that has great personal significance to you is fine; but remember you're going to have to live with, discuss, hear, and explain that name. Yes, you'll have to explain it often. And if your secret pet name for your wife is "Itsy Poo" or "Snugglebunny" or "Hot Lips," that is very appealing, I am sure, but are you ready to explore this intimacy over and over during the filly's entire racing career?

Here is a self-serving excerpt from *The Wall Street Journal* by Frederick C. Klein: "The best names are those that are fresh and stand on their own in addition to fulfilling their instructional function by playing off an animal's pedigree. Just about everyone's favorite is Native Dancer put together by Alfred Gwynne Vanderbilt from the names of the horse's sire, Polynesian, and dam, Geisha. Vanderbilt was the sport's longtime naming master.

"Vanderbilt's generally acknowledged successor is Cot Campbell, president of Dogwood Stable. He declines the honor, explaining that other employees of the Aiken, South Carolina, concern, encouraged by the lure of fifty-dollar bonuses, also offer their ideas when horses must be named. A committee, headed by Campbell, picks the winners.

"Dogwood has distinguished itself in recent years with such gems as Summer Squall (the 1990 Derby runner-up and Preakness winner) for the offspring of the sire Storm Bird and the dam Weekend Surprise, Oz from Ogygian and Sacred Journey, Hobgoblin from Exuberant and Halloween. And Garbo from Capote and the Private One."

By the way, we did not have the guts to submit this to The Jockey Club, but I share here this clever name suggestion from one of the boys in the barn. For a colt by Gulch out of Cold Hearted: Son of a Ditch.

You must name your horses by February 1 of their two-year-old year to avoid a charge. If you change a name, it will cost you $100, and if the horse has run, you cannot change it. If someone has tried unsuccessfully to name a horse and you bought the horse at public auction, a common occurrence, it will cost you $50 to name the horse.

It is not wise for people selling horses to name them. Part of the fun of owning a horse is naming it. Also, a name attached to a horse contributes to the personality of the horse — advantageously or otherwise.

Social Asset was our first horse, and she was woefully equipped to introduce colors that were someday to achieve some prominence in the racing world. But her debut — ignominious as it turned out to be more than thirty years ago — created among her connections a major league case of "first-race nerves," bordering on hysteria.

Her first race was at River Downs, near Cincinnati. In order to be on hand for this long-awaited event, I left work about three o'clock the previous day. Anne and I drove straight through from Atlanta to the "Queen City," arriving about midnight. After checking into a downtown hotel, I rushed out to get the "bulldog" edition of the morning newspaper — just to see the words "Social Asset" in print. What a thrill! She was certainly not picked nor written about in any meaningful way, but her name was set in print along with the other entries in this modest group of twelve maidens contesting a six-furlong race. And I wanted to gaze upon it.

The next morning moved with excruciating slowness. We arrived at the racetrack just as the gates opened for the first early birds. We had an interminable lunch. Thank God the filly was in an early race, or we would never have survived the wait.

Under the guidance of a rather untidy looking groom in an alarmingly soiled undershirt, Social Asset warily made her appearance in the paddock. An encouraging sign was that she was slightly less nervous than her owners — who incidentally were easily the best-dressed couple in all of River Downs.

Social Asset managing one of her few wins.

I am sure I have repressed much of the rest of the afternoon. Suffice it to say the filly ran horribly, as would be her custom during much of her career. She beat two horses (thank goodness). As the poor, mud-caked thing was being unsaddled, Anne and I hovered about to get some encouraging comment from her jockey. I remember that he muttered something about her being "green," and we all quickly agreed that OF COURSE she was BOUND to be green! What the hell! We did not address the fact that nine other green ones had finished ahead of us.

The return drive to Atlanta, I recall, seemed much longer than the drive up. However, much of it was spent analyzing the race, and by the time we had gotten home, the consensus was that Social Asset was an enormously talented filly who had shown incredible grit and determination. With that effort and education under her belt — and with a better ride from a different jockey — who knew what the future might hold!

So I am keenly aware of a new owner's anticipatory jitters and impatience prior to the first race. The truth is all owners are bound and determined to be on hand when their first horse runs its first race. And it is the worst possible race to attend. Invariably, a young horse is going to need a race or two or three (or more) before turning in a representative effort. Skip the first race (All right, I know you're NOT going to) and let the trainer describe it to you on the phone. If the horse should win, what a nice situation that would be, and if he runs unsuccessfully — more likely to be the case — a description will be just fine. Go the second or third time. Unless your trainer tells you, "This sucker will get the money!" Then go!

There are excuses after every effort — and there should be. It is useful to know that the horse didn't like getting dirt kicked in his face (Grass? Put him on the lead?), was "clocking" the horses around him (blinkers?), or on and on *ad infinitum.*

Some wag made up a list of 150 excuses for a horse not running well, with the suggestion that the trainer provide this list to the owner. Then after the race he could just call up and say, "Well, today it was sixteen, forty-seven, and a little bit of 108."

It is a good idea to wait twenty-four hours before one (trainer or owner) can legitimately assess the performance of a horse in a race — good or bad. The ravages of stress and deductions from emotions forged in the white hot heat of competition will have diminished, and a critique will play with much more clarity after a good night's sleep. Another invaluable tidbit: Schedule the celebration the night BEFORE the race. Do not plan a post-race function. If you win a big race, the post-race celebration will just "happen." If you lose, there is nothing deadlier, but you have to go through with it.

It was said earlier that an old racetrack adage is "Keep yourself in the best possible company, and your horse in the worst possible company." This is a wonderful thing to take very seriously. If you don't take anything else out of this book, do remember this advice.

It means taking advantage of conditions — the terms of eligibility for particular races. So until your horse wins a race, he will certainly compete in maiden races. Then go to the next condition: "non-winners of two races." Don't even consider anything else. Do not skip conditions! Two-year-old races are contested at four and four-and-a-half furlongs in April. The distance goes to five and five-and-a-half furlongs in May, June, and July. Six furlongs will be offered in late July and also August, and so will seven furlongs. Through the fall we move to a mile and more, and by December two-year-olds are running a mile and one-eighth. These distances are appropriate for young horses during their first year of competition.

If your horse should win in May, let's say, he may not get to run again for awhile. The reason is that he is no longer a maiden so he can't compete in that kind of race. The next step up is a "non-winners of two," but this early in the year not many have broken their maidens, so having enough horses to make up a race for non-maidens is highly unlikely. The race just "won't go."

This is why the first two-year-old stakes (which really begin in early summer) must be filled mostly by youngsters that have just broken their maidens.

You will probably want to run your two-year-old about six or seven times during the year, and some will say that is too much. Earlier in this book, I said the breed is not as hardy as it was thirty or forty years ago, and this certainly seems to be true. When I first came on the racetrack, it was considered fairly normal for a sound run-of-the-mill older horse to run once a week for a spell then get a breather. In other words, he might run twenty times in a year.

In the very old days, a horse might run twice in a week, even three times. The average work (breeze) schedule for a horse was every three or four days, with good long gallops in between.

Nowadays, if a trainer did not wait for at least two weeks — more like three or four — between races, he would be considered a butcher. The average work schedule is once a week. Horses walk for three or four days after a race. In days of yore, when Calumet was winning all those Derbys, the standard race schedule was to run in the Derby Trial on Tuesday afternoon (distance of one mile), then come back and win — or run damned well in — the Kentucky Derby on Saturday.

A good tune-up for the mile-and-a-half Belmont Stakes was the Metropolitan Mile, run five to seven days earlier. Now, let's say the breed is probably not as hardy as it was. Why, I don't know — and no one else can give you a definitive answer. But training is subject to fads, and when one successful trainer starts doing something, others (surreptitiously) start doing it, too.

And the disparity between the training and racing schedules of yesterday and today is situated somewhere between these two factors, with a slight drift toward fads. So I'm saying, the stock is not as hardy as it used to be, but modern-day trainers have also fallen into the pattern of giving horses a longer spell between races than is necessary in many cases. With a wary eye cocked toward their competitors, today's battle cry is conservatism. One of the theories — and a valid one — of the old-time trainers was if you ran a horse every two weeks, you really didn't have to do any training. The horse kept himself in peak condition. When he did exert himself it would be for the money, stimulated by his own adrenaline. In between, he would be kept fresh and happy. It might not be the best plan, but some of the greatest names of the American Turf practiced it.

When your two-year-old is ready to run, your trainer can give you a couple of weeks notice that there's a five-furlong maiden race for him on the 18th of June (info from the condition book). The morning of the 16th, the horse will be put in the entries. Around 1 p.m. that day, the "overnight" will be out. This is a mimeographed sheet that gives the entire card — all the races scheduled for the 18th. Hopefully, your horse's name will appear. Your trainer calls and tells you that he is in the fifth race, number six in a field of ten. Robbie Davis (one of America's best) has been named to ride.

If you go, either your trainer or the horsemen's relations department of the racetrack will have arranged for a table in the clubhouse dining room or box seats. At the end of the fourth race, you'll hotfoot it down to the paddock and stand nonchalantly in the middle of the walking ring. The groom leads the horse in and makes a few rounds, while you and your guests (probably) look on admiringly. Invariably you say to no one in particular, "Boy, he sure looks good, doesn't he?" We all agree: "UH HUH!" No one ever says, "Man, he looks terrible" (even if he does).

The paddock judge, whose job it is to get the horses saddled, the riders up, and the field out in time for the post parade and the official start of the race, tells the grooms to put the horses in their numbered stalls for saddling. If your horse is well-behaved, you (just you) might go in the stall for the saddling. If he's fractious, then don't complicate matters. Stay out in the middle of the walking ring.

The riders come out and stand by themselves in the grassy area. By now, the horses, fully tacked up, are all in the walking ring. The trainer joins you and your rider. Introductions are followed by tired old jokes about "the winner's circle," dreams from the night before, mutuel tickets to be cashed, and cute comments made by your grandchildren. The jockey, game to the core, laughs uproariously and seems to be having the time of his life. The paddock judge calls out, "Riders up!" The jockey says, "Well, let's go to work!" And the first race is about to begin.

Admittedly, I am more and more in the minority on this next issue. In a day when people travel on planes dressed as if they are going to compete in a track meet and attend the theater in outfits suitable for changing the oil in their automobile, I submit that running a horse at a big racetrack is an occasion that calls for dressing up. There needs to be at least a smidgen of pageantry in horse racing. There used to be a lot. Let's don't do away with it entirely.

Again, I admit I am part of a vanishing breed, and many a big-time horse owner likes to go racing in very casual style.

Some of the great racetracks insist on specific dress codes for certain areas of the facility. I applaud them.

By the way, who is supposed to go into the paddock? The owner and a reasonable number of his guests, the trainer and handlers of the horse, the jockeys, and racetrack officials. The truth is most people can come in if they look like they belong. And there are usually some in there who don't, I hasten to say. On big race days, paddock passes may be issued; the rest of the time admittance is pretty loosey goosey.

Do not take a drink into the paddock. Very bush league! Don't let children use it as a play area, and do display some decorum. The running of a race is an important occasion, and the fact that there are twelve or fourteen rather high-spirited, large animals present under stressful conditions would indicate a need for avoidance of boisterous behavior.

You'll probably sit with the trainer during the race, and hopefully you'll have something to yell about. Whether or not, the trainer — accompanied by you, if you like — goes down after the race, checks the horse, and gets the jockey's comments. This is very useful information, although until the rider knows you, he will be circumspect in his comments.

On the subject of yelling, let me own up to the fact that I am a major league screamer during the heat of the race. I always have been and always will be! And I don't understand those who find it unseemly.

When we ran Summer Squall in the Preakness, he was clearly going to be a favorite. ABC and Jim McKay asked if they could put a mike on me to record any colorful comments made during his stretch run. I agreed, and the network was ready to record my "observations" during this legendary race.

The race began. In the middle of the far turn, when the real running started, Summer Squall was laying third on the inside when he launched his bid. And it was Unbridled, our conqueror in the Derby, coming with a full head of steam on the outside. When they hit the top of the stretch, it was those two great horses in a hell of a horse race. Head to head they came. At that point I was definitely in the spirit of the occasion, and you could have heard me in Philadelphia.

From the quarter pole to the wire with our wonderful colt fighting his way to a two and a quarter-length win, I kept screaming one thing over and over: "Goddamn!" ABC decided early in the stretch run that "miking" me had not been such a hot idea!

With considerable help from me (vocally), Summer Squall won the Preakness. He had been second in the Derby. Unbridled won the Derby and was second in the Preakness. At the time, Chrysler Corporation offered a million dollar bonus to the horse that compiled the best record in the Triple Crown races.

So the two horses were tied in points following the Preakness. This meant that the horse that ran better in the Belmont Stakes, three weeks after the Preakness, would get the million-buck bonus. This brings us straight to the subject of medication — and to the hardest decision I ever had to make, and the one of which I am probably most proud.

Summer Squall was a bleeder. In a stiff workout in February of his wonderful three-year-old year he bled visibly from the nostrils, brought about by hemorrhaging of tiny capillaries in the lungs, induced by the stress of running. This is common and becoming more so, as a result of foul air perhaps.

Summer Squall was treated with Lasix (furosemide). This is a diuretic that thins the blood and significantly helps control the problem.

We then went on to run second in the Swale Stakes, win the Jim Beam, win the Blue Grass, run second in the Derby, and win the Preakness — treated with Lasix for every race.

At the time, all but one state permitted the use of Lasix. New York did not (they do now). And the Belmont Stakes is run in New York!

Did we risk another bleeding episode and try to win the Belmont, or at least finish ahead of Unbridled and pick up a cool million?

As manager of the syndicate and the horse's career, the call was mine. I felt that he had had a tough spring (on which he seemed to be thriving) and had done magnificently for us. But it did not seem right to ask him to give us one more monumental, gut-busting effort without benefit of this anti-bleeding medication.

I announced after the Derby — wishing to put the matter to rest at an appropriate time — that whatever he did in the Preakness, he would not run in the Belmont. Of course, when he did win in Baltimore, the press was all over me, but I stuck to my guns. I will say that the partners in the horse were absolutely magnificent. Not one of them ever put any pressure on me.

We literally handed the million to Unbridled. He ran, and ran fourth. I joked with Unbridled's trainer, Carl Nafzger — and we enjoyed a super-cordial relationship with that rival's camp — that he should at least have cut me in for a ten percent commission on the million!

The most frustrating thing about it was that on Sunday morning after the Preakness, which Summer Squall had run in the second-fastest time ever recorded, I went early to the barn to see the horse. That son of a gun was bouncing around the stall as if he hadn't done anything! I could have killed him. I said, "The least you could do would be to act tired!"

THE MEDICATION CONTROVERSY

You cannot open a racing periodical nowadays without reading something about medication. Regulating usage, banning usage, test result problems, it's all there in the headlines. Racing's venerated voice, Joe Hirsch, said in a column: "Medication is the issue of our time in racing, and because each state has jurisdiction within its borders, there

With longtime friend and Triple Crown rival, the trainer Carl Nafzger.

are many opinions. There are differences, too, among the various segments of racing, and most have had their say on the subject."

The subject is badly misunderstood, but an important factor is how the public perceives the situation. Racing probably does a darned good job of policing itself, all things considered. But the very nature of racing demands that the sport bend over backward to be as pure as the driven snow. Foes of the sport are always going to zero in on the medication angle, even when they don't know what they are talking about.

Unfortunately we do not have uniform, nationally-accepted testing procedures and parameters involving use of medication. How much is enough to influence the outcome of a race? Every state lab will give a different answer, much to the chagrin of trainers and owners. Negative headlines, suspensions, huge fines, and loss of reputation have resulted in a disturbing number of cases. There are many medications, drugs, and administering practices, but at this writing, four major names tend to stay in the news.

Lasix, a drug to control bleeding, is now legal in every state. But the levels allowed are different in every state, and the application times before a horse races vary widely, with some of the procedures being ridiculously complicated.

Bute (phenylbutazone) is a commonly used, highly effective anti-inflammatory agent for controlling musculoskeletal and joint pain. It has been around for a long time. Its proponents say that it simply permits a horse to run to his true potential. And with the modern day demands of racing, we've got to give the horse all reasonable help. Bute is widely used and has dramatic benefits for human athletes and non-athletes.

The critics say that drugs such as Bute cause us to keep a horse in training when he should be rested; that horses should run on "oats, hay, and water." Some say the decrease in durability of our horses can be traced to the fact that many of our studs and mares compiled illustrious records while being aided immeasurably by medication, and that no wonder we are turning out weakened and unsound horses.

Much in the news at the turn of the century are "milkshakes," a combination of sodium bicarbonate and sugar that is given to a horse shortly before post time. The bicarbonate is given to increase base (alkali) reserves of the horse and delay the increase in blood pH that occurs with exercise — and this is said to ward off fatigue. The sugar is added to give the horse an extra source of energy. In a much publicized event, Kentucky (known to be among the most lenient medication states) became the last state to ban milkshakes on race day.

Clenbuterol is a drug that relaxes the muscles of the airways. It is also an expectorant and aids in clearing out mucus. The rationale is that by dilating airways in the respiratory tract, it improves the horse's breathing efficiency. A very troublesome factor is that industry regulators have been unable to give trainers reliable advice about how close to a race to stop treatment so that the horse will not test positive.

The philosophy of medication is fraught with opportunities for wrongdoing. The trainer, anxious to win races, is keenly intent on getting the horse as good as he can make him. Veterinarians, for the most part honorable, ethical, and admirable men and women, want to provide the trainer (really you) with maximum help and position themselves on the legitimate cutting edge of the profession. But, sometimes "helping" a horse turns out to be excessive.

Having said that, I will now state that Thoroughbred racing struggles harder to police itself and stay clean more than any other sport. And none does a better job. It is devilishly hard to cheat in Thoroughbred racing.

POLICING THE SPORT

Stewards (deferentially referred to as "judge," especially by beleaguered jockeys), usually three at every racetrack and knowledgeable veterans of the sport, govern and referee the execution of the racing. Generally they do a fine job, adjudicating infractions and meting out punishment with great alacrity. The iron hand with which they should — and used to — rule is impaired, in my opinion, when lawyers and legal machinations (stays and injunctions) get into the picture. As in the days of Judge Roy Bean, whose law was the ONLY law "west of the Pecos," things would run better under the old, inviolable code when the stewards' rulings ended the matter — the ACLU notwithstanding.

Film patrols (cameras) and living, breathing human patrol judges are positioned at strategic points throughout the racecourse, and every inch of every race of every day is thus scrutinized. Every horse that is to compete on race day is examined and tested for soundness and the presence of illegal drugs beforehand. Following the race, the winner, a beaten favorite if there is one, and randomly selected horses are sent to the test barn ("spit box") to be tested for drugs.

Every human being that owns, trains, grooms, rides, or "hot walks" a horse (and all those in supportive roles) must be licensed and background checked. Jockeys are drug tested periodically. (Those with known problems are tested regularly.)

The Thoroughbred Racing Protective Bureau is the major security arm of racing and maintains surveillance on racetrack employees and people who frequent the racetrack — if there is the slightest indication that this is needed. Any irregular pari-mutuel wagering patterns are reported by the mutuels manager at the track, and these are investigated. With blood, DNA, and descriptive and photographic records of each horse as tools, the Horse Identification Department makes it virtually impossible to run a "ringer," or substitute a talented horse for one of proven meager ability, in order to pull off a gambling coup at juicy odds.

Veterinarians — God bless the good ones! — are there when you need them. And, I am convinced some are there when you DON'T need them! Vet bills are the bane of my existence, and the policing of vet charges is pretty much a "Catch-22" situation.

We have a rule of thumb that it costs about $35,000 per year to keep a horse in training. If that is true — and this is based on averaging miscellaneous costs at major racing centers — then about twenty percent of this amount is for vet charges. That is ridiculously high for horses that are ostensibly sound enough to be racing!

And I do not know the answer. When I have been worried about a horse and the vet is brought into the picture — and he usually is — and he says I think I can help him by doing so and so, I practically usher him into the horse's stall.

I know if I were a trainer I wouldn't be running into the shedrow yelling, "Oh, no, Doc! Don't be fooling with that horse." I'd be more inclined toward, "Go to it, pal." But certain trainers — God bless 'em! — are definitely more vigilant about keeping vet costs down than others. I believe there are veterinarians who walk into a racehorse barn with thirty-six occupants and can find something useful (maybe not necessary in every case) to do to just about every horse. And it can be done in a rapid, efficient (and profitable) manner.

But, loud and clear, I state that the overwhelming majority of vets are dedicated, reputable, exemplary professionals, and I strongly admire them. I am thankful for their existence. During my time in the horse business, I have had three internationally known veterinarians who have acted in a supervisory, consulting capacity for the Dogwood outfit. I have never had the slightest quarrel with the billing statements of any of them.

They have been — in proper chronology — Dr. D. L. Proctor of Lexington; Dr. Dewitt Owen of Franklin, Tennessee; and Dr. Robert Copelan of Paris, Kentucky. They have all been wonderful, and each has been my close friend. I have named horses for the first two and would like to name one for Dr. Copelan, but the famous centenarian horseman Fred Hooper beat me to it — and with a hell of a horse: Copelan.

But — vet bills are still the bane of my existence!

ONE HUNDRED AND FIFTY EXCUSES FOR LOSING A HORSE RACE

I know of no other athletes who work harder, risk their hides more often, demonstrate greater athleticism, and conduct themselves as becomingly as do jockeys. I am their staunch admirer.

And, understand this: a jockey is a member of a two-person team. His agent is the other member, and he is an interesting type indeed.

Think about it. Jockeys have no contract, no salary. Their living depends on their ability to get on horses, and when they do get on them, they'd better ride like their pants are on fire and win races.

If they take a vacation or get hurt, they simply lose — or are in jeopardy of losing — the business they have built up.

Jockeys must get up in the "middle of night," go to the racetrack, and make themselves available to trainers with whom they do business. This means breezing their horses in the morning. Sometimes a good horse is involved, and they're delighted to have the opportunity. But often it is just a horse for which the trainer needed a rider because he is shorthanded. Maybe an exercise rider is too hung over to get out of bed, so that trainer suddenly decides, "Oh, Mike, how about working this colt a half-mile — nice and easy, nothing fancy. I may want to put you on this colt when I find a good spot for him."

When 'Mike' is not working four or five horses during the wee hours, he and his agent are going from barn to barn making connections, doing "sales promotional" work, and sometimes mending fences. ("I'm sorry I had nowhere to go with that colt in the grass race the other day, boss. I know that sucker now, and I can win with him next time. I sure hope I get to ride him back!")

There's the traditional box of doughnuts to be left at barn 31, where the winner of yesterday's third race, ridden by our boy, is housed.

The agent points out that they should go by Picou's barn. "He's got that good grass horse in the stakes Saturday, and Velasquez (another jockey) is making noises like he might go out of town to ride Lukas' colt in Chicago. You know, we're sitting behind him. Who knows?"

At the end of the morning it's home for an hour or two before the

A winning combination: Craig Perret and Storm Song.

rider must report back to the Jock's Room to prepare for six rides (out of a possible nine) that afternoon. When the jock gets to "The Room," he peruses the *Daily Racing Form* to familiarize himself with the afternoon's competition and plan his strategy (which is sometimes: "Pray for a miracle"). All the while he is feasting on about four ounces of green salad "drizzled" with a thimble full of vinaigrette dressing, an orange for dessert, and a nice glass of cool water on the side. Yum yum!

Earlier our rider might have hit the sweat box to drop a pound or two and keep his body weight at 111, so that dressed and tacked out he can still "do" 113. If he "does" heavier than this, he will start to lose mounts.

Maybe, if time permits, he plays a little ping pong or a game of gin. His valet has laid out his equipment for the first race. This fellow — perhaps an ex-rider or current exercise boy in the mornings — handles two or three riders. His job is to check his riders' tack and keep it in top-notch condition (can't have any worn stirrup leathers!) and make sure that everything the rider is going to put on his body, and under it, is in good order (remember the yellow caps that had me so uptight?). The valet then helps the trainer tack up the horse.

A bell rings, indicating the horses are about tacked up and the riders should come out to the paddock. Out bounces this young man to ride a 15-1 shot. With a jaunty air, exuding confidence, he smiles, nods, waves, and shakes hands with every owner or trainer he encounters on his way to the number eight stall, where his horse is waiting.

The jockey shakes hands with the trainer and listens intently to instructions he knows damned well are completely useless. With a sincere frown of concentration, he nods his head vigorously, confirming his acceptance of the game plan.

He spies the owners standing nearby and rushes over to kiss the missus and press the flesh with the 'bossman.' They all agree that the horse looks good! The jock poses enthusiastically for a photo with the grandkids and hears for the 2,352nd time that they'll meet him in the winner's circle. He then scampers over to get on his mount (who cannot outrun a fat man), flashes one more brilliant smile as the post parade snakes its way out of the paddock, and goes out to take his life in his hands for the first of six times that afternoon.

After the race, he and his mount come back hot and dirty. He weighs in and then gives his report to the trainer and the owner (being careful not to insinuate in any way that the trainer has not done an incredible job on this horse): "Well, he didn't get off too good…and then when that dirt got to hittin' him I think he resented it. I tried to get him to the outside, but I was in too much traffic. He's got some ability, but he's just not giving it to us right now. He might not be crazy about this racetrack. I just don't know!" Back in the jock's room, he drinks three glasses of water, wipes the racetrack off his face, and gets ready for the next one.

The jockey often gets too much credit for winning a horse race and

No athletes work harder or take more risks than do jockeys.

far too much blame for losing one. It is so convenient to blame it on the jockey. How absurd that is — eighty percent of the time. And the writer has definitely been guilty of it.

That rider is out there on an 1,100-pound animal, surrounded by many other gigantic beasts, and they're all going about forty miles an hour with about a foot of leeway — hopefully — on either side.

Sure he deviates from riding instructions; sure he makes mistakes. Who wouldn't? Someone's got to make decisions in the midst of all that melee, and it better not be the horse (but sometimes it is!).

This vignette, essentially accurate, depicts a day in the life of a jockey. Even the greatest of our riders — while perhaps not quite as bright-eyed and bushy-tailed as an eager young apprentice trying to get started — must wade through all that tiresome drill. Can you imagine some sullen basketball player executing that paddock procedure? The owner of the team would be lucky if the player said "good morning" to him.

As some athletes in other sports rape, rampage, and pillage with all the gusto of Attila the Hun, the rider colonies at practically all our racetracks are relatively scandal-free. The men and women who ride racehorses are, for the most part, mannerly, decent, charity-minded citizens, and it would be grand if other influential sports figures emulated their behavior.

A great number of our riders are competing at weights that are unrealistically below what their bodies demand. Many jockeys who weigh in at 110 or 115 pounds would tip the scales at 140 or 145 if they ate like normal human beings. Try existing on 1,200 calories a day for much of your life and see how jolly that makes you on a hot July afternoon at Calder Race Course in Miami.

One of the greatest jockeys who ever drew breath is the immortal Lester Piggott. He rode for about forty years, starting at age sixteen. He was nearly five feet seven inches and should have weighed 150 pounds. He rode in England, where at least the scale of weights is heavier and mercifully more lenient at 120. He had a battleship-gray complexion, a face like a prune, and the disposition of a puff adder. He ate practically nothing. It was said that his dinner usually consisted of a leaf of lettuce, a glass of champagne (Dom Perignon, I am sure), and a cigar! But, oh man! Could he ride a horse!

The truth about jockeys is that about five percent of them are doing wonderfully financially. Another five percent are doing fair to middling. The other ninety percent are struggling.

A key factor in making a rider is his agent. Agents get about twenty to twenty-five percent of what the jockey grosses, and most of them more than earn it. If he is a successful agent, then you can bet he's "got a mind like a steel trap." A lot of agents are essentially gamblers. That's how they got interested in racing. When your money is on the line, the concentration tends to be very intense. Agents are fascinating characters. They're smart. They know every horse on the racetrack and have a pretty good idea of where those horses will run next. They have learned the idiosyncrasies of every trainer. They must also deal with the psyches of their bosses, who are often thirty or forty years younger.

While they certainly know their rider's opinion on horses he or she has been on, or wants to get on, agents are the ones who usually make the official commitment. Once they have given a "call," that engagement is inviolable. Agents must have "balls of brass." They cannot

The Master — Lester Piggott.

be shy and retiring about asking to ride a horse, but neither can they interrupt and irritate a trainer when he's struggling to get his horses trained in the morning.

When asked for a "call" on a horse, the agent — if he's a successful one — may well respond, "I THINK I can, but give me a few days to work it out." Translated, this means I want to wait and see if I can do better. Agents love to have close liaisons with certain trainers and may ride on a "first call" basis with a big outfit, in which case his response to such a request is more likely to be, "You got it!"

If you and your trainer have discussed riders and decided that you would like, let's say Jorge Chavez, a leading New York jockey, to ride your colt in his first race, the trainer will contact Richard DePass, "Chop Chop's" effervescent agent, and ask for the call. Richard, an ex-jockey who has made a superb agent, will have an idea of how this colt has been working, and he will also know whether trainers Smith, Jones, and Brown are likely to be starting any of their royally bred "scorpions" in this race. If the coast looks clear, you may get the call.

Agents cover for one another while at the same time being quite competitive. There exists a dog-eat-dog interplay among agents, but it does not result in a lot of hurt feelings and bitterness. Embracing the matter-of-factness of Mafioso, they live by the credo "It's just business." They're all hustling and doing their jobs. So, if they are tied up in an upcoming race, DePass (our intrepid agent) may point out to your trainer that "Migliore is open in that race." Migliore's agent will return the favor someday.

Riders have certain strengths and weaknesses. Laffit Pincay is known for his strong finishes. He can almost pick a horse up and hurl him forward. Some riders are especially good on two-year-olds, which require alert handling in the gate. "Cowboy" Jimmy Nichols, a long, lean "drink of water" from the Evangeline country of Louisiana, was one of the best two-year-old riders I've ever seen. He could out-break the field every time — not a bad idea when you're just running five furlongs. He just had that flair.

Eddie Arcaro was brilliant at "switching sticks." If a rider is engaged in a stretch battle and he is whipping right-handed, he can often exact a fresh response by switching to his left hand. However, this needs to be done speedily — without "missing a beat." Jerry Bailey is surely one of the great jockeys of our time. He is a fellow who could be president of a bank, sell life insurance, or excel at anything that interested him. Bailey is a fine athlete and a wonderful all-around jockey. However, his brain and demeanor are his greatest strengths.

Willie Shoemaker and Pat Day, the former retired and the latter not, will go down in history as having the greatest "hands." This means that when they communicated with the horse through their hands, they were able to instill confidence in the signals that were being sent. Both riders could rate (control) a horse without engaging in an energy-sapping tug of war, unlike some brute-strength riders who could "hold an elephant away from a bale of hay." Pat Day always "leaves something in the tank." Pat has the ability to nurse a horse along and ask him "the question" at just the proper time — right on the money. He is also a great one for "playing possum." He may let a horse run past him, the rider thinking that Pat has already played his trump card. But don't count on it! Chances are he has not, and he'll win the race. Pat is not a great "stick rider." When he "draws his sword," it is because he has run out of options. All in all, he is truly outstanding.

In the 1989 Preakness, Pat Day resorted to a tactic that to me captured the thrilling essence of Thoroughbred racing. Those two marvelous rivals Sunday Silence and Easy Goer were fighting their way down the stretch at Pimlico, neither willing to yield an inch to the other in a truly epic and heart-stopping drive.

Pat Valenzuela on Sunday Silence and Pat Day on Easy Goer had resorted to every riding tactic they knew, but no advantage had been gained by either horse. Forty yards from the wire, Day — on the rail —

put his stick away and shortened his right rein so as to pull Easy Goer's head right into the face of his gallant rival. Pat Day was saying to his horse, "All right now, look him in the eye, let him know you'll never back off — and then WIN THE RACE!"

It was a sound move backed by the kind of resolve he knew was there, and it should have won the Preakness.

It didn't. Sunday Silence won by inches.

But I loved the idea behind it!

Certain riders excel on the grass, and they are the ones who are patient — and optimistic. They are thinking that somehow, with just three-eighths of a mile left to go, if they don't panic and stay on the hedge, a hole will open up and they can win. The reason: They will have run a distance about thirty yards shorter than the rest of these guys. Jose Santos and Jean-Luc Samyn ('Samyn on the green.') are marvelous turf riders, and both are underrated. Which brings us to Angel Cordero, who had the personality and the charisma to charm the birds out of the trees when he was riding. And he had the talent, the gumption, and the unbridled will to win. He combined it with the keen understanding of the talents and eccentricities of most every horse in every race. And his personality dominated the Jockeys' Room.

When Angel sauntered into the paddock, before a big race, popping his whip on his boot and singing out his trademark greeting, "Hello there, Poppa!" — well, the battle was half won. You could see those other riders worriedly cutting their eyes over at him. Then, he would go out and ride his horse AND most of the others in the race.

If I had to take one shot with one rider for all the money, give me Cordero (who is now a jockey's agent after a stint as a trainer).

A word about whipping horses. Nothing is more disturbing in a horse race than to see a rider slashing away at a horse. The English have been in an uproar over this for some time, and some stiff punishments have been dished out for "excessive use of the whip." I am happy to say that there is increased awareness of this abuse now in this country. One of the most vocal foes is the fine California race caller Trevor Denman. His condemnation of whipping has brought about a lessening of it.

A certain amount of "encouragement" is often necessary if a horse is to win the race, and I do not think it is particularly painful (especially in the heat of battle) or as punishing as it appears to be. It gets the horse's attention. But mostly, I think it sends a message of urgency to the animal. Still, it is overdone and often not necessary.

Piggott was the most legendary hitter of all time, and in a fierce stretch drive he would almost knock a horse sideways (and in the process, with his windmill stroke, perhaps intimidate his rival alongside).

Such an occasion took place in the Prix Vermeille at the storied Chantilly Race Course, outside of Paris. Big money was involved (always stimulating to Lester), and the horse next door, refusing to give way in this ding-dong battle, was being ridden by a jockey Lester absolutely despised. As the riders slashed and scrubbed away in this furious stretch run, Lester dropped his whip! Perhaps losing his cool for once, Lester reached over and jerked the whip out of his rival's hand, cocked it, and renewed his efforts to win the race. He did. And as they galloped past the wire, Lester returned the purloined whip with a flourish and an oily, infuriating smile.

Of course, the stewards took a dim view of this and called both riders in immediately after the race. When queried about this tactic, Lester simpered innocently and explained, "I just borrowed it. And I DID return it!"

He did not get by with it, and his mount was disqualified. But the caper had panache!

The native origin of jockeys has tended to parallel that of prizefighters, with the exception of the late part of the 19th Century when most of the great jockeys were black (Isaac Murphy, Jimmy Winkfield, et al.). This was certainly not the trend among fighters of that era.

Ireland was the predominant spawning ground of both jockeys and fighters early in the 20th Century. In the '20s and '30s, Italians — perhaps many of them poor immigrants — were seen on racetracks and in prize rings with great regularity. Since then, Hispanics — a gang of them from Panama — and Cajun riders from Louisiana are seen in much of the action. Jockeys do come from everywhere, but, incredibly, the parishes (counties) of Vermilion, Acadia, Iberia, and Lafayette in southwest Louisiana have turned out more great riders than most continents!

This Cajun country of Louisiana is a hotbed of Quarter Horse racing. It's rough, tough, and anything goes in these wild and woolly quarter- to half-mile "explosions." Those Frenchmen put their babies on Quarter Horses as soon as they can walk efficiently, so the rider colonies in Cajun country consist of kids as young as eight. And can they horseback! Breaking from the gate is their specialty. Some of the rustic tracks or "courses" just disappear into the pine thickets! Riders terminate the terrifying trip by simply falling off or bailing out!

The gifted jockeys move on to big-time Quarter Horse tracks and then into more lucrative Thoroughbred racing.

At present, the Jockeys' Guild has on its rolls about 132 Louisiana riders. Some of the most celebrated jockeys in the history of Thoroughbred racing have come from Cajun beginnings: Desormeaux, Delahoussaye, Sellers, Albarado, Broussard, Romero, Melancon, Nichols, and the redoubtable Craig Perret — one of my all-time favorites.

Perret, an immensely likable, entertaining guy now in the shank of a great career, emerged from Quarter Horse tracks hacked out of the cane fields, bursting on the national scene as a sixteen-year-old riding phenomenon.

He plied his trade primarily in New Jersey for years, but he was everywhere. He has been a major factor on the national racing scene for more than thirty years. He can ride with anybody, and he can talk

In the winner's circle with Craig Perret after the Breeders' Cup Juvenile Fillies.

with anybody. He can provide vital information about a horse he has just ridden, and he does it in the most entertaining way, with no paucity of material. After a race, Craig will practically follow you back to your box, gesticulating wildly, and elaborating on the race ("When I axed the question, he just didn't…").

He rides when he wants to now and is not one to greet the dawn of a new day looking for horses to work. But when big money is on the line, you could not have a better man in your corner. He's ridden many horses for Dogwood, including Dominion, Proctor, Impeachment, and Storm Song, our champion filly of 1996, on whom he won the Breeders' Cup Juvenile Fillies ($1 million).

He's also delivered a few hurtful beatings. Craig Perret was the regular rider of Unbridled, who won the Kentucky Derby when we were second with Summer Squall. In the race, in which Summer Squall was co-favorite, we laid third or fourth during most of the running. Then around the final turn, the front runners simply died, and our colt just inherited the lead much sooner than we wanted, for we had that long, punishing stretch in front of us. At that point, turning into the stretch and idling on the lead, that popular colt heard the indescribable roar of 125,000 frenzied fans.

The Dogwood colt had cruised to the front so effortlessly that his mind was not exactly on the urgency of the race, and when he heard that ear-splitting pandemonium, he threw his head over toward the grandstand in wonderment. At that point, Unbridled, with Craig Perret pounding a tattoo on his glistening flanks, was "balling the jack" on the outside. He roared past the mesmerized Summer Squall before that colt could collect his wits. He blindsided us, and he went on to win the Derby in very convincing fashion. Several years later, I was discussing that race and in the crowd was my friend Craig Perret. I covered that part about Summer Squall being startled by the noise and becoming "mesmerized." When I paused, Craig Perret looked over at me with a big grin on his face and said, "Cot, I'll tell you what 'mesmerized' Summer Squall! IT WAS WHEN ME AND UNBRIDLED CAME RUNNING PAST HIM!"

His point was well taken.

When you think about it, the jockey is the most logical promotional device for the racetrack to reach existing and potential racing fans. The horse is ideal, but he is really not on the scene very long. If he or she becomes a star, it behooves the owner, for economic reasons, to retire the animal to stud and cash in on that lucrative aspect of his career. The horse vanishes from the spotlighted arena. But because he is not physically big, the jockey cannot compete well for the adoration of youngsters, as can such behemoths as Shaquille O'Neal, Michael Jordan, Dan Marino, Ken Griffey Jr., and — to border on the ridiculous for a moment — Hulk Hogan or Stone Cold Steve Austin. Size truly has a lot to do with riders being handicapped as heroes for kids.

THE CHALLENGE FOR RACETRACKS

Some racetracks in this country are doing fabulously; others are falling on their faces. Their degree of success depends to a certain extent on promotion. But for the most part it depends on geography, and whether they are bucking competition from riverboats, casinos, lotteries, harness tracks, dogs, jai alai, or whatever else rears its ugly head.

Back in the '40s, '50s, and '60s, racing was the only game in town. If you wanted to gamble, you went to the racetrack — and people went in droves. Other than Las Vegas, the only place you could make a legal bet was the track. Now the competition for the gambling dollar, and also the entertainment dollar, is fierce.

The toughest job in the world to me would be running a racetrack. And it is conceivable that the nation's brightest managerial talent has figured this out, and, consequently, not gravitated toward running racetracks. There are, however, some fabulous track managers. Managers and their staffs are preoccupied with getting money through the pari-mutuel windows. That's what it's all about!

The racing secretary is the person whose job it is to attract dollars to the premises. His job is to card races that will draw the maximum number of horses (more to the point: betting interests), enticing recreational and serious players to come to the track or, at the very least, play his races from a simulcast site.

To put on the show, he needs owners like you to run your horse at his track (often, he hopes). In the process, management wants you to come out, partake enthusiastically of food and drink, and bet a lot of money on your horses and others in action that day. And bring pals.

As a result, you, as an owner, are going to be courted to some extent by the racetrack, whereas thirty years ago booming times at the turnstiles and betting windows caused management to demonstrate little, if any, interest in making you comfy. Nowadays, enlightened racetracks do a good job of providing the horse owner with a place to sit, something to eat (if you are running in a stakes), and, in general, laying on some niceties to show their appreciation.

Some of the most successful tracks of today are the ones — and it is with a heavy heart that I acknowledge this — that offer slot machines in areas where many pari-mutuel windows once beckoned.

Tracks such as Charles Town, Delaware Park, Prairie Meadows, and Louisiana Downs were struggling several years back. And now, with slots legalized in their states, these tracks are packing them in and have been able to raise purses for the horsemen. The dreaded, defiled slots are now looked upon with beneficence — by some, that is. The purists among us adore the old traditional tracks. Saratoga is like stepping back into 1890. One can almost see Lillian Russell, Diamond Jim Brady, John L. Sullivan, and Bet-a-Million Gates schmoozing among the elm trees in the paddock.

Saratoga is the greatest racing in the world. And if there is anything like a national convention in racing, it happens at Saratoga. The yearling and two-year-old sales take place there. Every racing organiza-

The Saratoga racing experience is unrivaled.

tion schedules its directors' meetings at "The Spa." Everyone who wants to throw a party, throws it in Saratoga. Most of the big decisions and momentous deals involving the business side of racing and the sporting side — the running and breeding of racehorses — come to fruition in this small upstate New York town. If you want to sell or buy a horse, gamble, engage in some world-class carousing, or just be seen, you'd better show up at Saratoga!

The fictitious character Elwood P. Dowd (played by Jimmy Stewart) in the play *Harvey*, a production about a pleasant but consistent boozer and his imaginary companion, a six-foot-tall rabbit named Harvey, sagely proclaims, "No one ever brings anything unimportant into a bar." So do I say nothing unimportant ever happens in Saratoga in August.

Saratoga is like taking a year of your life and stuffing it into one unforgettable six-week period. The great trainer Woody Stephens once said about Saratoga and its thirty racing days, "It ain't the 30 days that gets you. It's those 30 NIGHTS!"

I have adored my ventures into West Coast racing. Del Mar is one of the most charming places I've ever been. Santa Anita, with its backdrop of the San Gabriel Mountains, is absolutely breathtaking. Some of racing's greatest moments have taken place there. The horses, owners, trainers, and jockeys that have operated in California are unsurpassed.

Woodbine has colorful and meaningful racing in Canada; the storied old Fair Grounds in New Orleans has an unforgettable personality and festive spirit and is becoming one of our more important tracks; Arlington Park in Chicago is probably the most painstakingly manicured and architecturally impressive racing plant in America and offers topnotch racing fixtures on dirt and turf; Monmouth Park on the Jersey shore, with its flower-bedecked parterre boxes, is so comfortable, so relaxed, and so very delightful.

While Dogwood has raced all over America and has started horses from Rome to Tokyo, most of our concentration has been in the East and Midwest. And the latter region takes me to Keeneland ("Racing as it was meant to be!").

Situated in the heart of the lovely bluegrass country of Central Kentucky, a few miles outside of Lexington, it was originally built as a small track at which Kentucky hardboots could race their horses. No track in this country has the elegance, the class, and the personality. Keeneland caters to the true essence of the Thoroughbred horse.

The crowds are the best dressed and the most enthusiastic. Keeneland is run by racing people for racing people, with enormous appreciation of the accomplishments of the horse. Keeneland Association is a non-profit organization that channels much money into a wide variety of charities in Kentucky. It has a very short meeting in the spring and another (about sixteen racing days) in the fall. These race meetings, therefore, are among the most eagerly awaited events in that part of the Midwest. Keeneland is synonymous with

Keeneland is run by racing people for racing people.

April and October in the region.

This racetrack now offers the highest purse structure in America. Dogwood in 1971 won the prestigious Alcibiades Stakes, which offered a very respectable (at the time) purse of $25,000-added and attracted the finest fillies in the land. At the start of the new millennium, a two-year-old maiden race lured unraced babies with the staggering purse of $50,000!

Ninety miles west of Lexington, in another town that appreciates the racehorse, is Churchill Downs. That enormous, old ramshackle racetrack has operated for a century and a quarter but has an eon of tales to tell.

Irvin S. Cobb, the charming writer and humorist, once said, "Until you've been to Louisville and seen the Kentucky Derby, you ain't never been nowhere, and you ain't never seen nothin'!"

He may have been right. For a week of the year it is truly the most exciting track of them all, and one of the most celebrated venues in all of sports. Churchill Downs is the one place in all of racing that EVERYONE knows about. On the first Saturday in May, most all of the nation stops and gets involved with the Kentucky Derby!

Every racetrack has its own personality, its own charm, or lack of it, maybe. And, no matter what your personality, your degree of sophistication, your comfort requirements, your pocketbook, your yen for status or desire for anonymity, there are a place and a modus operandi for you at each of them.

The writer has experienced — and adored — racing at both the top and bottom.

We have won a classic, a Breeders' Cup race, two Eclipse awards, and have represented this nation in several important foreign international races. Speaking objectively, our outfit is a factor in racing.

Certainly, I am known in the industry. At this point, I have access to the finest facilities at practically every major racing site in this country. I am sure to be "taken care of" wherever I go. After thirty years, I have simply paid my dues.

But it was not ever thus. I recall those early days quite well. Anne and I would rush out to Keeneland at 10:30 in the morning on a race day, just so we could find a spot down on the rail near the wire so we could see the races three hours later.

When we made eye contact with "famous" jockeys such as Bill Carstens, W. D. Lucas, Johnny Heckmann, or Kenny Church, it was an electrifying moment. Perhaps at dinner in a restaurant one might actually be in the same room with a noted Keeneland trainer like Tennessee Wright!

It was too much to ask!

I remember driving all night to get to Louisville for the Derby, chattering excitedly every mile of the way with my friend Chuck Baldi (who actually had met — I mean SHAKEN HANDS WITH! — Margaret Glass, office manager at Calumet!). We examined and re-examined every horse, owner, trainer, and rider that would compete the next day. When we arrived, we sometimes had decent seats, but there were years when the accommodations permitted us to HEAR the Derby, but we sure as hell could not SEE it! But I was there. Man, I was there!

All of this takes me to Gulfstream Park near Miami, for which there is a warm spot in my heart. As the child of a horse owner, I had been to a number of racetracks as a kid — Ak-Sar-Ben in Nebraska, Oaklawn Park in Arkansas, and Churchill Downs. But, the Florida racetrack offered me my first steady exposure to racing as a "grown-up" (to use the term loosely). And that experience is stamped as indelibly in my memory as a first adolescent romance.

This would have taken place in what might be termed euphemistically as my "unsettled days." I was in Miami for the purpose of learning to speak Portuguese so that I could go to Peru (or was it Chile?) and seek my fortune. Reasons for this venture seem very cloudy at this time — as, believe me, they were bound to have been then! They probably don't even speak Portuguese in Peru (or was it Chile?).

While I awaited acceptance at the Berlitz School of Language, an enrollment procedure mired in the red tape of the G.I. Bill, it was necessary to support myself. I found employment parking cars at night at one of the world's most famous night clubs, "Copa City" on Miami Beach.

Every night we tended to the vehicles of such as Walter Winchell, Sophie Tucker, Joe E. Lewis, Jimmy Durante, Sugar Ray Robinson, and many lesser, but still flashy, ladies and gentlemen, including many of the racing crowd.

The doorman, my superior, upon whose largesse I depended, was a horse player and later a very successful jockey's agent. He, other employees, and patrons (horse players are very democratic) discussed endlessly each evening the results, what might have been the results, and the ensuing financial rewards (never the failures certainly) of that day at the track. An inevitable routine soon evolved for me. I would sleep until noon at my modest boarding house — my

Gulfstream Park is where the action is in the winter.

occupation was entirely nocturnal, you understand — then catch the Greyhound bus for a thirty-minute ride to Hallandale for most of the afternoon's sport at Gulfstream Park. Then I would hook a ride back into town and report for duty in time for the early supper trade at "Copa City."

I loved those days at Gulfstream, handicapping the horses, talking the talk with the wise guys and critiquing the horsebacking of "Jersey Joe" Culmone, Chuck Burr, "Cowboy" Jimmy Nichols, Logan Batcheller, Tommy Barrow, and, by all means, Jimmy Stout ("When you're in doubt, go to Jimmy Stout!"). I spent much more time there than was good for me, but in that era I wasn't likely to be whiling away my hours at the Miami Public Library.

In late spring the nightclub closed for the season. Next door was a funeral home, and I had become acquainted with the owners during slack periods for both establishments. They had me sized up as a rather clean-cut youth — outwardly, at least. They knew from observation that I could drive a car. They were in need of a young man who perhaps owned a dark blue suit, could drive the ambulance or hearse, and could deliver proper sympathy and support in the process. I was offered a job working nights.

I accepted with alacrity. My Berlitz School application had not yet been approved, and I was verging on a serious case of the "shorts."

In those days, three funeral homes on the beach rotated taking emergency ambulance police calls throughout the night. The mortuaries, naturally, found this arrangement highly productive, and many a fine "client" developed from these calls. I always prayed for a quiet night (while the proprietors prayed against me), but there were not many.

My evenings, for the most part, consisted of pulling inebriates — dead and alive — out of canals, administering oxygen to heart attack victims, doing what could be done to get other unfortunates to the hospital (or to our place?!), and generally driving around Miami Beach with the siren wide open at very rapid speeds, much to my delight.

Again I slept late, caught "Big Blue" to the racetrack and thus stayed very current with the entire Gulfstream meeting of 1950, though the action was slowing and some of the horses, horsemen, and my hand-icapping pals were breaking camp and heading north.

And, alas, my days at the funeral home were numbered. The owners were looking for a bit more of a commitment from me. If the relation-ship was to continue, they wanted me to be groomed as an apprentice mortician. This program was not going smoothly, and they sensed that my heart lay at Gulfstream Park and not in the mortuary.

Then too, I definitely did not relish some of the nitty-gritty of the embalming procedure. One day, when called upon to do some particu-larly untidy chores on an exceedingly unattractive cadaver, I "gave notice," thus striking a meaningful blow for the future of "undertaking."

I did not get a chance to return to Florida racing for some years. And when I did, thankfully I was introduced to a culinary ritual that has become deeply embedded in the overall experience of going rac-ing in Florida.

In February of 1963, a friend from the advertising business and I flew down from Atlanta to see the running of the Widener Handicap. That day Beau Purple defeated my hero, the great Kelso. That night my friend took me to dinner at Joe's Stone Crabs. I was introduced to my favorite restaurant in the world.

Since then, winning days with Dogwood horses, crushing defeats, long days at the two-year-old sales — every racehorse day in South Florida — have been capped off by dinner at Joe's. Practically every waiter there is a horse player. And for a third of a century, a succession of great maitre d's — Roy, Dennis, and Billy — have followed our hors-es, sans any touts from me. This establishment and the evening dining ritual have become as essential a part of the racing routine as going to the barn in the early hours for training — and just as delicious.

While every racing town has its own version of Joe's Stone Crabs, the heartbeat of any racetrack is best heard in the racing secretary's office.

From eight to eleven each morning it is swarming with trainers and jockeys' agents entering horses, scratching horses, and hustling riders onto mounts. They are going through machinations that will crystallize into the presentation of nine horse races, involving about 100 horses, probably thirty different jockeys, in front of thousands of people wagering many millions of dollars.

THE CONDITION BOOK

The "bible" is certainly the much cussed and discussed condition book, a small pamphlet that describes the races that are available in the upcoming twelve-day period. This book can be pleasing to the trainer, or it can be irritating if it doesn't hold races suitable for the horses in his barn.

If there are no races for certain of his horses, he will without doubt let the secretary know. If he is a trainer with a lot of clout (in that he customarily provides a lot of horses for races at the meeting), then the racing secretary will listen with a most sympathetic ear, and he will put up an "extra," describing this race in the mimeographed "overnight" sheet that comes out. This sheet, issued about 1 p.m. on Wednesday, say, will cover the races on the card for Friday, and the described extra will be proposed for Saturday. Therefore, you're seeing it on Wednesday so you'll have ample notice to enter it Thursday morning. Got all that?

After the first condition book is well under way, it may become apparent to the secretary, and trainers certainly, that there are too many three-year-old races going long, for instance, and not enough sprints for older allowance fillies, and also a shortage of maiden races in the $30,000 to $50,000 claiming range. When "book two" comes out, this balance will be corrected. The condition book contains other useful information.

There's the stakes schedule. We all yearn to cogitate about this list of important feature races, offering significant money, for the best horses on the grounds and others who may ship in. Stakes races are usually run on Saturday or Sunday, but important meetings, of short duration, such as Keeneland, Saratoga, or Del Mar may have a stakes race every day, or close to it. These are the marquee races that bring in the stars, and folks to watch them.

You pay to nominate (make your horse eligible) for a stakes race, and this is usually done a month or several weeks in advance. You put up another $1,000, typically, on Thursday when you enter, and another $1,000 if you start. Since you are paying to run, you may scratch your horse at any time.

This is not true of the regular run-of-the-mill overnight races in the condition book. There is no entry fee for any of these. And, therefore, the stewards are plenty picky about scratches. We get back to the fact that the racetrack is trying to present a card that will be enticing to the bettors. This means plenty of entries. Scratch time is normally the morning before a race. The reason for scratching a horse is that he is sick, the track conditions have changed (it rained, and the track is sloppy — not to your liking), or a "bearcat" drew into the same race with you, and you don't want any part of him.

The stewards will review your scratch card. They will be sympathetic about sickness, as long as a veterinarian supports it. They will cooperate to a certain extent with your abhorrence of track conditions, especially if you can demonstrate that your horse has some bad wheels, and an "off" racetrack is asking for trouble. On the avoidance of the tough horse, they'll be expecting a torrent of excuses for not running against him, and you'll pay hell getting out of the race. Your trainer can just refuse to lead your horse over to the saddling paddock. He'll certainly be scratched then, but that is a sure way to get fined, suspended, and put in rather permanent hot water with the people who run the racetrack.

If a race is carded on the grass and the rains come, the race is probably going to be moved to the main track to protect the turf. This means that turf specialists are now being asked to run on a sloppy main track — not their cup of tea, usually. Stewards are inclined to be lenient when reviewing scratches under these circumstances.

A solution to this problem in recent years is that entries to grass races are now permitted on the basis of "MTO" — main track only. So when the program is printed, ten horses may be in the "body" of the grass race, and, at the bottom, horses designated MTO may occupy numbers eleven through fourteen. If the race moves to the main track, these horses will run, and the stewards can be more accommodating about letting some of the grass runners out. The race will go with a decent-sized field and will not have "fallen apart." Sometimes an MTO horse will luck into a very advantageous situation and knock out a win because he was in the right place at the right time.

When entries are taken for any race, the entry slips are placed in a box. About 11 a.m. one racing official steps up to the counter, numerous agents and trainers arrayed before him. He takes the first slip "in the dark," while another associate takes a pill (number ball) out of a leather Kelly pool bottle. They then know that the horse, Arrival Time, will be in post position three, if that was the pill that came out. And so on, until twelve horses have been entered. Then they will draw up to four to six more, and they will become "also eligibles." This provides a reservoir of horses in case of scratches. If your horse is on the "also eligible" list, he may draw in (some tracks take them at random, some in numerical order) but his post position will automatically be on the outside. You're glad you drew in but sad that you are breaking from the highly undesirable "12 hole."

The entries are usually closed by noon, and the overnight is then printed. However, the entries stay open until the card is firmed up. Sometimes, there's a desperate struggle to close. The secretary may have to get on the phone and "hustle" a horse. He'll call a trainer and say, "Look Bill, I've got five horses in the filly allowance race going long. How about running Waltzing? There's not much in there, and you'd have a good shot, I think." He's asking for a favor. If the trainer feels that it wouldn't hurt Waltzing and she might, indeed, have a shot, then he may say, "OK, put her in." Now the secretary owes him one, and this is always a nice situation to be in.

In cases where there is a critical shortage of horses, closing a race may drag on until late afternoon. This is inconvenient to all concerned and is quite embarrassing to the racing office.

Now is a good time to discuss Kentucky Derby eligibility, which is widely misunderstood. The deadline for nominating horses to the Triple Crown races (the Derby, Preakness, and Belmont Stakes) is January 15, about fourteen weeks before the Derby, which is held on the first Saturday in May. You put up $600 at that time. And any three-year-old that is showing promise usually gets nominated. About 350 nominations will be received. If you forget, or your horse has done a big turnaround, then there is a second deadline, and the fee is $6,000. The next step — and this is what surprises so many laymen — is simply to enter your horse seventy-two hours before the race is run. This costs $15,000. Then, if and when you run, it will cost you another $15,000.

There is no invitation, no series of qualifying races, per se, as is commonly presumed. However, the size of the field is limited to twenty horses. If twenty-two are entered, Churchill Downs will permit only the top twenty in order of graded-stakes earnings. Rarely do this many enter, so a horse that has never won a race could join the crème de la crème of Thoroughbred racing in the lineup.

Occasionally this happens. One misguided incentive for entering is the desire for the Derby boxes, the super-celebrity treatment, and the hype and notoriety that go with running a horse in the Derby. The $30,600 tab tends to control such a harebrained undertaking — that, and the desire not to make a complete ass of yourself. There have been cases, I repeat, where neither deterrent has done the trick.

It is possible to pay a $150,000 supplemental fee right up to the last week and make your horse eligible to enter. If you had just won the $750,000 Blue Grass Stakes with a horse that had not been nominated, maybe you would put up this awesome amount. At least the horse would have paid for it, and then some.

The condition book covers other useful information: post time; entry preference rules and regulations; stable area regulations (housing for help, acceptance of dogs); eligibility rules; information on the scale of weights; the distribution of purses; names of jockeys, their agents and telephone numbers; recommended restaurants and lodging in the area; and blank forms for nominating for stakes.

WEIGHTS

Weight allowances in racing are used to account for the horse's sex and age, and for apprentice jockeys. Weight is also added or subtracted in allowance races based on the horse's winning record since an arbitrarily assigned date, the theory being that horses coming off long layoffs or those not enjoying current winning form would tend to get a helpful weight break. Weight in horse racing is a vital factor and a rather involved and slightly complicated subject. If you like to bet on horses, you are vigilant about observing weights. Two great sayings in racing are "Time is only important if you're in jail" and "Weight will stop a freight train."

Let's consider an allowance race at Churchill Downs in May for fillies and mares three and up that have not won two races other than maiden, claiming, or starter. One mile and one-sixteenth. This is a specific race in the book.

The word "allowance" has to do with weights.

Three-year-olds carry 111 pounds. Older horses carry 123 pounds. The difference in the horses is that in May the former are still not mature and deserve a twelve-pound break. As the year progresses, this disparity will diminish. The conditions go on to stipulate that "non-winners of $17,360 twice since September 30" are allowed three pounds off; "$14,260 twice since May 30," five pounds off; "$11,780 twice in 1999 or 2000," seven pounds. The apprentice jockey allowance (known as "the bug") is an incentive for trainers to use young, inexperienced riders ("bug boys") trying to get started. Weight allowances for apprentices range from seven down to three pounds. Until the "boy" has won five races, he offers the trainer a seven-pound weight break; until he has won ten races, it is five; and from then until he completes his first year of riding, he gets three pounds off. Let's say we have a three-year-old filly that broke her maiden in November of her two-year-old year. She has run well since but has not won. She is entitled to get in the race at 104 — exceedingly light. And now we are toying with the idea of riding an apprentice who has only won four races in his brief career. We get seven more pounds off, so we can now run and carry 97 pounds.

We're "in with a feather," for sure.

But these weight allowances and their advantages to us are almost academic. Where can you find a human being small enough to do ninety-seven pounds? And can he control a racehorse? Most apprentices could do 104, because they are quite young. Rarely do you see an older journeyman rider who would weigh in as light as 108. Pat Day and Joe Bravo are two of them.

If you elect, you can take the overweight if you have a rider that can't tack out at 104. However, five pounds is the limit to the overweight you can take. You could not ride a jockey if he weighed 110. In addition to all that rigmarole, running a three-year-old filly against older fillies and mares in May is probably not a good idea anyway. There are too many races for three-year-old fillies exclusively. Use one of those.

The boys have to give the girls a weight concession because colts tend to be a tad bigger and stronger (not always correct). In the spring, when many fillies and mares have their minds on romantic activities and tend to be distracted, they receive a five-pound break. Later in the year the difference is only three. In the Derby, fillies carry 121 and colts tote 126.

It can't be proven, but many racing experts feel that one pound can mean a length; that is if you're running a mile and a quarter to a mile and a half. And this premise is the basis for the establishment of handicap races in our sport. Some of our most famous stakes races are handicaps. This means that the racing secretary — in all his wisdom — takes a list of the horses that are eligible to run in the Santa Anita Handicap, and he assigns weights based on past performances and current form that would cause all the horses to hit the finish line in a dead heat — THEORETICALLY, of course. Cigar is assigned 127 pounds; Devil His Due is given 122; Colonial Affair, 121; Del Mar Dennis, 113; Wallenda, 113; Valley Crossing, 111; West by West, 110; Sir Vixen, 108; and so forth.

The top weights squawk like hell, threaten not to run, while the beleaguered racing secretary (who has been there many times) listens patiently. When the weights come out several weeks before the race, a lot of posturing and gamesmanship plays out. The trainer with the "big horse" says, "Good God! ONE HUNDRED AND TWENTY-SEVEN POUNDS! Hell, I'll fly him to Belmont and run there with 125 before I stay in California and run against Devil His Due carrying only 122! That's ridiculous!"

He usually stays there and runs, but racing secretaries do compete against one another for the big stars with attractive weight assignments. They'd better not be too attractive, or else the other horses in the race won't run.

Then, too, there's always the consideration of next time. "If I win this race with 127 on my horse, how much are they gonna put on me in the Pimlico Special?" So jockeys are told to win it if they can, but don't show off. ("I don't want to see no five lengths!") There are "weight-for-age" races where all three-year-olds in the race carry 122, say, and older horses carry 126. This type of race — usually seen in the fall of the year — often gives an attractive advantage to the truly high-class horses. The Breeders' Cup races are all weight-for-age.

Some horsemen favor the abolition of handicap races, but I find fault with this thinking. Generally, without handicaps, just a few horses would dominate the sport and the others would have no shot at the big races. Sometimes they dominate anyway. Kelso, Forego, Discovery, Exterminator — they were all legendary weight carriers.

Track Conditions

You hear much talk nowadays — too much perhaps — about "track bias." Dyed-in-the-wool handicappers talk endlessly about "speed-favoring" tracks, or the fact that "speed on the rail is holding." Or "the racetrack is honest today." Or "speed is dying today." The consistency of a racetrack is a rather remarkable subject. And moisture, temperature, humidity, and certainly the renovation process of the maintenance crews and their equipment can have a lot to do with the nature of the track.

A fast track, without much cushion, can be beneficial to a horse whose tactics are to break, go for the lead, and "never look back."

Deeper racetracks take their toll on front runners, and favor the come-from-behinders who perform best when "the speed is coming back to them" (tiring). Track bias is a factor but not of the exacting nature that it is cracked up to be. As this is written, discussions of "track bias" are IN. Just as leisure suits, "Kilroy Was Here," Karaoke, or Cowboy bars are OUT. Racetracks are rated from "fast" to "good" to "sloppy" to "muddy" to "heavy" to "slow." The last three are tracks that are in varying degrees of drying out after taking a great deal of water. They tend to be gummy, sticky, and quite fatiguing. Sometimes, however, they can be beneficial to a tender-footed horse that may find this condition quite forgiving. A "sloppy" racetrack is one that has had a sudden deluge of water, and horses are actually splashing through it. Sometimes they are cutting through to the base, and this can be "sloppy-fast." Front runners do well on a surface of this sort, if for no other reason than they are inconsiderately kicking back a great deal of gluey mud — quite discouraging to jockey and horse when planning a spirited advance!

Fast turf courses are termed "firm." Water-starved courses can border on "hard" — a condition that can cause a runner to need shock absorbers. The English refer often to a horse having gotten "jarred up" on a hard or firm turf course.

"Good" is the ideal condition, and this means that there is some "cut in the ground" to borrow another of the Brits' quaint little expressions. We don't deal much with "yielding" or "soft" over here because races are then taken off the turf, usually because it behooves the racetrack to protect its grass course if it is to be used heavily over a period of two or three months. A place like Keeneland, which operates only a few weeks twice a year, probably would go ahead and run on the turf when it is in that soft condition.

Firm turf favors a horse with a "daisy-cutting" action — one whose stride skims over the ground. The efficiency of this action would be nullified by soft grass, in which the foot sinks several inches. However, a horse with normally undesirable excessive action would be flattered because he picks his feet up high and plunks them down into the turf. Sometimes this is referred to as "round action."

Racecourses, their consistency, and the poor track superintendent whose unenviable job it is to maintain them, are disparaged and analyzed endlessly by horsemen. The racing strip is the ideal whipping boy for those trainers whose stables are in a slump. They blame the heat or the cold or the wind or the racetrack. But, of course, they're all competing under the same conditions!

Remember earlier, we said there existed a handy list of 150 different excuses for losing a horse race? Well, numbers eighty-five to 137 deal with the condition of the racetrack!

WHEN AN IMMOVABLE OBJECT MEETS AN IRRESISTIBLE FORCE

Imagine a southbound freight train, highballing down the railroad tracks, and a northbound freight, with the throttle wide open. They're on the same track. They collide!

You have just witnessed the mating of a Thoroughbred stallion with a Thoroughbred mare.

With five people usually in attendance to make sure things go as smoothly as possible, it is still an undertaking that — to the random observer — generates incredible force, exuberance, and determination.

The breeding of Thoroughbreds is a gigantic agri-business that spreads out across this continent and flourishes in most foreign countries.

So why wouldn't life in the horse breeding industry be a lot simpler, and just as productive, if Thoroughbred breeders used artificial insemination (AI). It would be. Simpler. And it might be just as productive. But it's not going to happen, and I, for one, am glad.

Practically all livestock, including every other equine breed but Thoroughbred, is reproduced by the practice of AI. But the

Thoroughbred still operates in a world of tradition mixed with a little mystique.

This is one small factor. But, more importantly, artificial insemination would create a major economic upheaval within this industry. It would virtually eliminate the important, tertiary level of the breeding industry, which, for the most part is concentrated in states like Georgia, South Carolina, Michigan, Nebraska, Oregon, and plenty of others.

Suppose you could breed 600 mares to Storm Cat, currently our hottest stallion. The stud fee would theoretically be $30,000 instead of $300,000. This means that a significant but lesser stud now standing for $30,000 would be bred to 300 mares, we'll say. His fee would be diluted to $7,500. Then, the stallion standing for $7,500 today would be worth only $1,000.

And many of today's lesser stud horses would be eliminated entirely. No market for these individuals, whatsoever.

Could The Jockey Club speak to this problem by restricting the number to 200, for instance? Sure, for awhile, until the legal eagles got into the picture and the courts ruled that this would be "restraint of

A lot of action takes place in the breeding shed.

trade." Which they did in 1948 with the Angus cattle breeders.

Another reason for not going to AI would be the tendency to restrict the gene pool, thereby emphasizing undesirable characteristics in the breed. This would become tantamount to an intense form of inbreeding. Imperfections in stallions would be magnified. For instance, a subfertile stallion, while benefiting from this exacting technique that would permit greater conception rates, would nevertheless pass along this flaw to numerous offspring.

The breed would simply not benefit.

Further, there are several other factors that, while not paramount, are significant. There's the matter of security. When one pays a $50,000 stud fee, you want to send your man with your mare to the breeding shed and see that specific coupling take place (freight train collision notwithstanding!).

This may be an "old wives' tale," but some great horsemen have felt strongly that a natural cover by a stallion imparts vigor in the foal. And we're all looking for vigor.

A "pro" factor for AI is that it would be beneficial in controlling disease.

But at this point, the "cons" greatly outweigh the "pros." Breeding is a beguiling aspect of our business. It immediately conjures up visions of Walter Brennan, Mickey Rooney, Fay Bainter, and perhaps good old grinning, shuffling Stepnfetchit — all struggling wholesomely (from Hollywood) to deliver a foal that will win the Kentucky Derby three years hence and eliminate hard times on this Bluegrass farm.

Many readers of this book are primarily interested in the breeding side of the Thoroughbred game. It is most appealing, completely charming, but with its own unique set of headaches, problems, and snares. Easy it is not.

When starting a breeding program, it takes a long time to fill up the pipeline. Commercial breeding (producing weanlings, yearlings, and two-year-olds for the auction sales) succeeds best when it has numbers on its side. The breeder struggles with infertility, abortions, the fickle nature of the market, foals with bad conformation. He has many moments of exhilaration and triumph; times of despair, discouragement, and distress. Just as much of each as does the race-tracker, just a different set of contributing factors.

If you're breeding for the market, and you have four mares, it is quite possible that one could have aborted, two didn't get in foal, one produced a very crooked-legged, commercially unattractive foal. Your "crop" is non-existent. However, if you have a band of twenty mares, six may not have produced a marketable foal for whatever reasons, but fourteen did, and your "harvest" will have been bountiful enough.

But remember this: whether you like racing or breeding, all of it ends up at the finish line. The end use of a racehorse is winning money by running well in horse races. The racetrack may not be your cup of tea, but if you deal in the world of Thoroughbreds, you absolutely cannot get away from it. But breeding racehorses does have a unique and lovely dazzle about it, heightened by the lure of the land and nature.

One of the finest and most respected veterinarians of recent times is Dr. D. L. Proctor of Lexington. He has the conformation of a pulling guard — which he was in younger years. He has a marvelous personality, wonderful sense of humor, and spotless integrity. D. L. is a confident, hearty, decisive man with a keen love of animals and an unmistakable — but bluff and practical — kindness about him. He has spent a lifetime working with and helping the breed's most humble and the breed's most exalted representatives. It matters not to him.

Proctor had a client named Bill Hatfield who was a small market breeder in Woodford County. This horseman was a staunch member of the little Methodist church in Midway, Kentucky. And that church had just retained a new pastor from out of state — a very young couple, his wife pregnant for the first time.

The new minister was most intrigued with the horse business, and since he was slap-dab in the middle of one of America's leading Thoroughbred producing counties, he was most anxious to accelerate his orientation in this unfamiliar world of breeding racehorses.

It was in the middle of foaling season, and Hatfield thought it would be nice if the young couple could actually be a part of the birthing process. This would be especially poignant since the couple was about to experience the wonderful miracle of bringing their own new life into the world.

Bill had an older mare who was due to foal. She showed all the right signs, and she was regular as clockwork. He figured that very night she would deliver, so he called the minister and said, "Preacher, my old mare, Flower Bonnet, is sure to drop a foal tonight. Why don't you and the missus come out for supper, and I think before the evening is over, you all will see a truly wonderful sight — one you'll never forget!"

The preacher and his wife were thrilled, and accepted.

They came out, had a delicious supper, and sure enough, about eight o'clock the night watchman called from the foaling barn and said that time was drawing nigh. Flower Bonnet was ready to deliver. They all left the table and rushed down to the barn.

About an hour later, Proctor got a phone call. It was his friend Bill Hatfield, and he was in a frenzy.

"Oh my God, Doc, you gotta get out here. Flower Bonnet's trying to foal, and she's all messed up. I don't know what's going on, but the foal is turned around, and I'm afraid we're going to lose 'em both. Hurry!"

Proctor headed for Woodford County. He drove straight to the foaling barn, ablaze with lights, and when he hurried in, there were the Hatfields, the young preacher and his wife, the foaling man, and the night watchman, worriedly peering into the large foaling stall. He quickly confirmed that Flower Bonnet was indeed in serious trouble.

Dripping with sweat, the old mare had partially delivered the wrongly turned foal. She was clearly hemorrhaging and was in complete panic — on her feet and rushing frantically around and around the stall.

Now, the night watchman was an eccentric old fellow — as horse farm night watchmen often are — with a fetish for martial paraphernalia. He was the absolute Rock of Gibraltar, but he gloried in carrying out his duties — unnecessarily — while in military garb, and rigged with a .45-caliber pistol on one side, and a huge, razor-sharp Bowie knife sheathed on the other.

Proctor went into the stall, and saw immediately that the mare would be dead in minutes. And neither would the foal survive, unless something was done immediately. He had about ninety seconds to try to save the foal. The mare had no chance.

Man of action that he was, Proctor suddenly focused on the night watchman, reached over, snatched the .45 out of the old man's holster, and when the mare came around the next time, "POW," right between the eyes. He killed her immediately; she dropped like a shot.

He then grabbed the Bowie knife, and with incredible speed, he slit her belly open from her chest to her hindquarters. He reached in and with all his strength, and just in the nick of time, brought out her almost strangled baby!

It wasn't pretty, but he did what he had to do — the only thing he could do! He saved the life of what was to be a handsome and healthy colt.

The hapless audience to this grisly saga was absolutely stunned, demolished, speechless.

Except for the young minister who had brought his pregnant and trusting wife to witness what was to be an awesomely inspirational miracle. With his face wreathed in anguish, he clutched both her hands, turned his eyes toward the heavens, and promised, "Oh, Lord, if You'll let this dear girl survive having this baby, I can tell You she'll never have to have another one!"

While many go into Thoroughbred breeding, knowing from the

outset that this is the side of horse racing that is for them, there are others who gravitated into breeding because they started out owning a female racehorse. If she was good, then the move probably made sense; if she couldn't run, and you went into breeding because you liked her or your wife did and you couldn't bear to get rid of her, then that is understandable and appealing, but may not be commercially sound. In fact, it is not.

When one ends up with a bad horse in this game, the best advice is to cull that individual. Beware of postponing the inevitable, of putting off an unhappy course of action. Usually that is really what is behind the decision to breed a poorly pedigreed failure of a race filly. I have been guilty of it.

This writer strongly recommends that basically you do that which makes you happy and gives you enjoyment in this sport and industry, as long as you can afford it. However, it would be helpful, and would be exceedingly pleasing in the long run if it could make some economic sense.

What does not make sense is breeding sorry mares to sorry stallions. The result will be sorry offspring. What gives that practice an infinitesimal bit of blue sky to gaze at and yearn to reach, is that, once in a decade, along will come some ill-bred colt or filly that is faster than the word of God! And maybe has some class in the bargain. The greatest example of modern times has been John Henry. He was a plain brown gelding — long-bodied, high-headed, and short-legged — sired by an ignominious stallion named Ole Bob Bowers and out of a pretty common mare named Once Double. Appropriately, he sold at auction as a yearling for $1,100.

But John Henry was a running machine who went on to win $6,591,860.

The old tried and true adage in Thoroughbred breeding is "Breed the Best to the Best!" Brilliant advice, but who can follow it? A more practical adaptation of that motto would be, "Breed the best you've got to the best you can afford." That we comprehend.

There are, of course, two breeding theaters on whose stages you can make your presentations, and they are quite different.

If you are breeding to race your own horses, then you can certainly indulge yourself. You can breed mares that you are fond of to stallions whose accomplishments, looks, and personalities ring your chimes, inexplicable to the rest of the world though it may be.

If you are breeding commercially, then you MUST put yourself in the place of buyers, and produce horses that have commercial appeal. You don't have to guess at what those matings may want to be. There is a massive amount of research material that will give you sales averages, rates of success of certain crossings, and various other indicators. If you are breeding for the market, you simply cannot indulge your whims, unless, of course, you are prepared to back them up on the racetrack.

The commercial market has undergone several changes in the last two decades — and will undergo plenty more. This demands that commercial breeders have the ability to zig and zag, realign, and be resilient.

There was a time in the early '80s when you could breed practically anything to anything, lead it over to the sale pavilion, and make money. That bubble burst, the over-production of horses brought about cutbacks, and in the late 1980s and '90s, four out of five sale yearlings did not make money.

Nowadays we stand there applauding from a front row seat, as monolithic home runs sail out of the ball park and into store windows down the street! But we also observe nervously that they are interspersed with many strikeouts, little dribblers in front of home plate, and, every now and then, maybe a broken-bat single. As this is written in early 2000, a handful of exceptionally well-heeled players are for the most part making possible the increasing sales averages. But the overall picture of results at horse sales is creating a false sense of prosperity. A few consignors are "wearing diamonds," but plenty more are taking too many horses home. Many horses are not reaching their reserves, and consignors are struggling to sell them privately.

Incidentally, the home runs we do see are powered by conformation and — in the case of two-year-olds — speedy works of ridiculously short duration. Pedigree is not as much of a factor at this stage of the game.

What is the key to the great triumphs of the legendary breeders of these and earlier times? Numbers, quality, and luck. They DO breed the best to the best, they've got plenty of them, and quite often, naturally, they turn out super-successful racehorses. They combine all of the above with sound animal husbandry. And, skillful promotion of one sort or the other.

What ludicrous mumbo jumbo to think that a certain farm or individual possesses the secret to being able to turn out a steady stream of fine racehorses! There is no genius behind this. Smarts maybe. Reread the previous paragraph — that's what it is all about. You can talk about "nicks," outcrosses, line breeding, inbreeding, dosages, measurements, pedigree analysis until you are cross-eyed, but there's no magic behind breeding good horses.

When you're visiting Lexington and you're driving down Old Frankfort Pike amidst all the great horse farms, you may see a kindly looking old fellow, with flowing white hair. Full mustache; hat pushed back on his head; crinkly, heavy-on-the-crows-feet eyes. His arms are leaning across the top of a board fence, and he's peering thoughtfully out at a field full of broodmares. That must be a famous racehorse breeder planning his matings for the future, waiting for the decades of wisdom, lore, and know-how to show him the way.

No. It is a famous racehorse breeder, but he's wondering where to pick up a pair of tickets to the Kentucky-Tennessee basketball game Friday night!

Just so you know: **Inbreeding** refers to a pedigree in which a common ancestor appears in two or more places in the first four generations. An example would be for the paternal grandfather and the maternal great grandfather both to be Seattle Slew. This individual would be inbred 2x3 to Seattle Slew. A little too close many would feel. Three by three would be the conservative minimum. Our example is a trifle on the intense side. If a certain stallion was known for his fiery nature, close inbreeding to that horse would get you a handful of trouble. Fire on fire!

Out-crossing is the opposite, with there being no repeat names throughout every generation. This avoids concentration of bad characteristics; also good ones.

"Nicks" are simply crosses that seem to have worked. Northern Dancer on the top with Secretariat on the bottom. This is one of the most beloved in the industry.

Line breeding is the mating of animals of common ancestry, but definitely several generations removed, and much less intensified than inbreeding.

Dosage is a system for weighting pedigrees, developed independently by several sages in our industry, each with his own wrinkles. Oversimplified, various *chefs-de-race*, dominant stallions within the last several decades, are assigned classifications, which are designed to describe the characteristics they bring to a pedigree (speed, stamina, and varying degrees of each). Numbers are then assigned to each and an index is thus derived. Generally, sprinters will have high numbers and routers low numbers.

The high visibility aspect of dosage has to do with Kentucky Derby participants. At one point, many pupils felt that the dosage had to be right or there was little confidence that the subject could get a mile and a quarter the first Saturday in May. Several winners sporting "impossible" dosages have knocked the theory into cocked hats on a few occasions. But it ain't dead yet, and the Dosage Boys are strong in number. Other observers gnash their teeth and rent their garments at the very mention of the word!

THE BREEDING SEASON

Life in Central Kentucky in the springtime revolves around Keeneland racing — and ovulation.

The latter is not as much fun as the former; but the truth is, to the Thoroughbred breeder, ovulation is a matter of more urgency. His world turns on it.

It behooves a mare to ovulate (to produce and discharge eggs from an ovary) within forty-eight hours of the time she was bred; if not, she won't conceive and the stallion's "cover" will have been wasted. When the mare is worth millions, the stud fee could be a quarter of a million, and the prospective yearling could fetch a couple of big ones, then it is awfully pleasing if the ovulation occurs on schedule.

For some years now, breeders have been trying to put one over on the mares — to sell them on the idea that the breeding season should really begin early in the year!

Left to their own romantic ruminations, most mares would come into heat around May and then stop cycling sometime in August. This is what God and Mother Nature intended. Since the gestation period for the horse is eleven months, this means that the babies would arrive around April — when the weather is warm and the grass is green.

But, in view of the fact that January 1 is the birthday of all Thoroughbred racehorses (in the Northern Hemisphere), breeders reasoned that it would be highly desirable if the foals arrived sooner and were, consequently, a little bigger when they were presented for sale. There is a great deal of size difference in the foal born on January 20 and the one whose foaling date was May 25.

So, because of the demands of the marketplace, modern broodmare management techniques have altered the mares' heat cycles — pushing the breeding season as far forward as possible. Believe it or not, one way to make the mares think spring has come sooner than it has is to increase the amount of "daylight." Voila! The days are getting longer!

"Programming" a mare involves keeping the lights on in the stall until the middle of the night. "Spring must be coming! I've got to get ready!"

A dirty trick in a way, but you can also look at the glass as being half full. Exciting times will get here sooner. Along with the lights, hormones are often used to change a mare's natural cycle and bring about the magic word: "Ovulation."

There is no question about what qualifies as the lousiest job on any breeding farm. It is that of the "teaser." The teaser is a stallion, and he may be any breed — even a dead-game Shetland pony! — just so he is optimistic, resilient, dumb, energetic, and possessing an unshakable libido.

It is his job to determine, by LIMITED physical contact, if the mare — soon to be palpated by a veterinarian to determine the ripeness of her ovaries — is in heat. This will be indicated by the manner in which she reacts to the teaser's ardent overtures. She will demonstrate her readiness in a variety of ways. She also will express her lack of readiness by striving enthusiastically to kick the living hell out of the teaser. One way or another, just as the teaser is beginning to think he is going to get lucky, he is led away. The mare then is prepared for her date with "The Big Guy." If anyone is going to be kicked on this farm, let it not be a member of the "Varsity."

Lest you worry too much about the teaser's mental equilibrium, be advised that he is permitted to consummate the sex act every now and then — usually with a nurse mare or other working type. That's fine with the teaser! Any port in a storm!

Most mares will stay in heat for six or seven days, then go out. Ordinarily, they will come back in heat every twenty days until fall. If they do not, they are pregnant.

However, there are speedier methods of determining this — in fifteen days, and quite reliably — through ultrasound. A probe is inserted rectally, and it can take a picture of the mare's uterine horns and detect a forming fetus. It also can detect TWO forming fetuses, and

The breeding shed can be like the control tower at a busy airport.

these are bad news: twins, a dirty word in the racehorse game. Live twins are a rarity in Thoroughbreds. Not only do twins make delivery hard for the mare, they usually are weaker and smaller if they do survive. When twin fetuses are detected, one twin is usually aborted, so that the mare can produce a foal that will be healthy and strong and vigorous.

Once the season is in high gear, stallions at the farm are hopefully fully "booked." The stallion's book is comparable to the appointment book of a popular doctor. Mares do not just show up at the door of the breeding shed.

The mare has long since been approved for the mating. If the stallion is one for which there is strong demand, then the syndicate manager is going to be very picky about booking only those mares with good race and/or produce records, and he will certainly avoid mares that have histories of bad conception rates.

Now that all her systems are ready and raring to go, the mare's home farm manager calls the stallion farm's booking secretary to inform that "our mare is in heat, and we need to book her." If it is a big, efficient farm — which may be scheduling as many as three breeding sessions in a day (with the last one probably around 8 p.m.) — you might be able to put her on a van and bring her right over; or at least the next morning, or afternoon. Both parties are plenty anxious to expedite this liaison.

The breeding shed on a big farm is quite a misnomer. It is hardly a "shed." More, it looks like a decent-sized planetarium. Its level of activity at the height of the breeding season approximates that of the control tower at O'Hare Airport. It is deadly serious. With a normal crew of five working in smooth harmony, the atmosphere is all business. One understands that with a ton of excited (an inadequate word, in some cases) horse flesh flinging itself about, it is no time for high jinks!

The stallion foreman handles the stud horse during the act of breeding. There is another key person holding the mare (usually with a twitch on her nose in case she doesn't realize how enjoyable this is!). Or someone may be holding up her front leg, so she can't kick. I know,

Breeding shed personnel are crucial to the completion of the act.

she's supposed to be IN HEAT, receptive — and she is! Still, she can express herself in some violent ways.

There's the "tail man." This is the guy or gal who holds the mare's tail to the side so that it doesn't interfere with the stallion's job at hand. Some stallions breed as soon as they mount. And everything is over in a minute. Another will like a little foreplay. He jumps up, slides off, and repeats this several times, biting the mare's mane, slapping her sides with his front legs, squealing, grunting, and generally making a complete ass of himself. Sound familiar?

By the way, this erotic activity is becoming more and more unisex. And these people might just as well be canning pickles for all the titillation that accompanies their direction of this sex act. Men and women work together to govern this operation, and others may be observing it casually, yet there is no self-consciousness whatsoever in the breeding shed.

After these animals are bred, a sample of the stallion's semen is collected for testing, and there is a precise and important routine of hygienic post-breeding practices.

Other mares are actually lined up in the staging area, and other stallions are being readied for their turn. A stallion might be doubled in a day (bred twice), or if he is unusually fertile and has strong libido, he might be tripled. Most stallion managers — the big bosses in this entire operation — have a policy that a mare may be bred twice during her heat cycle, but only if it does not interfere with another booking, and no more than twice.

STALLIONS — A NUMBERS GAME

So back to the comparison to O'Hare. On a big farm with twenty-five stallions, there could be forty "covers" in a busy day.

Stallion managers have become much more aggressive about the number of mares in a young, fertile stallion's book. Thirty years ago it was around forty-five. Fifteen years ago, it was normal to breed a stallion to approximately sixty mares. Around 1992, some innovative farms jumped to 100 and more, while being criticized sharply in certain quarters for overusing their studs and trying to flood the market with runners. This practice has calmed down a bit, and the average book of a popular stallion is now seventy or seventy-five.

Of course, now we also have dual-hemisphere stallions. As you may know, Southern Hemisphere countries have breeding seasons that are opposite to ours. Their breeding — and foaling — season is in the fall, when our stallions are fallow and have absolutely nothing to do except contemplate the joys of the next breeding season. Some aggressive fellow conceived the idea of putting certain popular stallions on planes in midsummer and sending them and their sperm to New Zealand, Australia, or South America, and breeding to another fifty mares during that season. It makes wonderful sense economically, and it seemingly has not harmed the stallions.

Dogwood retired a wonderful racehorse, Wallenda, then sold sixty-five percent to a farm in Kentucky. And he became a "shuttle stallion," zipping gaily back and forth from Australia each year and having the time of his life! After several years, the Australians bought out our partnership's thirty-five percent, rather than paying annual stud fees to us. He still does double duty, and has no wish to discontinue the arrangement!

The stallion manager is the impresario behind the career of the stallion. If the horse going to stud has been a great racehorse, has a marvelous pedigree, is beautifully conformed, and attractively priced, then the stallion manager's job will be confined mostly to screening the quality of mares whose owners will be granted the right to buy a season to him.

If some of these ingredients are deficient, then life becomes more difficult for him, and he may have to hustle the stallion, promote him to the hilt, and maybe make some deals (breed three mares for the price of two, or maybe let you breed to another red-hot stud on the farm, if you'll agree to send a nice mare to this new stallion).

There is often strong interest in a newly retired racehorse going to stud for the first year. Then, when his foals arrive a year later, their appearance can be a stimulus to breed to him. However, the second season at stud is a drag. Nothing much is happening and people are becoming bored with him and it is the toughest part of his career to promote. While his yearlings will be going to market that year, the breeding season precedes the closely watched auction season. So, even if they sell like hot cakes at the summer and fall sales, it cannot have an effect on the stallion's book until the following breeding season (his third).

And, then, the two-year-olds go to the races, and the connections of the stallion hope and pray that one of those babies comes out and "scorches the earth" in late spring, or early summer. Positive or negative reaction tends to be much too premature, but it's there and must be reckoned with. If the stallion has a couple of two-year-old winners in the summer, and perhaps a stakes winner, the market jumps all over him — at the sales and in the breeding shed. This may be a flash

"Making" a stallion's career requires canny forecasting.

in the pan, but it's a wonderful flash in the pan to have! And the flash tends to stay in the pan.

If, on the other hand, the horse goes into September and has had only a winner or two, the breeding and buying public will drop him like a bad habit. Very fickle and very unfair, but those are the facts of life. Horsemen claim to be looking to develop good three-year-olds, but woe be to the stallion that doesn't come up with some speedy two-year-olds!

The stallion manager strives constantly to create the sweet smell of success for his charges. It is devilishly difficult to "make" a stallion. Most of them simply don't succeed. When you read that Black Beauty has been sold to Japan, or South Africa, or moved from Lexington to Texas to "give him more opportunities" it translates that he's on the "downhill run." But it is an old joke in the breeding business that as soon as an American stallion is sold to Japan his progeny start "breaking up the game" with numerous wins on U.S. racetracks.

The severity of a stallion contract is in direct proportion to the popularity of the stallion. If he's Northern Dancer, Mr. Prospector, Danzig, Seattle Slew, Gone West, Sadler's Wells (England/Ireland), Storm Cat, then chances are "No Guarantee" is a term that has been bandied about. This means that you will pay a fee — a damned big one, by the way — up front. And you take your chances. You are not guaranteed a live foal. If this works out, the strength of this prominent sire will bring you many shekels at the yearling sales (if the individual produced by this union is sound and attractive). If the mare does not get in foal, after three tries, it is "Sayonara, and thank you very much!"

Most stallion contracts are "Live Foal," meaning that when the foal "stands and nurses" the dough is due. In many contracts, the fee is paid in September, and it is refunded if the mare "slips" (aborts) the foal or if, for any reason, the baby is unable to stand and nurse. Live Foal is the only kind of contract that all but the most sophisticated and heavily armed breeder should undertake, in my opinion.

But I am not a breeder. I started to be during the boom years in the mid-1980s, then decided I'd better do that which I knew best and leave the breeding to the breeders. On top of that, breeding presented a messy conflict with my major operation of forming racehorse partnerships. It is much cleaner and more attractive if I go to the auction and buy someone else's offerings. It would not play well to say, "We bred this horse, he's worth $100,000, and we're going to syndicate him for that."

Much more appealing is the concept that I went to a sale that offered 350 horses, and I bought six, and — while the whole world had a chance to bid on them — this is what I bought them for; and these are now their marked-up prices.

BREEDING RULES OF THUMB

Breeding horses successfully is mostly a matter of applying common sense.

A common mistake often made by newcomers has to do with the pedigree. If the broodmare or broodmare prospect is the great-granddaughter of Northern Dancer, that is very nice, but there needs to be a great deal in between. Do not be beguiled by distant quality. Good Lord, they ALL trace back to some illustrious ancestor. Let your pedigree philosophy be "What have you done for me lately?" Don't look too far beyond the mamma and daddy.

There are several schools of thought on this (as there are on practically every subject having to do with horses, Thoroughbred or otherwise), but it is logical to me that you would try to weave into the design of your breeding tapestry desirable threads of conformation.

For instance, I would not breed a big "camel" of a horse, to another tall "drink of water." What you should expect from such a mating is the possibility of a coarse, ungainly individual.

Neither would I breed two small, short-coupled horses, for fear I would get a little fireplug of a thing that churned up the ground and went nowhere.

The argument in favor of breeding like to like is that if a mare was small, and a darned good racehorse, then don't fight nature and try to get her to deliver to you characteristics and talents that she herself did not combine. In other words, "If you don't like my peaches, why do you shake my tree?" Or, she was good being small, so don't fight it.

I repeat though, my desire would be to try to get a bit more scope and size into the offspring by breeding her to a larger stallion, who had a tendency to "stamp" his get ("get" means babies).

Some valuable economic rules of thumb are these:

• A satisfactory production record for a broodmare is one blank, or fallow, year out of every four.

• When breeding to a stallion, calculate that you would expect the foal to bring four or five times the stud fee. We're not talking home runs here, but this should simply be a solid, attainable return on your invested stud fee. You would not go broke taking this small but not-to-be-sneezed-at profit.

• When you buy a broodmare in foal, you should be convinced that the future yearling would bring about seventy-five percent of what you paid for the "package."

• If you are offered a SHARE — not a season — in a stallion that is being syndicated, the scenario that makes it attractive was covered in Chapter 5.

This share, negotiable always, just like a share of common stock, carries with it the right to breed one mare per year, or you can sell your right, or season, for whatever it will bring — presumably the published stud fee.

Another popular and logical practice is that of foal sharing. The original Summer Squall partnership still owns — at this writing — nine shares in the stallion, which the author manages.

Since our Dogwood partnership is essentially not in the breeding business, we ask Lane's End Farm to sell our annual breeding rights for the published stud fee. It very kindly does this. However, on occasions where fine mares are involved, we "foal share."

You supply the mare; we supply the stud season. You bear the expenses of the package up to six weeks before the yearling is to sell, at which time we share expenses and profits on the basis of sixty percent to you and forty percent to us.

If the yearling brought $180,000 at the Saratoga sale, we have done a far better thing financially than selling the stud season for $35,000, although we certainly have waited for a while to get it, with some risks involved.

State Incentive Programs

To encourage the breeding and racing of Thoroughbred horses in its state, the Maryland General Assembly in 1962 created an incentive program called the Maryland Fund. It was the first state to take this progressive action.

Since then, twenty-four other states have developed some form of state-bred incentive programs, and they vary widely in scope and significance.

Some swear by them, and say they are a blessing. Some say they are a curse to the improvement of the breed because they put a premium on mediocrity.

Generally, these incentive programs work in four ways: (1) purses for races exclusively for horses bred in that state; (2) awards for owners of stallions that have sired successful state-breds; (3) awards for owners of horses that have won or placed in state-bred races; (4) and awards for breeders of successful state-breds.

The Kentucky Thoroughbred Development Fund certainly tends not to be an example of rewarding the breeding of bad horses, because Kentucky is truly the cradle of the industry and the source of most of the world's high-caliber horses. The KTDF is most appealing, and as this is written a decent allowance race at Keeneland offers the staggeringly high purse of $59,000. Of this, $8,850 comes from the fund. If your horse was not bred in Kentucky, the purse he's competing for is $50,150 — not exactly peanuts either.

New York has a most attractive program, awarding premiums to breeders and owners of New York-breds which earn money in open races. The program also stipulates that a certain number of races at each meet must be carded EXCLUSIVELY for New York-breds. And the pots for those races are quite juicy. There are, of course, breeder awards for those races also.

As a buyer looking to maximize earning potential, I prefer to buy a Kentucky-bred, and next a New York-bred. I like Maryland-breds because that state offers some lucrative stakes races exclusively for Maryland horses. The same is true for the Florida Stallion Series. California has a similar offering — Cal Cup Day, with well over $1 million in purses for California-breds. After that, any incentive for buying horses just because they were bred in a certain state goes down pretty rapidly for me. That is not to say that good horses can't come from anywhere.

Every state that races — and some that don't, like Georgia and South Carolina — has Thoroughbred associations. These organizations work toward the promotion and betterment of the industry within that state. They are constantly lobbying local and state governments, pushing state breeding and/or racing, trying to establish a market for state-breds, and administering the incentive programs.

Each can provide you with specific details on the programs within that state. The Thoroughbred Owners and Breeders Association (TOBA) in Lexington can give you the name and address of any such organization in your state.

I owned up to the fact that I was not a breeder, and I do not think like a breeder. However, I must point out with mammoth pride that I bought, named, and campaigned one of the greatest broodmares of modern times! The key word in that sentence is "named."

She received the honor of "Broodmare of the Year" for 1999 by the Kentucky Thoroughbred Owners and Breeders, joining other legendary producers who mothered the greatest horses in history and have made an indelible impression on the breed.

The mare so honored was "Anne Campbell."

At the 1975 January Keeneland sale, Claiborne Farm, as agent for Mill House Farm, was selling a big, bay two-year-old filly, slightly pigeon-toed and otherwise not entirely correct in her front limbs. She was clearly a cull, despite the fact that she was sired by the illustrious Never Bend, and out of a swift Saratoga stakes-placed filly named Repercussion.

I bought her for a paltry $6,500, and named her for my wife, Anne, because this filly — cull though she might have been — represented class in the American Thoroughbred, and one of the first opportunities for Dogwood to step up into this realm of equine aristocracy.

We broke Anne Campbell at Dogwood (Claiborne had not put her under tack the previous fall), sent her to the races, and she could run. She won the Old Hat Stakes at Gulfstream Park, and placed in the prestigious Jasmine and Poinsettia Stakes.

She was owned by a partnership, and when her racing days were over, we bred her to Elocutionist and she produced a foal for us. We then sold the mare for $125,000 — a pretty good lick at the time.

Anne Campbell went on to produce Desert Wine ($1.6 million), Menifee ($1.7 million), Arsaan (English stakes winner), and is the granddam of the European two-year-old champion, Fasliyev.

During the mare's lifetime she sold several times for prices in the millions. But for some years she has been part of the great broodmare band of Arthur Hancock, one of Kentucky's finest horsemen, who bred and co-owned Menifee. The mare has been pensioned at Stone Farm for the last few years of her life.

Anne and I are proud of the mare, and delighted to have had this slightly oblique association with a great achievement in Thoroughbred breeding.

But the introduction of this subject is mostly a device — admittedly contrived — to write a few paragraphs about what MUST be covered somewhere in this book — the human Anne Campbell, and her contributions to my life and to our wonderful, unorthodox odyssey through the world of Thoroughbred racing.

I first met her in 1958. She was a senior at Agnes Scott College near Atlanta, and I was an impecunious and struggling young advertising agency copywriter, a year away from his last drink and trying to overcome what had been a pretty badly tarnished reputation.

Since that day to the present I have found Anne Campbell to be nothing but stupendous in every conceivable way, exuding sheer goodness, joy, and fun into every life she has touched, with Cot

Anne Campbell and Anne Campbell — both stars!

Much of Dogwood's success rests with Anne.

Campbell being the major beneficiary. She is the finest human being I have ever known, seen, or heard about. And I know whereof I speak!

I am known to be a perfectionist and the most critical of judges, and the actions of family connections and blood relatives have never blinded me from disapproval when warranted.

She has believed wholeheartedly in everything I have ever done; her judgment has contributed significantly to any successes we have earned and enjoyed. The slightest look or word of caution from her sets off bells, whistles, and flashing red lights within me, and I am quick to take back and reassess, whatever the situation.

I have been fortunate enough to have succeeded in two different ventures in my business life, and I think I would have done so without my wife. But I am not sure about that. With her, it has been so much easier, and has it ever been fun!

Imagine this scene. Anne and I are at a big racetrack and we're running an important horse. There are clients in the box with us, and you could cut the tension with a knife. The horse is favored, supposed to win. The race begins and he is cruising on the lead midway into the turn. Now the real running starts; the challenges come. Our horse throws his head in the air, quickly gives up the fight, and starts to "go in the wrong direction." He finishes way up the track. There is a sickening, stunned silence in the box. Lord, what do we do now?

I'll tell you what I do. I get the hell out of there! I'VE GOT TO TALK TO THE JOCKEY! Then, I've got to see the re-run, analyze the race, review the situation! This is important stuff!

Fifteen minutes later I return to the box, hoping like hell the people have all gone home.

Who wouldn't be grateful for an Anne, and all those wonderful attributes, at a time like that?

Anne Campbell. To me, she is "The Broodmare of the Millennium."

CHICKEN ONE DAY...
FEATHERS THE NEXT

Where is horse racing headed? Well, where racing is going is bound to be more complicated than where it's been. That's for sure.

The Horse is what it's all about! Yet the breeding and racing of horses — like most other endeavors in our world — have become disturbingly complex.

If horse racing is going to be your game, be warned that it becomes more and more difficult to "keep your eye on the horse," and avoid losing your perspective. The fiscal and economic side of the business can get the upper hand.

The media, which once wrote wonderful stories about thrilling horse races and colorful horse people, now must tackle simulcasting, medication, Internet gambling, the fluctuations of various racing-oriented stocks, the travails of our industry "league office" (National Thoroughbred Racing Association), slot machines (love 'em or hate 'em), and a wide variety of competitive factors that threaten racing's future.

A steady stream of this wearisome stuff does besmirch the wonderful enchantment that goes with running good horses in fine races at great racetracks. Thoroughbred horse racing leads the league in the formation of study groups, seminars, and committee meetings, and conventions of organizations that collectively use practically every letter in the alphabet. Not much has been accomplished in the recent past — with the exception of the formation of the Breeders' Cup — until a combination of some smart, young marketing guys from Atlanta and some of the wisest heads within the horse business got together and hammered out the aforementioned NTRA.

The NTRA is meant to be like the Professional Golfers Association, baseball's National and American Leagues, the National Basketball Association, National Football League — a central governing body for all of the many, badly fragmented segments of horse racing. It is now in its second year, and, like the new stallion in his second season, it is boring its constituents, and they are beginning to pick at it.

In a magazine column in the summer of 1999, I wrote:

"One of the most desperately needed, astonishing miracles of modern times occurred when a group of visionaries in the Thoroughbred racing industry did the impossible and created for the first time ever a cohesive, central promotional organization to try to bring our sport and business out of steady decline and back into national prominence.

"And now, after 18 months on the job, with attendance and handle at many racetracks on the rise, much more racing on television, the creation of the brilliantly conceived partnership with the TVG Network, and so many other wonderful accomplishments, comes the distressing, illogical news that the promotional budget for racing must be cut because of lack of support. This, when the sweet smell of success is detectable in the air!

"I am disappointed and incredulous that any buyer, breeder, seller, or trainer of horses would balk at helping to fund this absolutely vital campaign to reinvigorate racing."

Racing needs this organization to be successful. There are many barometers that point to a bright future. But, the NTRA has had to spend much of its time stroking and hand-holding some of the recalcitrant members of this industry. Already it has been necessary to cut the promotional budget several times, and the natives are restless.

The media in racing is like it is in every other industry: invaluable and responsible in some quarters and self-serving and seeking sensation in others. One of the most interesting publications in racing is the *Daily Racing Form*, which assimilates and serves up to the bettors (primarily) an incredible amount of data on a daily basis. In this age of computers, it is not as remarkable as it was ten years ago, when the same multiplicity of informational minutiae was moved nightly in time to present horse players with practically every detail one would need prior to making a wager on a horse at Arlington Park, Del Mar, Pimlico, Philadelphia Park, Calder, Woodbine, or whatever racetrack was operating the next afternoon.

The *Form*, never a publication for sentimental contemplation of the performers, or preoccupation with "improvement of the breed," has today adapted what seems to be a pronounced "in your face" editorial policy, almost going out of its way to ignore the names of the people who pay for and own the horses. Some of their writers are marvelous, most are plenty good, but this particular attitude is disappointing, and not in the best interest of the sport. You could make the point — and they probably would — that "the best interest of the sport" is not their lookout.

But I make the point that the ownership of a horse by such as Bob and Beverly Lewis, Ogden Phipps, Frank Stronach, Rick Pitino, Queen Elizabeth, and, yes, even Dogwood Stable, is a salient news factor in a racing news story, and the omission of it seems almost studied.

The point of all this is that the diminution of racing's romance and pizazz and the continued emphasis on the gambling and fiscal side of the sport (business!) by the media are undesirable. I understand that gaming funds the sport. But so do the people who buy the horses and maintain the racing stables. They put on the show, and we need more of them. I am naturally in their corner.

The future of racing, "they" say, lies in in-home wagering, and this is probably the one thing on which NTRA has staked its life. NTRA has formed an alliance with TVG, the yet-to-mature television network, owned by *TV Guide* and backed by vast millions, that is expected to bring racing into thirty million homes. Understandably, this project is fraught with thorny legal problems, and working them out has been

Former jockey Julie Krone, interviewing trainer Bob Baffert, is part of the TVG "talent."

tedious. Thus, the progress of this project, so vital to racing and the viability of our central "league office," has been running behind schedule, much to the satisfaction of many of racing's naysayers.

In an earlier Chapter, I lamented the stultifying legal and regulatory requirements imposed on the structure of limited partnerships by the Securities and Exchange Commission. Well, I looked around one day, and it hit me that I was letting the tail wag the dog. I had drifted away from the wonderful essence of the horse business and I was mired down in the business side of things.

Because we were selling limited partnerships, several members of my staff and I had found it necessary to become members of the National Association of Security Dealers (membership in which interested me about as much as would belonging to the Nazi Party) and I was spending most of my time with lawyers, accountants, and bankers. I was having to struggle even to SEE a horse. The wonderful animal that had enticed me into the business had faded into the distance, and I might as well have been dealing in toilet seats, grommets, or widgets.

Man, I put the brakes on!

I decided to get the accent back where it belonged — and what led me to the horse business in the first place: racehorses. Dogwood Farm — all 433 acres of it in West Central Georgia — was put up for sale, and the game plan was to move the horses to Aiken, South Carolina, lease a barn, and train at the great Aiken Training Track.

This we did. Shortly after we got the horses settled in Aiken, Anne and I began falling in love with the charming old horse town. We bought a house there, and moved, lock, stock, and barrel out of Atlanta — a great town that was now getting awfully big and complicated, and losing its personality.

Further streamlining took place in Aiken. I asked Ron Stevens, our longtime head trainer (and employee) to open up his own operation, with the idea that Dogwood would be his "soupbone" account. He would use our equipment and the barn would retain something of the Dogwood personality, but he would be an independent contractor.

Then we quit doing limited partnerships and went to general partnerships, which enabled us to get rid of the ghastly restrictions imposed by the National Association of Security Dealers. Each partnership would consist of Dogwood and four other partners.

How much simpler life suddenly became! Gone for the most part were the bankers, accountants, and lawyers. We got ourselves in a wonderful groove, and we've jealously guarded that groove ever since.

Ron Stevens has been an integral part of Dogwood's success.

The only time in my life when I wearied of the horse business came — inexplicably — about ten years ago. I decided that managing an operation with sixty horses was more of a job than I wanted, and I was going to cut down the roster by one third. So I announced to the local and national press that Dogwood was going to cut back, that the demands were too great, and that I was going to "smell the roses" a little more than I had been doing; that a simpler, easier life was called for. Of course everyone immediately decided that I had some terminal illness and that my days were numbered.

The new scaled-down Dogwood sallied forth. A couple of weeks later I went to my next horse sale and bought half as many horses. When I got back to Aiken, and thought about the joys and happiness that would be brought about by fewer horses, less racing, and less action, it hit me like a ton of bricks! What the hell is wrong with me? The last thing in the world I really want is to cut back.

Full speed ahead.

The big cutback had ended, and I was slightly embarrassed that I let the subject come up in the first place.

The thing I find most fascinating about Thoroughbred racing is that there is practically no problem that cannot be corrected by winning a horse race. You win a race and cold-hearted bankers suddenly begin oozing charm, and accountants who haven't smiled in years start bubbling with enthusiasm. And the bigger the race — the more the oozing and the bubbling.

The horse business keeps you young. Just look at the vast number of octogenarians that are active participants in the game. There's the proof of it.

I maintain that when you own a horse it becomes an extension of your own persona. And, no matter what life has dealt you — and it has been mighty good to me — that horse gives you the chance to get ahead of the rest of the world. As long as you've got that horse — that dream — you've got a chance to shoot the moon. You won't be involved with horses long before you hear the old maxim, "Nobody ever committed suicide with an untried two-year-old in the barn!"

On the rare moments when I do become nettled by the business side of the Dogwood operation, I have a simple practice to get un-nettled. I go to the barn. I start each day there anyway, but maybe I'll go over in the quiet of the afternoon or evening and walk down the shedrow and visit a little with the horses. Feed a peppermint or two. Works wonders for your perspective.

But in the racing and breeding of horses your perspective had better be adjusted to the fact that it's likely to be chicken one day, chicken feathers the next. When it's going good, you think, "Man, we're going to keep rolling. This is never going to end!" When the stable is mired down and nothing is going right, you also think, "This is never going to end." They both do.

The success of my life depends on winning races, developing good horses. Never was Dogwood as strong as in the beginning of 1988. Our outfit came out of 1987 with a North American champion in the fine steeplechaser, Inlander; the stakes-winning Southjet with $1,040,483 in earnings; and other stakes winners Law Court and Atlas, plus plenty of depth on the bench.

Within a six-week period in late February and April, Inlander, Southjet, Atlas, and Law Court were dead! So was another nice horse.

On February 28, Southjet was making a brilliant move in the $300,000 Pan American Handicap at Gulfstream Park when he took a bad step and was quickly pulled up by his jockey, Jean-Luc Samyn. He had badly torn the support ligaments in his ankle. He was removed from the course in a horse ambulance. In his stall that night, a team of vets, his trainer, his groom, and I saw him through a critical post-injury period. With a gel cast on his ankle, and an intelligent patient (who knew he was in bad trouble) to work with, he appeared salvageable for stud duty. However, the blood supply system in the injured joint was so badly damaged that he soon took a turn for the worse. Within several days he had deteriorated, and was in great pain. The insurance adjusters approved euthanasia. I gave the final word and Southjet was gone.

On April 6, Law Court, an evil-tempered import from England, but a hell of a racehorse, died of colic in his stall at Hialeah. Still more. On April 9, Inlander broke a shoulder when he got careless going into a jump in the $100,000 feature at the Atlanta Steeplechase. He took off early, struck the jump and somersaulted over it. An eerie, collective gasp rose up from the tremendous crowd. It was clear to all of us that he had come to grief. When I got to where he lay, helpless, I immediately authorized his destruction.

A few days later, Atlas was on the lead at the top of the stretch in a stakes at Fair Grounds racetrack in New Orleans. Oddly, he, too, took a misstep, broke a leg, and plunged crazily on the grass course. As I had done with Southjet, I vaulted the railing and jogged to where he lay. He was destroyed there and then.

During that same period in April, I got an early morning phone call (never a good sign) from a trainer in Hot Springs, Arkansas (Oaklawn Park). Our colt, Buckhead, while galloping, had been struck by a panicked, riderless horse. He and the other horse were killed and our exercise boy was badly hurt.

I hasten to say this intense streak of bad luck was incredibly odd. Chicken one day, feathers the next.

I am first and foremost a horseman, and you can't imagine the emotional trauma of losing quality performers and individuals who mean so much to your life. You're losing great friends who have done so much for you. Certainly when it happens, when you're making the long trek down the racetrack to where the distressed animal is, you rise to the occasion. You don't weep and wail and carry on. You quietly deal with the situation, discuss what needs to be discussed, and then try to move on without a lot of useless post mortems. No "what ifs," no "why did it happens?" A defense mechanism kicks into place.

You show no emotion; in fact, you go to great lengths not to. You go about your business and activities outwardly unaffected and you do not discuss it. Believe me, this is the only way to handle it; for me to handle it, at least.

But, oh God, when you wake up at three o'clock in the morning, the tragedy and the significance of it engulf you. Six months later you may have an illogical, weird reaction to some completely unrelated situation. You're surprised at yourself, but you know the reason.

Because you don't demonstrate emotion does not mean you don't feel as much pain. But, for your sanity, you must try to move on away from the dreadful disappointments and occurrences as efficiently as possible.

"Professionalism?" If the doctor who tells his young patient he has a terminal disease spends the next two days anguishing over that situation, he's done a terrible disservice to his other patients, his family, and himself. He cares, though.

After being a horseman, I am next a businessman. Good news stimulates the sale of shares in Dogwood racehorses. Bad news creates a bear market. And, in the spring of 1988, we had on our hands "the Mother of all bears!" Our racing stable was like, say, the Notre Dame football team which won the division championship with a bunch of sophomores in 1987. But when all of the team reported for the 1988 season a freak accident had wiped out the starting backfield, in which there had been several All-Americans.

It was demoralizing to all of us who worked at Dogwood. Certainly it was plenty demoralizing to our clients who owned the horses. And it sure as hell was hurting business.

On top of the disasters which had struck the five horses, an all-encompassing black cloud seemed to settle over all of Dogwood and our horses. Nothing seemed to go right. If there was a photo finish, we lost. If a young horse had shown promise during the winter in Aiken, when he got to the races, he failed to deliver. A minor, but time-consuming virus epidemic hit several racetracks where we had divisions, and it seemed to be flying the colors of green and yellow. Nothing went right.

As the old country song complained, "If it weren't for bad luck, I'd have no luck at all."

I think all of us in racing understand luck — or at least we believe in it and don't understand it. We sure believe in it. When it's running badly, all you can do is keep on truckin', doing what you're doing, and hang on tight. It will change when it changes. You can't make it happen. But when your luck turns and the good streak starts, be like the veteran crapshooter — double up and crowd your luck.

July came and Dogwood was still floundering and I was faced with a big time dilemma: the Keeneland July summer yearling sale.

This was the first of the four sales at which I buy my "inventory" of yearlings, and normally I would spend several million dollars on five or six of the 300 crème de la crème individuals that would be offered. They would be the finest physical specimens, sporting the choicest bloodlines, and selling at one of the most glamorous and exciting happenings that take place in the world.

I am one of the biggest domestic buyers, but definitely a "boy among men" when compared to the truly top players such as the Arab sheikhs, Robert Sangster, the Japanese consortiums, Stavros Niarchos, Americans like William T. Young, Allen Paulson, D. Wayne Lukas, and others in their horse-buying heyday in 1988.

Dare I not show up? What sort of message would that be, in an industry that is thirsting for juicy gossip?

Despite my usual normal optimism, I did not arrive in Lexington with an air of invincibility, nor, indeed was one warranted. Whether I knew it or not, the year had taken its toll on my confidence. And why not? Horses were not running well, and the phone was not exactly ringing off the hook with clients calling to chat about the upcoming sale. Each year I've been able to sense and measure the electricity among my clients. In 1988, the voltage was low; in fact, we might have blown a fuse! And, believe me, I did not want to buy too many young horses if there was a bleak market for their syndication. The idea of launching my own personal racing stable with several millions of dollars worth of young horses did not seem fiscally sound.

But I have always felt that when your back is against the wall, the best plan is to charge. And I did.

By Sunday afternoon — in the sweltering heat of July — before the first sale session, Ron Stevens and I had seen every horse we wanted to see and had culled the list down to about twenty.

I had spent a good bit of time at Will Farish's sale barn. He had three or four that I was keen on. One was an elegant-looking filly from the first crop of a Derby winner, Spend a Buck. There was a Danzig colt that I liked. He was a little on the dumpy side, but I thought he would improve. Finally, there was another colt, by Storm Bird (by Northern Dancer), and the first foal from the fine race mare Weekend Surprise, a daughter of Secretariat. This was a great breeding "nick."

I loved the pedigree, and I fancied the colt — with reservations. He was of average size, nicely balanced, had good bone, but was a little crooked in the left front ankle (which I could live with). He also had a way about him. He definitely got people's attention.

In fact, that was also my main objection. When I first asked for him to be brought out, he was exceedingly obstreperous, dragging his poor showman all over the viewing area. And he was very studdish. He definitely had his mind on the fillies in the adjacent walking ring. Much to the embarrassment of the Lane's End people, he came out of the stall with — and maintained doggedly — a huge erection. No amount of slaps with the shank or cold water from sponges aimed at the strategic area could correct the situation. Overall, he was not "presenting himself" well.

However, on return visits to see him he improved markedly as the newness and excitement of the sale grounds wore off. On Sunday, he was behaving decently. But another thing worried me a little. He did not have a good walk, and this is the only demonstration one gets of athleticism at this early stage of the game.

There were eight or nine other horses at other consignments that I was going to take a shot at. And by now I was sufficiently caught up in the spirit of the sale so that my mind and judgment had been cleared of the cobwebs of gloom.

At one o'clock Monday, the seats in the pavilion were almost full. The auctioneer's rat-a-tat-tatting gavel established some semblance of order. The announcer made the obligatory opening announcements having to do with the conditions of sale, and the action began when Hip Number One was led into the tanbark-filled ring in front of an audience of about 1,000.

Much of the process of buying horses at sales is waiting. I waited, because I had particular interest in Hip Number 66, due in the ring about 3:30.

This was the naughty Storm Bird—Weekend Surprise colt. This time, perhaps mesmerized by the light, the auctioneer's noisy chant, and the murmuring crowd, his conduct was quite exemplary. No erection, not even a hint of one!

He opened at $50,000, bumped along in $25,000 increments, and at $175,000 when the bidding slowed, I jumped in and bid $200,000. I thought I had him, but a young English agent, representing one of the lesser Arab sheikhs, bid $210,000. We seesawed back and forth with me bidding quickly now, faking strength and resolve. I bid $300,000 and bought him. I hoped I had not bought $300,000 worth of trouble.

While in Kentucky, I bought seven more — colts by Alydar, Danzig, Nijinsky (two), and Nureyev, and fillies by Spend a Buck and Nijinsky. I had bought a total of six at Keeneland for $1,300,000, plus two at the Fasig-Tipton July sale for a total of $285,000.

We arranged shipping to Aiken, and the horses and Ron and I headed home. The first chapter had been completed. There were many more to be written. The Alydar colt we bought was named Autocracy. The Spend a Buck filly became Pinch Penny, the Danzig colt was called Zig Zag Zig, the Nureyev colt was named Hither, the Nijinsky colts were Hitchcock Woods and Ivan the Terrible, and the Nijinsky filly, Reno Sweeney.

The Storm Bird colt was named Summer Squall.

And he would turn out to be faster than the word of God!

He would be undefeated as a two-year-old, winning four stakes.

He would win the Preakness, the Blue Grass, the Jim Beam, and the Pennsylvania Derby as a three-year-old.

He would finish ahead of his arch rival, Unbridled, four of the six times they met in their careers; and earn $1,844,282, while winning thirteen of twenty starts.

Three-fourths of him was sold by the partnership, while he was racing, for $6 million. We still own one-fourth of him, and he has sired a

Summer Squall — catching "lightning in a jar."

Horse of the Year/Kentucky Derby winner and a champion filly and is one of most highly regarded stallions in all of the Thoroughbred racing industry.

I had caught "lightning in a jar!"

ACKNOWLEDGMENTS:
THE ANATOMY OF A BOOK

When it was first suggested that I write this book, a major stumbling block — I am ashamed to say — was the fact that I did not know how to use a word processor. I am one who has not embraced the computer age, and in August of 1999 did not even have a nodding acquaintance with it.

As an ex-newspaper reporter, I had typed, of course, but it had been a while. Even that "skill" had been developed in an unorthodox and agonizing manner, and speed and glibness on the typewriter had never been my strongest suit.

After flunking out of college, I had worked in Florida as a boat driver, pruner of citrus trees, house painter, and master of ceremonies of the water ski shows at Cypress Gardens.

I decided — somewhat illogically — that it was clearly indicated that I become a newspaper reporter. There were several obstacles in the path of my cutting a wide swath as a member of the Fourth Estate, but I did not worry too much about them at the time. One, never having graduated from grammar school, high school, or college, I was really not very well educated. Two, while I had read a lot, I had never written anything. Three, I could not type.

I did not concern myself with One or Two. I solved Three by going to a pawn shop and purchasing for five dollars a very old and tired portable typewriter, along with a dog-eared chart that explained the "touch system." I practiced and learned, while concocting colorful reportorial treatments concerning the running of recent Kentucky Derbies, heavily laced with references to "banana-nosed Eddie Arcaro."

Then, armed with a rather vague letter of introduction from one of the South's greatest journalists, Ralph McGill (who really said little more than here was a young man seeking a job on a newspaper in Florida), I began beating the bushes in search of a job. I found one on the now defunct *Tampa Times*, and hung on by the skin of my teeth for about a year. Then, I became sports editor of the small *Winter Haven News Chief*, where I worked for several years.

Two things happened. My education blossomed — relatively speaking. And I learned how to type, noisily and heavily on an old Royal.

I am thankful that I did hone my skills on the word processor ("It's so easy to make corrections!") and tackle the writing of this book, because I have enjoyed it immensely.

It is now time to thank those people who have helped me and most of the gratitude is expressed to those who provided technical knowledge so that I could become "computer literate," to use the term very loosely.

First, I engaged the services of Tony Waters, a computer guru, troubleshooter, and instructor. Tony had taught Anne what she knows on the subject (she is a world-class authority compared to her husband). With Anne acting as somewhat of a buffer and translator, Tony sought to teach me the necessary skills. And he did. He demonstrated patience akin to that of the legendary Annie Sullivan when she taught her deaf and dumb pupil, Helen Keller, to read, write and speak.

Certainly I thank Sharon (dot.com) Williams, Dogwood's resident computer expert. She helped me immeasurably, although most of my problems would have been like asking Einstein the sum of nine times nine.

My wonderful secretary-assistant of thirteen years, Diane Smith, has heard through the walls in our adjacent offices my plaintive cry, "Oh, Diane"!?!? over and over, and has never failed to respond quickly, cheerfully and productively. She has borne the major technical brunt of producing this book, on this end.

Mary Jane Howell has been invaluable, assembling research material with the speed of summer lightning. She has shown remarkable creativity and aptitude in finding all sorts of facts and figures. She has proof-read with dogged determination, and has made many fine suggestions. I thank her.

Jack Sadler has backed me up — and backed me down — and been a superb double check on many of my equine observations.

So has Bill Victor, Dogwood's treasurer, in the realm of finances, partnership structure, and taxation. I have been in good hands with Bill.

I have sent chapters to my two daughters for their expert playback. Both Cary Umhau, in Chevy Chase, Maryland, and Lila Tindall in Atlanta, have played important roles in the Dogwood story. They were little girls when it started, and at one time or another they have both been valued employees. God Bless them both and thanks for their never-ending support and enthusiasm.

Anne urged me to write the book, selling me on the idea at a time when I was unenthusiastic. She has been a major performer in the Dogwood adventure, and shares with me the feeling that it is enormously rewarding to inject into one's life from time to time new and challenging undertakings. They will wear you out perhaps, but they will also keep you young.

Anne has been the major cheerleader and critic in any endeavor I have tackled since July 25, 1959. Without her — well I shudder to think!

This book — and everything in my world — is dedicated to her.

RESOURCES

For ownership information, contact:

National Thoroughbred Racing
Association
230 Lexington Green Circle
Suite 310
Lexington, KY 40503
(859) 245-6872
Web Site: www.ntraracing.com
E-Mail: ntra@ntra.com

Thoroughbred Owners and Breeders
Association
P.O. Box 4367
Lexington, KY 40544-4367
(859) 276-2291
Web Site: www.toba.org
E-Mail: toba@iglou.com
(TOBA is a clearinghouse for
state associations)

For sales information, contact:

Barretts Equine, Ltd.
P.O. Box 2010
Pomona, CA 91769
(909) 629-3099
Web Site: www.barretts.com
E-Mail: barrettseq@aol.com

Fasig-Tipton Company
2400 Newtown Pike
P.O. Box 13670
Lexington, KY 40583-3610
(859) 255-1555
Web Site: www.fasigtipton.com
E-Mail: info@fasigtipton.com

Keeneland Association
4201 Versailles Road
P.O. Box 1690
Lexington, KY 40588-1690
(859) 254-3412
(800) 456-3412
Web Site: www.keeneland.com
E-Mail: keeneland@keeneland.com

Ocala Breeders' Sales Company
P.O. Box 99
Ocala, FL 34478
(352) 237-2154
Web Site: www.obssales.com
E-Mail: obs@obssales.com

For periodicals, supplements, and books, contact:

The Blood-Horse, Inc.
P.O. Box 4038
Lexington, KY 40544-4038
(859) 278-2361
(800) 866-2361
Web Site: www.bloodhorse.com
E-Mail: editorial@bloodhorse.com; subscribe@bloodhorse.com

INDEX

PHOTO CREDITS

Chapter 1 — Courtesy of Cot Campbell: p. 16, 21; Paul R. Anderson: 18; Calder Race Course: 20

Chapter 2 — Matt Goins: 24; Barbara D. Livingston: 27; Keeneland-Cook: 29; Hollywood Park: 32

Chapter 3 — Anne M. Eberhardt: 39, 51; Cot Campbell: 42, 46

Chapter 4 — Jim Jernigan: 61; Cot Campbell: 72, 82, 86; Barbara D. Livingston: 64, 65, 68; Anne M. Eberhardt: 70, 74, 75, 76

Chapter 5 — Turfotos: 91; Michael Burns: 94

Chapter 6 — Cot Campbell: 113; John Crofts: 115; Bob Coglianese: 117; The Blood-Horse: 123, 137; Trevor Jones: 124; Jim Raftery-Turfotos: 126; Anne M. Eberhardt: 132

Chapter 7 — Cot Campbell: 145; Anne M. Eberhardt: 148, 156, 169; Barbara D. Livingston: 155, 171; The Blood-Horse: 164, 165

Chapter 8 — Barbara D. Livingston: 179; Anne M. Eberhardt: 191; Skip Dickstein: 194

Chapter 9 — Milt Toby: 200; Ginny Southworth: 202; Anne M. Eberhardt: 205; Barbara D. Livingston: 209; Cot Campbell: 214; Tony Leonard: 222

Chapter 10 — Skip Dickstein: 228, 238; Anne M. Eberhardt: 230; John Crofts: 232; Barbara D. Livingston: 241, 243, 246

Chapter 11 — Anne M. Eberhardt: 259, 270, 271, 274; Cot Campbell: 281; Lista's Studio: 282

Chapter 12 — Barbara D. Livingston: 287; Ginny Southworth: 289; Skip Dickstein: 297; Suzie Picou-Oldham: 298

Back Cover — Suzie Picou-Oldham

Editor — Jacqueline Duke

Assistant editor — Judy L. Marchman

Cover and book design — Beth S. McCoy

Copy editing and research — Rena Baer, Diane I. Viert

Cover photo — Dan Dry

ABOUT THE AUTHOR

W. Cothran Campbell is a pioneer of Thoroughbred racehorse partnerships, founding Dogwood Stable in 1969 for that purpose. Since the stable's inception, Campbell has introduced more than 1,200 people to racing and Dogwood has purchased more than $100 million worth of bloodstock.

Dogwood Stable clients include numerous current and former chairmen or presidents of Fortune 500 corporations and stars from the entertainment and sports industries. Among North America's most successful racing stables, Dogwood has campaigned such top horses as Preakness Stakes winner Summer Squall, two-year-old filly champion Storm Song, and steeplechase champion Inlander.

Campbell formerly served as chairman of Burton-Campbell, Inc., one of the South's largest advertising agencies, before taking up the reins of Dogwood Stable full time. He has served on numerous Thoroughbred industry boards and is a trustee of the Thoroughbred Owners and Breeders Association and board member of the National Museum of Racing and Hall of Fame. In addition, he is a founding member of the National Thoroughbred Association and a co-founder of the Georgia Thoroughbred Breeders Association. In 1992, Campbell received the John W. Galbreath Award for entrepreneurial excellence and leadership in the horse industry, presented by the University of Louisville.

He and his wife, Anne, live in Aiken, South Carolina. They have two daughters and five grandchildren.

OTHER TITLES

from
Eclipse Press

Baffert: Dirt Road to the Derby

Cigar: America's Horse (revised edition)

Country Life Diary (revised edition)

Crown Jewels of Thoroughbred Racing

Dynasties: Great Thoroughbred Stallions

Four Seasons of Racing

Great Horse Racing Mysteries

Matriarchs: Great Mares of the 20th Century

Olympic Equestrian: The Sports and the Stories from
Stockholm to Sydney

Thoroughbred Champions:
Top 100 Racehorses of the 20th Century

Thoroughbred Legends series:

Citation: Thoroughbred Legends

Dr. Fager: Thoroughbred Legends

Go for Wand: Thoroughbred Legends

Man o' War: Thoroughbred Legends

Native Dancer: Thoroughbred Legends

Seattle Slew: Thoroughbred Legends